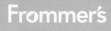

Frommer's

Montreal
day BY day®

3rd Edition

by Leslie Brokaw, Erin Trahan
& Matthew Barber

FrommerMedia LLC

Contents

14 Favorite Moments   viii

1 The Best Full-Day Tours   7
The Best in One Day   8
The Best in Two Days   12
The Best in Three Days   16

2 The Best Special-Interest Tours   23
Historic Montréal   24
Cultural Montréal   30
Gastronomic Montréal   34
Romantic Montréal   38
High Design Montréal   42
Millennial Montréal   46
Montréal's Parks   50
Montréal with Kids   56

3 The Best Neighborhood Walks   61
Vieux-Montréal   62
Downtown Montréal   66
Plateau Mont-Royal   72
Parc du Mont-Royal   76

4 The Best Shopping   81
Shopping in Montréal   82
Shopping Best Bets   84
Shopping A to Z   85
Exploring the Underground City   91

5 The Best Dining   93
Dining Best Bets   94
Dining in the Plateau & Mile End   95
Dining in Downtown & Vieux-Montréal   96
Restaurants A to Z   98

6 The Best Nightlife   105
Nightlife Best Bets   106
Nightlife in Plateau Mont-Royal
    & the Village   107
Nightlife in Downtown Montréal   108
Nightlife A to Z   110

7 The Best Arts & Entertainment 115

Arts & Entertainment Best Bets 116
Arts & Entertainment A to Z 117
Arts & Entertainment in Montréal 118

8 The Best Hotels 123

Hotel Best Bets 124
Accommodations in Vieux-Montréal 125
Accommodations in Downtown Montréal
 & the Plateau 126
Hotels A to Z 127

9 The Best Day Trips & Excersions 133

Québec City 134
Québec City: Where to Stay 140
Québec City: Where to Dine 142
The Laurentians 144
The Laurentians: Where to Stay in
 Mont-Tremblant 148
The Laurentians: Where to Dine in
 Mont-Tremblant 149
Cantons-de-l'Est 150
Cantons-de-l'Est: Where to Stay 153
Cantons-de-l'Est: Where to Dine 154

The Savvy Traveler 155

Before You Go 156
Getting There 159
Getting Around 160
Fast Facts 162
Montréal: A Brief History 170
The Politics of Language & Identity 172
Useful Phrases & Menu Terms 173
Websites 176

Index 178

Published by:

FrommerMedia LLC

ISBN: 978-1-628-87296-5 (paper); 978-1-628-87297-2 (ebk)

Editorial Director: Pauline Frommer
Editor: Lorraine Festa
Production Editor: Donna Wright
Photo Editor: Meghan Lamb
Cartographer: Elizabeth Puhl
Indexer: Maro Riofrancos

Front cover photos, left to right: Oratoire St-Joseph/Click Images; Place d'Armes/Tourisme Montréal, Mario Melillo; Ice skating in Atrium Le 1000/© Atrium Le 1000.

Back cover photo: Place d'Armes.

For information on our other products and services, please go to Frommers.com.

Frommer's also publishes its books in a variety of electronic formats. Some content that appears in print may not be available in electronic formats.

Manufactured in China

5 4 3 2 1

About This Guide

Organizing your time. That's what this guide is all about.

Other guides give you long lists of things to see and do and then expect you to fit the pieces together. The Day by Day guides are different. These guides tell you the best of everything, and then they show you how to see it in the smartest, most time-efficient way. Our authors have designed detailed itineraries organized by time, neighborhood, or special interest. And each tour comes with a bulleted map that takes you from stop to stop.

Hoping to soak up the atmosphere of Vieux-Montréal, visit the magnificent collections of the Musée des Beaux Arts, or shop in the city's famous Underground City? Planning a stroll through Park Mont-Royal, or a whirlwind tour of the very best Montréal has to offer? Whatever your interest or schedule, the Day by Days give you the smartest routes to follow. Not only do we take you to the top attractions, hotels, and restaurants, but we also help you access those special moments that locals get to experience—those "finds" that turn tourists into travelers.

The Day by Days are also your top choice if you're looking for one complete guide for all your travel needs. The best hotels and restaurants for every budget, the greatest shopping values, the wildest nightlife—it's all here.

Why should you trust our judgment? Because our authors personally visit each place they write about. They're an independent lot who say what they think and would never include places they wouldn't recommend to their best friends. They're also open to suggestions from readers. If you'd like to contact them, please send your comments our way at feedback@frommers.com, and we'll pass them on.

Enjoy your Day by Day guide—the most helpful travel companion you can buy. And have the trip of a lifetime.

About the Authors

Leslie Brokaw has been writing for Frommer's since 2006 and is co-author of the most recent editions of *Frommer's Montréal & Québec City* along with Erin Trahan and Matthew Barber. She is based in Boston.

Erin Trahan is a Boston-based writer and editor. She has contributed to six previous Frommer's books thanks to her co-authors and her easygoing travel companions, Nate and Iris.

Matthew Barber has contributed to four previous Frommer's books, and lives in Boston with his wife, Leslie Brokaw, and their son and dog.

An Additional Note

Please be advised that travel information is subject to change at any time—and this is especially true of prices. We therefore suggest that you write or call ahead for confirmation when making your travel plans. The authors, editors, and publisher cannot be held responsible for the experiences of readers while traveling. Your safety is important to us, however, so we encourage you to stay alert and be aware of your surroundings.

Star Ratings & Icons

Every hotel, restaurant, and attraction listing in this guide has been ranked for quality, value, service, amenities, and special features using a **star-rating system.** Hotels, restaurants, attractions, shopping, and nightlife are rated on a scale of zero stars (recommended) to three stars (exceptional). In addition to the star-rating system, we also use a **kids icon** to point out the best bets for families. Within each tour, we recommend cafes, bars, or restaurants where you can take a break. Each of these stops appears in a shaded box marked with a coffee-cup-shaped bullet.

A Note on Prices

In the "Take a Break" and "Best Bets" sections of this book, we have used a system of dollar signs to show a range of costs for 1 night in a hotel (the price of a double-occupancy room) or the cost of an entree at a restaurant. Use the following table to decipher the dollar signs:

Cost	Hotels	Restaurants
C$	under C$100	under C$15
C$$	C$100–C$200	C$15–C$25
C$$$	C$200–$300	C$25–C$60
C$$$$	over C$300	over C$60

Frommers.com

Now that you have this guidebook to help you plan a great trip, visit our website at **www.frommers.com** for additional travel information on more than 3,600 destinations. We update features regularly to give you instant access to the most current trip-planning information available. At Frommers.com, you'll find scoops on the best airfares, lodging rates, and car rental bargains. You can even book your travel online through our reliable travel booking partners. Other popular features include:

- Online updates of our most popular guidebooks
- Vacation sweepstakes and contest giveaways
- Newsletters highlighting the hottest travel trends
- Online travel message boards with featured travel discussions

An Invitation to the Reader

In researching this book, we discovered many wonderful places—hotels, restaurants, shops, and more. We're sure you'll find others. Please tell us about them, so we can share the information with your fellow travelers in upcoming editions. If you were disappointed with a recommendation, we'd love to know that, too. Please write to: Support@FrommerMedia.com.

14 Favorite
Moments

14 Favorite Moments

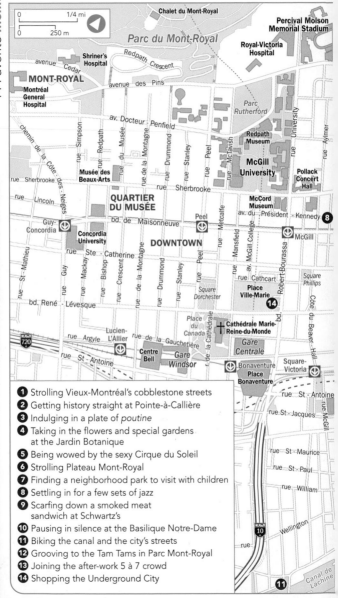

1 Strolling Vieux-Montréal's cobblestone streets
2 Getting history straight at Pointe-à-Callière
3 Indulging in a plate of *poutine*
4 Taking in the flowers and special gardens at the Jardin Botanique
5 Being wowed by the sexy Cirque du Soleil
6 Strolling Plateau Mont-Royal
7 Finding a neighborhood park to visit with children
8 Settling in for a few sets of jazz
9 Scarfing down a smoked meat sandwich at Schwartz's
10 Pausing in silence at the Basilique Notre-Dame
11 Biking the canal and the city's streets
12 Grooving to the Tam Tams in Parc Mont-Royal
13 Joining the after-work 5 à 7 crowd
14 Shopping the Underground City

Previous page: Step back in time along Vieux-Montréal's cobblestone streets.

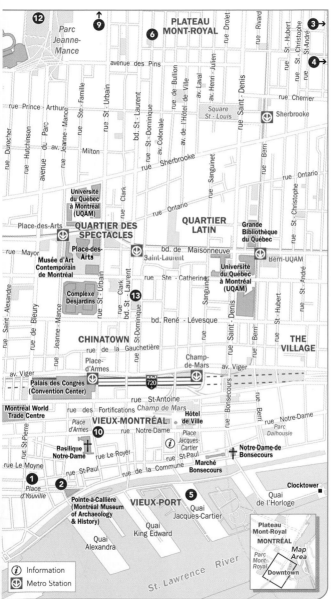

PLATEAU MONT-ROYAL

Parc Jeanne-Mance

avenue des Pins

rue Prince-Arthur

Milton

Square St-Louis

Sherbrooke

rue Cherrier

rue Ontario

Université du Québec à Montréal (UQAM)

rue Ontario

Place-des-Arts

QUARTIER DES SPECTACLES

Place-des-Arts

Musée d'Art Contemporain de Montréal

rue Mayor

QUARTIER LATIN

Grande Bibliothèque du Québec

bd. de Maisonneuve

Saint-Laurent

rue Ste-Catherine

Université du Québec à Montréal (UQAM)

Berri-UQAM

Complexe Desjardins

bd. René-Lévesque

CHINATOWN

rue de la Gauchetière

THE VILLAGE

Place-d'Armes

Champ-de-Mars

av. Viger

av. Viger

Palais des Congrès (Convention Center)

Montréal World Trade Centre

rue des Fortifications Champ de Mars

rue St-Antoine

Hôtel de Ville

rue Notre-Dame

Parc Dalhousie

Place d'Armes

VIEUX-MONTRÉAL

rue Notre-Dame

Place Jacques-Cartier

Notre-Dame-de-Bonsecours

Basilique Notre-Dame

rue Le Royer

rue St-Paul

Marché Bonsecours

rue Le Moyne

rue St-Paul

rue de la Commune

Place d'Youville

Pointe-à-Callière (Montréal Museum of Archaeology & History)

VIEUX-PORT

Quai Jacques-Cartier

Clocktower

Quai de l'Horloge

Quai King Edward

Quai Alexandra

St. Lawrence River

Plateau Mont-Royal

MONTRÉAL

Map Area

Parc Mont-Royal

Downtown

ⓘ Information

Ⓜ Metro Station

An enormous joie de vivre pervades Montréal, which celebrates its 375th anniversary in 2017. It's the largest city of the Québec province and the most French region of North America. Modern in every regard, Montréal has a beautifully preserved historic district, skyscrapers in unexpected shapes and colors, and sprawling neighborhoods of artists' lofts, boutiques, and cafes. Cold and snowy a good 8 months of the year, Montréal's calendar is packed with festivals and events that bring out natives and guests in every season. Here are 14 favorite moments in taking in this humming, bilingual metropolis.

Montréal's main square, Place Jacques-Cartier, by night.

❶ Strolling Vieux-Montréal's cobblestone streets and forgetting what year it is. Horse-drawn carriages (calèches) add to the ambience, but it's the old-world feel of the buildings that really transports you back to the 18th century. In summer, find a cafe table on the Place Jacques-Cartier, the main square. In the winter, lace up some ice skates and twirl while the snow gently falls. *See p 62.*

❷ Getting history straight at Pointe-à-Callière. In English it's called the Montréal Museum of Archaeology and History, and a first visit to Montréal might best begin here. Built on the very site where the original colony (called Pointe-à-Callière) was established in 1642, this modern museum engages in rare, beguiling ways. *See p 26.*

❸ Indulging in a plate of poutine. Unofficially the comfort food of the Québec province, *poutine* is french fries topped with cheese curds and gravy. Packed with flavor (and calories), it comes plain or dressed up

Live entertainment at the Montréal Museum of Archaeology and History.

An outdoor event at the popular Cirque Festival.

with bacon, hot peppers, or even foie gras. La Banquise in the Plateau Mont-Royal neighborhood is open 24 hours a day and has two dozen varieties to feed your need. *See p 100.*

4 Taking in the flowers and special gardens at the Jardin Botanique. The city's marvelous botanical garden spreads across 75 hectares (185 acres) and is a fragrant oasis 12 months a year. Spring, naturally, is when things really kick in, with lilacs, tulips, and glorious blooming crabapple trees. Year-round greenhouses are humid quarters to orchids, vanilla plants, and rainforest flora, while specialty areas such as the wooded First Nations Garden provide private spots to tuck away. *See p 40.*

5 Being wowed by the sexy Cirque du Soleil. The world-famous circus troupe has its home base in Montréal and usually sets up tents each spring on the quays (piers) of Vieux-Port, the Old Port district of the city. If you're in town when they are, don't pass up the chance to see the magical, mysterious, sensual show. *See p 117.*

6 Strolling Plateau Mont-Royal. Thick with boutiques, restaurants, and sidewalk cafes, the main drags of boulevard St-Laurent (known to all as "the Main") and rue St-Denis are where to find the city at play

and to join in. A directory of events and shops—from thrift stores and fashion boutiques to bakeries, nightclubs, and galleries—is online at www.boulevardsaintlaurent.com. *See p 48.*

7 Finding a neighborhood park to explore with children. Montréal's residential neighborhoods, such as the Plateau, Mile End, and Outremont, the neighborhood west of Mile End, all have well-maintained parks. Many have playgrounds that provide a bilingual oasis for children who are maxed out from sightseeing. *See p 59.*

8 Settling in for a few sets of jazz. Jazz may be the most American of art forms, but it is widely embraced by America's neighbor to the north. The monster Festival International de Jazz de Montréal celebrated its 37th year in 2016, and is an annual highlight for 11 days in July. Finding good, live jazz is easy year-round, too. *See p 113.*

9 Scarfing down a smoked meat sandwich at Schwartz's. Even with world-renowned gourmet restaurants at their beck and call, returning visitors make it a priority to get to this modest storefront for the Hebrew delicatessen's unique smoked meat. Tables are communal and packed tight. Take-out is an option, as is a midnight snack: Schwartz's is open until 12:30am

Throngs of fans descend upon Montréal for July's Festival International de Jazz.

during the week and later still on weekends. *See p 103.*

⑩ **Pausing in silence at the Basilique Notre-Dame.** Once you see the basilica's ornate and breathtaking altar, you might understand why the church's Protestant architect converted to Catholicism. *See p 63.*

⑪ **Biking the canal and the city's streets.** The Lachine Canal was inaugurated in 1824 so that ships could bypass the Lachine Rapids on the way to the Great Lakes. After much renovation, it reopened in 1997 for recreational use. It's lined with 19th-century industrial buildings (many now converted to high-end apartments) and bike paths on both sides. Meanwhile, the city boasts an expanding network of more than 600km (373 miles) of bike paths for

The mall at Place Montréal Trust in downtown's Underground City.

commuting and relaxing. Bikes are available at rental shops and from the BIXI short-term rental kiosks around the city. *See p 52 and p 161.*

⑫ **Grooving to the Tam Tams in Parc Mont-Royal.** Every Sunday in warm weather, Montréalers in the upper Plateau neighborhood wake to the sounds of hundreds of bongos at an event called Tam Tams. This weekly pandemonium of percussion draws both musicians and sunbathers. It's a Montréal tradition, so stop by in the early afternoon and sprawl out on the grass with everyone else. *See p 54.*

⑬ **Joining the after-work 5 à 7 crowd.** Happy hour here is called 5 à 7 (five to seven), and many bars have bargain drinks and appetizers. One option is Labo Culinaire (Foodlab) in the Quartier des Spectacles, on the top floor of the Société Des Arts Technologiques. It has an outdoor terrasse that in warm months is among the nicest in the city. *See p 110.*

⑭ **Shopping the Underground City.** Large shopping complexes built below many of Montréal's busiest buildings are connected by a huge maze of pedestrian tunnels—there's a subterranean town down there. It's a public project where everyone benefits: the city, the vendors, the shoppers. It's an especially appealing option during the bitterest of winter days. *See p 91.* ●

Sherbrooke

MUSÉE DES BEAUX-ARTS DE MON

The Best **in One Day**

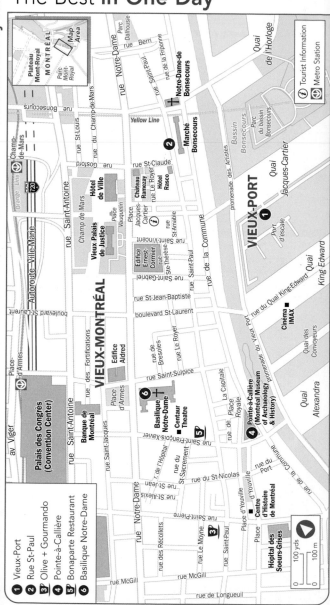

Previous page: Montréal's grand Museum of Fine Arts.

Center your first day in Montréal around the sites and atmosphere of the oldest and most historic part of the city: Vieux-Montréal. The city was born here in 1642, down by the river at Pointe-à-Callière. Its southern boundary is Vieux-Port (Old Port), a waterfront promenade that provides welcome breathing room for cyclists, in-line skaters, and picnickers, and it extends north to rue St-Antoine, once the "Wall Street" of Montréal. Read up ahead of time at the neighborhood's official website, www.vieux.montreal. qc.ca. START: **Take the Métro to the Place d'Armes station and head down rue St-Sulpice to the river.**

Canada Day celebration at Vieux-Port.

❶ ★★★ kids **Vieux-Port.** Montréal's Old Port has been central to its commercial and economic status

Montréal's charming and historic rue St-Paul is home to numerous galleries, shops, restaurants, and bars.

over the last 200 years, but the port was a dreary area of town until it got a facelift in the 1990s. Now the converted waterfront and its piers, or quays, are a playground year-round for families, strolling couples, and outdoor athletes. In winter, ice skating rinks are set up here. The popular children's science museum, **Centre des Sciences de Montréal,** is located on Quai King Edward, and includes good special exhibits and an onsite IMAX theater (p 121, bullet ❶). From June to September, **a miniature electric train** (board in in front of the museum) scoots along the length of the port, and in 2015 Canada's first **urban zipline** circuit set up shop here. **Cruise companies** also leave from here on daytime trips along the St. Lawrence River. Bikers can pop into **ÇaRoule/Montréal on Wheels** (27 rue de la Commune est; ☎ 877/866-0633 or 514/866-0633; www.caroulemontreal.com) and pick up a bike to head out on the path along the adjacent Lachine Canal. Activities continue in the cold months, when an expansive **ice skating rink** becomes the focal point. ⏱ *At least 2 hr. www.oldport ofmontreal.com.* ☎ *800/971-7678 or 514/496-7678. Mini train rides C\$4. Zipline \$C20. Ice skating C\$7 adults, C\$5 children 6–12, free 5 and under. Skate rentals available. Métro: Champ-de-Mars, Place d'Armes, or Square Victoria.*

❷ ★★★ **Rue St-Paul.** The quaint main street of Vieux-Montréal (in English, Old Montréal) is full of bistros, shops, bars, art galleries, and historical venues. Start at the eastern end, near the **Marché Bonsecours** (350 rue St-Paul est). Built in the mid-1800s and first used as the Parliament of United Canada, Bonsecours market is now home to restaurants, art galleries, and boutiques featuring Québécois

Re-enacting the New France period in Old Montréal.

products. As you travel west on rue St-Paul you'll pass through **Place Jacques-Cartier**, the neighborhood's main square. At the northern end of the plaza is the green turreted **Hôtel de Ville,** Montréal's City Hall. In recent years, many decent art galleries have sprung up alongside the loud souvenir shops on the street, and some of our recommended restaurants are right here, too (see chapter 5). *Important navigational note:* Street numbers will get lower as you approach boulevard St-Laurent, which is the north-south thoroughfare that divides Montréal into its east and west halves. Numbers will start to rise again as you move onto rue St-Paul ouest (west). ⏱ *At least 1 hr. Métro: Champ-de-Mars.*

The impressive Hôtel de Ville, Montréal's old City Hall, sports a new bronze roof.

It started out as an earthy bakery painted in reds, pinks, and gold curlicues, but now ❸ **Olive + Gourmando** is a full-fledged cafe offering up croissants, scones, and hearty fare such as its Cuban sandwich, truffle mac & cheese, and fancy grilled cheese The only pity that this eminently appealing spot is only open for lunch, Tuesday through Saturday. *351 rue St-Paul ouest.* ☎ *514/350-1083. www.oliveetgourmando.com. \$.*

❹ ★★★ **Pointe-à-Callière.** A first visit to Montréal should include a stop at this Museum of Archaeology and History. Evidence of the area's many inhabitants—from Québec's earliest native tribes to French trappers to Scottish merchants—was unearthed during archaeological digs here, the site of Montréal's original colony. Artifacts are on view in display cases set among the ancient building foundations and burial grounds below street level. After starting with the 16-minute multimedia show in an auditorium that actually stands above exposed ruins of the earlier city, you can wind your way through the subterranean complex until you find yourself in the former **Customs House,** where there are more exhibits and a well-stocked gift shop. ⏱ 1½ hr. 350 Place Royale. www.pacmuseum.qc.ca. ☎ 514/872-9150. Admission C$20 adults, with discounts for seniors, students, and children, free for children 4 and under. June to mid-Oct daily 9:30am–6pm; mid-Oct to May Tues–Fri 10am–5pm, Sat–Sun 11am–5pm. Métro: Place d'Armes.

At the elegant ❺ **Bonaparte Restaurant,** adroit service is provided by schooled pros who manage to be knowledgeable without

The stunning Basilique Notre-Dame de Montréal.

being stuffy. Highlights have included snails and oyster mushrooms in phyllo dough, Dover sole filet with fresh herbs, and mushroom ravioli seasoned with fresh sage. Look for the table d'hôte specials for the best deal: C$16 to C$26 in the evening. 447 rue St-François-Xavier. www.bonaparte. com. ☎ 514/844-4368. $$.

❻ ★★ **Basilique Notre-Dame de Montréal.** This magnificent structure was designed in 1824 by James O'Donnell, an Irish-American Protestant architect from New York—who was so profoundly moved by the experience of creating this basilica that he converted to Catholicism after its completion. The impact is understandable. Of Montréal's hundreds of churches, Notre-Dame's interior is the most stunning, with a wealth of exquisite details, including carved rare woods that have been delicately gilded and painted. ⏱ 30 min. 110 rue Notre-Dame ouest. www. basiliquenddm.org. ☎ 514/842-2925. Basilica admission C$5 adults, C$4 children 7–17, free for 6 and under and for those attending services. Daily at least 7:30am–4pm. Métro: Place d'Armes.

The old Customs House.

The Best **in Two Days**

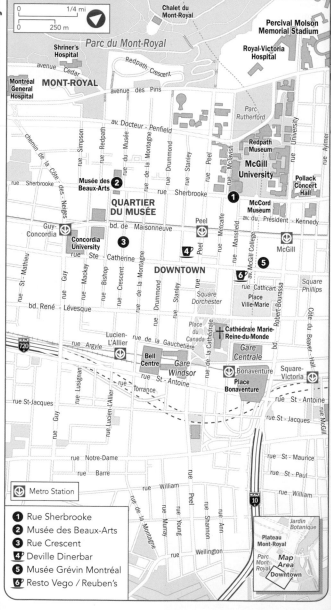

| 0 | 1/4 mi |
| 0 | 250 m |

Chalet du Mont-Royal

Percival Molson Memorial Stadium

Parc du Mont-Royal

Shriner's Hospital

Royal-Victoria Hospital

avenue Cedar

MONT-ROYAL

Redpath Crescent

Montréal General Hospital

avenue des Pins

Parc Rutherford

av. Docteur - Penfield

chemin de la Côte - des - Neiges

rue Simpson
rue Redpath
rue du Musée
rue de la Montagne
rue Drummond
rue Stanley
rue Peel
McTavish
University
Aylmer

Redpath Museum

McGill University

rue Sherbrooke

Musée des Beaux-Arts ❷

rue Sherbrooke

❶

Pollack Concert Hall

QUARTIER DU MUSÉE

McCord Museum

av. du - Président - Kennedy

Guy-Concordia 🔘

bd. de Maisonneuve

Peel 🔘

rue Metcalfe
rue Mansfield

🔘 McGill

Concordia University

rue Ste - Catherine

❸

Peel

4⁴

av. McGill College

5

DOWNTOWN

6⁶

rue Cathcart

Place Ville-Marie

Square Phillips

rue St-Mathieu
rue Guy
rue Mackay
rue Bishop
rue Crescent
rue de la Montagne
rue Drummond
rue Stanley

Square Dorchester

Côte - du - Beaver - Hall

bd. René - Lévesque

Place du Canada

Cathédrale Marie-Reine-du-Monde

rue de la Cathédrale

Robert-Bourassa

720

rue Argyle

Lucien-L'Allier 🔘

rue de la Gauchetière

Gare Centrale

Square-Victoria 🔘

Bell Centre

Gare Windsor

🔘 Bonaventure

rue Lusignan
rue Lucien-L'Allier

rue St-Antoine

Place Bonaventure

rue Torrance

rue St - Antoine

rue St-Jacques

rue St - Jacques

rue McGill

rue Guy

rue Notre-Dame

rue St - Maurice

rue Barre

rue St - Paul

rue William

rue Peel
rue Shannon
rue Ann

rue William

10

Jardin Botanique

🔘 Metro Station

rue de la Montagne
rue Murray
rue Young

rue Wellington

Plateau Mont-Royal

Parc Mont-Royal

Map Area

Downtown

❶ Rue Sherbrooke
❷ Musée des Beaux-Arts
❸ Rue Crescent
4⁴ Deville Dinerbar
5 Musée Grévin Montréal
6⁶ Resto Vego / Reuben's

After soaking in the sights and sounds and tastes of the oldest section of the city on day one, spend day two in the heart of Montréal's business district. Here you'll find the bustle and energy of a city at work, and some of Montréal's grand promenades and cultural offerings. START: **McGill station, and walk north 2 blocks on rue University to rue Sherbrooke.**

❶ ★★ kids Rue Sherbrooke. This broad boulevard is the heart of what's known as Montréal's "Golden Square Mile." This is where the city's most luxurious residences of the 19th and early 20th centuries were, and where the vast majority of the country's wealthiest citizens lived. (For a period of time, 79 families who lived in this neighborhood controlled 80% of Canada's wealth.) Starting at the cross street rue McGill and heading west on rue Sherbrooke, the main campus of Canada's most prestigious school, **McGill University,** is on your right. Inside the campus is the

Palatial buildings abound along rue Sherbrooke—many were once residences of Montréal's wealthiest citizens.

well-regarded **Redpath Museum,** the oldest building in Canada (1882) built specifically as a museum. At 690 rue Sherbrooke ouest is **Musée McCord,** a museum of Canadian history that has a contemporary, playful zest. It maintains an eclectic collection of photographs, paintings, and First Nations folk art, and its edgy special exhibits make it especially worth a visit. ⏱ *At least 15 min. Musée McCord www.mcgill.ca/redpath.* ☎ *514/398-4086. Free admission (contributions of C$5 adults and C$2 children suggested). Mon–Fri 9am–5pm; Sun 11am–5pm (summer Sun 1–5pm).*

❷ ★★★ Musée des Beaux-Arts. Montréal's grand Museum of Fine Arts, the city's most prominent museum, was Canada's first building designed specifically for the visual arts. Enter through the modern annex on the left side of rue Sherbrooke, which was added in 1991; it is connected to the original stately Beaux Arts building (1912) on the right side by an underground tunnel that doubles as a gallery. The adjacent church, which has Tiffany windows, was converted in 2011 into an addition to the museum, although it can only be visited on guided tours or when attending a classical concert there. The permanent collection is extensive, but many come for the temporary exhibitions, which can be dazzling. Past highlights have included the dazzling glassworks of Dale Chihuly, treasures of Catherine the Great, including her

Canada's prestigious McGill University.

the afternoons and evenings. The party spills over onto nearby streets, with both **Maison du Jazz** (2060 rue Aylmer; ☎ 514/842-8656; www.houseofjazz.ca) and **Upstairs Jazz Bar & Grill** (1254 rue Mackay; ☎ 514/931-6808; www.upstairsjazz.com) presenting great music options. ⏱ *At least 30 min. See chapter 6 for venue details. Métro: Peel.*

The splashy downtown restaurant **4** ★ **Deville Dinerbar** is packed with businesspeople at lunchtime and a partying crowd at night. It claims to take its cue from American diners, but that goes only as far as its use of booths for some of the seating and its enormous portions; you'd be hard pressed to find an American diner with a marble bar, sparkly chandeliers, or a reputation for killer fish tacos. Choices include salads, sandwiches, burgers, pastas, and specialties such as lamb shanks, diver scallops, and chicken schnitzel with spaetzle. *1425 Stanley St. www.devilledinerbar.com.* ☎ *514/281-6556. $$.*

spectacular coronation coach, and a show on the opulence of Pompeii. ⏱ *2 hr. 1380 rue Sherbrooke ouest. www.mmfa.qc.ca.* ☎ *514/285-2000. Permanent collection C$12 adults 31 and over, free for ages 30 and under; free for adults 65 and over on Thurs. Admission to temporary exhibitions (includes entrance to permanent collection) C$20 adults 31 and over, C$12 ages 13–30, free for children 12 and under. Wed 5–9pm C$10 ages 13 and up. Tues–Sun 10am–5pm plus Wed until 9pm. Métro: Guy-Concordia.*

3 ★ **Rue Crescent.** Downtown's party central. Crescent's most northern block is stocked with boutiques and jewelers, but the next 2 blocks are a gumbo of terraced bars and dance clubs, inexpensive pizza joints, and upscale restaurants. **Newtown** (no. 1476), **Sir Winston Churchill Pub** (no. 1459), **Hurley's Irish Pub** (no. 1225), and **Brutopia** (no. 1219) are among the venues that draw hundreds (and often thousands) to the street in

The jardin de sculptures at Musée des beaux-arts de Montréal.

Popular rue Crescent is home to trendy shops and restaurants, and it's the heart of downtown Montréal's nightlife.

❺ ★★ Musée Grévin Montréal.

An offshoot of the popular Musée Grévin wax museum in Paris, this Canada-rich version opened in 2013 and has become a top attraction. The tone is set with a dimly lit hallway with thousands of color-changing fiber optic threads hanging from the ceiling and a 5-minute video of psychedelic nature scenes accompanied by booming music. The goal is to disorient you from the outside world, and that it does. Sound effects and music play as you visit with lifelike replicas of figures that are grouped by theme. Early on there's a heavy focus on Canadian personalities and historic New France characters dating back to Québec's beginnings in the 16th century, while in the Ballroom entertainers including Céline Dion, Lady Gaga, and Brad Pitt fill a star-studded room. If you're traveling with kids below age 5, we recommend having a backup plan—we witnessed several young children who got spooked by the unmoving but lifelike statues. ⏱ *at least 30 min. 705 rue Ste-Catherine ouest. www.grevin-montreal.com.* ☎ *514/788-5211. Admission C$20 adults, with discounts for students and seniors; C$14 for children ages 6–12; free for children 5 and under. Mon–Sat 10am–6pm; Sun 11am–5pm. Métro: McGill.*

☕ **Resto Vego** presents vegetarian fare buffet style, and you pay by weight—about C$12 for an ample portion. Dishes include garbanzo curry, veggie lasagna, salads, and so on. A second-floor location at the corner of rue Ste-Catherine lets you watch the world go by. Directly downstairs is the well-regarded meat-centric deli ☕ **Reuben's** if you're traveling with someone tofu-adverse. *Resto Vego 1204 av. McGill College. www.restovego.ca.* ☎ *514/871-1480. $. Reuben's 1116 rue Ste-Catherine ouest. www.reubensdeli.com.* ☎ *514/866-1029. $.*

Sir Winston Churchill Pub.

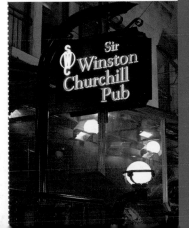

The Best **in Three Days**

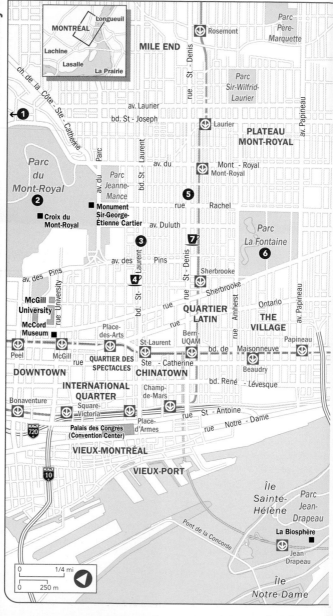

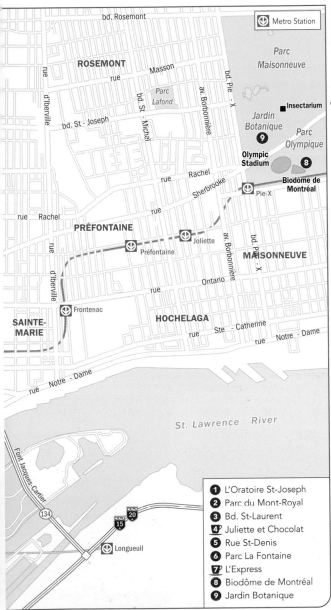

bd. Rosemont

🔽 Metro Station

Parc Maisonneuve

ROSEMONT

rue d'Iberville

rue Masson

bd. St - Michel

Parc Lafond

bd. St - Joseph

av. Borbonnière

bd. Pie - X

■ Insectarium

Jardin Botanique ⑨

Parc Olympique

Olympic Stadium

⑧

Biodôme de Montréal

rue Rachel

Sherbrooke

🔽 Pie-X

rue

rue Rachel

PRÉFONTAINE

rue d'Iberville

🔽 Préfontaine

🔽 Joliette

av. Borbonnière

bd. Pie - X

MAISONNEUVE

rue Ontario

🔽 Frontenac

SAINTE-MARIE

HOCHELAGA

rue Ste - Catherine

rue Notre - Dame

rue Notre - Dame

St. Lawrence River

Pont Jacques-Cartier

(134)

🛣 20 15

🔽 Longueuil

① L'Oratoire St-Joseph
② Parc du Mont-Royal
③ Bd. St-Laurent
④ Juliette et Chocolat
⑤ Rue St-Denis
⑥ Parc La Fontaine
⑦ L'Express
⑧ Biodôme de Montréal
⑨ Jardin Botanique

The first two recommended days of sightseeing are focused around two relatively compact neighborhoods of the city. For the third day, pick and choose among some of the best parks and strolling areas north of the city's downtown. Like with any great city, people-watching and soaking up its outdoor spirit are as rewarding as visiting its cultural institutions.

❶ ★ L'Oratoire St-Joseph.

This enormous copper-domed structure is one of the most recognizable in Montréal, although to see it in person you'll need to trek to the northern side of Mont-Royal (the small mountain just north of downtown, from which the city derives its name). Consecrated as a basilica in 2004, it came into being through the efforts of Brother André, a lay brother in the Holy Cross order who earned a reputation as a healer. By the time he had built a small wooden chapel in 1904 on the mountain, he was said to have performed hundreds of cures. He performed his work until his death in 1937. In 1982, he was beatified by the pope—a status one step below sainthood—and in 2010 he earned the distinction of sainthood, too. There's a Facebook page in his name maintained by the church, at www.facebook.com/saintfrereandre. Many still visit in the hopes of a miracle, sometimes climbing the 99 steps on their knees. Others come to hear the 56-bell carillon, which plays Wednesday to Friday at noon and 3pm, Saturday at noon at 2:30pm, and Sunday at 12:15 and 2:30pm. A new visitor's center and an observatory at the top of the basilica's dome are expected to be complete by the end of 2017. ⏱ *1 hr. 3800 chemin Queen Mary (north slope of Mont-Royal). www.saint-joseph.org.* ☎ *877/672-8647 or 514/733-8211. Free admission to most sights, donations requested; oratory museum C$4 adults, C$3 seniors and* students, C$2 children 6–17. Open daily 10am–4:30pm and weekends July–Aug until 5:30pm. Métro: Côte-des-Neiges.

❷ ★★ Parc du Mont-Royal.

Renowned landscape architect Frederick Law Olmsted (1822–1903), who designed New York's Central Park, left his mark on Montréal in Parc du Mont-Royal (Royal Mountain Park). The 232m (761-ft.) peak for which the city is named provides Montréalers with a slew of options for recreational activities. Strollers and joggers trek the miles of paths that snake through the park and sunbathers hang out near man-made Beaver Lake in summer. In winter, there's cross-country skiing and tobogganing. Shutterbugs can snap panoramic photos from the

Religious pilgrims flock to the L'Oratoire St-Joseph in search of miraculous healing.

The view from Parc du Mont-Royal is one of the best in the city.

Chalet du Mont-Royal's terrace at the crest of the hill. **Maison Smith** (1260 chemin Remembrance; www. lemontroyal.qc.ca. ☎ 514/843-8240), an information center on the road that runs between the park and the Notre-Dame-des-Neiges Cemetery to the north, has maps for hiking or birding and a sweet cafe. We offer a suggested walking tour on p 76. 🕓 *At least 2 hr. There are several entry points to the park, including at av. des Pins and rue Peel. Métro: Peel for the south side, Côte-des-Neiges for the north. Bus: #11 travels along chemin Remembrance.*

❸ ★★ **Boulevard St-Laurent.** Also known as "the Main," St-Laurent hums with offbeat boutiques, bars, and restaurants, drawing shoppers, students, and sightseers. Spend some time snacking and people-watching your way along the boulevard, perhaps starting at rue Sherbrooke and heading north. When the sun goes down, the street becomes a 20-somethings' playground—the bars and dance clubs here are popular with the city's college undergrads. Note that St-Laurent is the dividing line of the city: Addresses to its left are all on the west side, and to the right all on the east. 🕓 *At least 1½ hr. Bd. St-Laurent, north of rue Sherbrooke to av. du Mont-Royal. Métro: St-Laurent.*

Street art murals line the streets of Montréal, especially along Boulevard Saint-Laurent.

4 **Juliette et Chocolat** fills the broad need of coffee house, luncheonette, and purveyor of exceptional chocolate desserts. You can also order wine or beer, and savory options, too, such as buckwheat crêpes and a salad with dark chocolate vinaigrette. Chocolate comes in all forms: as hot and cold beverages, in crepes, in dense brownies (11 kinds!), as sauce over ice cream, in fondue. Take-home goodies like chocolate shaped into fried-egg or avocado forms add to the fun. *3600 bd. St-Laurent. www.julietteetchocolat. com.* ☎ *438/380-1090. Sun–Thurs 11am–11pm; Fri–Sat 11am–midnight. Métro: Sherbrooke. $.*

5 ★★ **Rue St-Denis.** Parallel to boulevard St-Laurent and 8 short blocks to the east, rue St-Denis also runs the length of the Plateau Mont-Royal district. It is to Montréal what boulevard St-Germain is to Paris, with shopkeepers and people on the street more likely to speak just French here than on other major boulevards in town. It extends from the Quartier Latin straight north, with some of the most interesting blocks between rue Sherbrooke and av. du Mont-Royal. ⏱ *At least 1½ hr. Rue St-Denis, north of rue Sherbrooke to av. du Mont-Royal. Métro: Sherbrooke.*

6 ★ **Parc La Fontaine.** One of the city's oldest and most popular parks, this park is especially pretty and well used on its northern side. Illustrating the traditional dual identities of the city's populace, half the park is landscaped in the formal French manner, the other in the more casual English style. A small, picturesque lake is used for ice skating in winter, when snowshoe and cross-country trails wind through trees. In summer, these trails are well-used bike paths. ⏱ *1 hr. The park can be entered anywhere on its perimeter. Métro: Mont-Royal.*

Open for breakfast, lunch, and dinner 7 days a week, **7** **L'Express** is the most classic of Parisian-style bistros. From the black-and-white-checkered floor to the grand, high ceilings to the classic cuisine, this is where Old France meets New France. Popular dishes include the homemade ravioli, the croque-monsieur, and maple sugar pie. *See p 101.*

The captivating rainforest section of the Biodôme de Montréal.

Montréal's botanical gardens are among the largest and most beautiful in the world.

❽ ★★★ kids Biodôme de Montréal. A terrifically engaging attraction for children of any age, the delightful Biodôme houses replications of four ecosystems: a tropical rainforest, a Laurentian forest, the St. Lawrence marine system, and a polar environment. Visitors walk through each and hear the animals, smell the flora, and, except in the polar region, which is behind glass, feel the changes in temperature. The rainforest area is the most engrossing and includes golden lion tamarin monkeys that swing on branches only an arm's length away. (Bats, fish, penguins, and puffins are behind glass.) It's next to the Stade Olympique (Olympic Stadium). ⏱ *2 hr. 4777 av. Pierre-de-Coubertin (next to Stade Olympique). www.espacepourlavie.ca/en/biodome.* ☎ *514/868-3000. Admission C$19 adults, C$18 seniors, C$14 students, C$10 children 5–17. Check the website for hours, which change seasonally. Métro: Viau.*

❾ ★★★ Jardin Botanique. Montréal's sprawling 75-hectare (185-acre) botanical garden is home to 10 themed exhibition greenhouses. One houses orchids; another has tropical food and spice plants, including coffee, cashews, and vanilla; another features rainforest flora. In a special exhibit each spring, live butterflies flutter among the nectar-bearing plants, occasionally landing on visitors. Spring is when things really kick in: lilacs, tulips, and blooming crabapple trees in May, lilies in June, and roses from mid-June until the first frost. The garden has hosted a popular **Gardens of Light Chinese Lantern Festival** in autumn, with magical colored lanterns lighting the paths; check the calendar to see if this program is scheduled. Otherwise, take in the **Chinese Garden,** a joint project of Montréal and

Kids love the Botanical Garden's playground.

City of Festivals

Few cities in North America can rival Montréal when it comes to celebrations. Throughout the year, the city is home to some of the biggest and most heralded festivals in the world, and attending one can make for a very memorable vacation. Among the options to plan around: **Montréal Bike Fest,** which includes a nocturnal bike ride (Tour la Nuit) and the grueling Tour de l'Île, a 52km (32-mile) race around the island's rim (May); **Les FrancoFolies de Montréal,** featuring French-language pop, hip-hop, electronic, and world beat music (June); and the city's signature event, the **Festival International de Jazz,** which hosts huge acts and free outdoor performances, many right on downtown's streets and plazas (July). Book a hotel room well in advance if you're visiting during these big parties. For details, see "Festivals & Special Events" on p 156.

Shanghai, which evokes the 14th- to 17th-century era of the Ming Dynasty and was built according to the landscape principles of yin and yang; the serene **Japanese Garden,** which has tea ceremonies and a stunning bonsai collection with miniature trees as old as 350 years; or the wooded **First Nations Garden,** which highlights Native knowledge of plants and the agricultural focus on the "three sisters" of corn, beans, and squash. The grounds

are also home to the **Insectarium** (p 60, bullet **9**), designed especially for kids. ⏱ *At least 2 hr. 4101 rue Sherbrooke est (opposite Olympic Stadium). www.espacepourlavie.ca/ en/botanical-garden.* ☎ *514/872-1400. Admission C$19 adults, C$18 seniors, C$14 students, C$10 children 5–17. Check the website for hours, which change seasonally. Admission includes access to the Insectarium. No bicycles or dogs. Métro: Pie-IX.* ●

2 The Best Special-Interest Tours

Historic Montréal

0   1/4 mi
0   250 m

Parc Jeanne-Mance

Jardin Botanique

Plateau Mont-Royal

Parc Mont-Royal

Map Area DOWN-TOWN

Royal-Victoria Hospital

Percival Molson Memorial Stadium

avenue des Pins

Parc Rutherford

rue Prince - Arthur

rue Ste - Famille

rue St - Urbain

rue St - Laurent

rue St - Dominique

av. Coloniale

rue de Bullion

rue de l'Hôtel de Ville

av. du Laval

Redpath Museum

McGill University

rue Aylmer

rue Durocher

rue Hutchinson

avenue du Parc

avenue Jeanne - Mance

Milton

Pollack Concert Hall

rue Sherbrooke

rue Clark

Musée McCord (McCord Museum) **1**

2

Université du Québec à Montréal (UQAM)

rue Ontario

QUARTIER LATIN

av. du Président - Kennedy

Place-des-Arts

QUARTIER DES SPECTACLES

rue Metcalfe

rue Mansfield

av. McGill College

bd. de Maisonneuve

McGill

rue Mayor

Place-des-Arts

Saint-Laurent

rue Ste - Catherine

Musée d'art contemporain

rue Ste - Catherine

rue Cathcart

Square Phillips

Alexandre

Bleury

Mance

rue St - Urbain

Clark

St - Laurent

rue St - Dominique

Place Ville-Marie

Robert-Bourassa

Côte du Beaver - Hall

rue Saint-

de

Jeanne -

Complexe Desjardins

rue

bd. René - Lévesque

Cathédrale Marie-Reine-du-Monde

CHINATOWN

Gare Centrale

rue de la Gauchetière

Bonaventure

Square-Victoria

Place Bonaventure

av. Viger

Place-d'Armes

Champ-de-Mars

720

rue St - Antoine

Montreal Convention Centre

rue St-Antoine

Champ de Mars

720

rue St - Jacques

Montreal World Trade Centre

rue des Fortifications

Hôtel de Ville

rue McGill

rue St-Pierre

Place d'Armes

VIEUX-MONTRÉAL

rue Notre-Dame

5

Place Jacques-Cartier

rue Notre-Dame

Basilique Notre-Dame

rue St - Maurice

rue Le Royer

rue St - Paul

rue Le Moyne

rue St-Paul

rue de la Commune

10

rue William

Place d'Youville

4 2

3

Montreal Museum of Anthropolgy & History

VIEUX-PORT

Quai Jacques-Cartier

Quai King Edward

Quai Alexandra

St. Lawrence River

1 Musée McCord
2 Site of the Amerindian Hochelaga Settlement
3 Pointe-à-Callière
4 Marché de la Villete
5 Musée du Château Ramezay

(i) Information
(Metro) Metro station

Previous page: Sightseeing ships and a view of the Montréal skyline.

irst Nations vs. Europeans. French vs. British. Peace vs. war. Montréal history is thick with both tranquility and strife. The city wears its history proudly on its sleeve: In no other place in North America does the richness of 400 years of nation building continue to be as discussed, dissected, and celebrated as it is in Montréal and its sister city, Québec City, to the north.
START: **Métro: McGill.**

❶ ★★ Musée McCord. This museum is fresh at each visit and boasts two appealing permanent exhibitions: "Montréal: Points of View," touching on the lives of first inhabitants and the spirit of the city today, and "Wearing Our Identity: The First People's Collection," which presents a respectful look at the relationship of the region's First Nations to their clothing, which often is made of animal pelts. Temporary exhibitions are edgier and have included the first major retrospective of fashion photographer Horst (a frequent contributor to *Vogue* in the 20th century) and a collection of "queer baroque" ceramics works. The museum has a collection of online exhibits that give a taste of its playful voice. A strong museum shop features locally made bags and jewelry, aboriginal artwork, and children's toys. Each exhibition is small, and

"Burning of Hayes House, Dalhousie Square, Montreal," by James Duncan, at Musée McCord.

won't take most visitors more than 15 minutes each, but there usually are at least two temporary shows in addition to the permanent displays. ⏱ *1 hr. See p 13, bullet* ❶.

Catch a glimpse of Canadian history at Musée McCord.

Today's First Nations

Native sovereignty and "the land question," notes prominent filmmaker Alanis Obomsawin, "have been issues since the French and English first settled the area. A lot of promises were made and never kept." A member of the Abenaki Nation who was raised on the Odanak Reserve near Montréal, Obomsawin provides unflinching looks at that tension and at the lives of contemporary Native Americans, who are referred to collectively in the Québec province as members of the First Nations. She began making movies for the National Film Board of Canada in 1967 and has produced more than 30 documentaries about the hard edges of the lives of aboriginal people. Termed "the first lady of First Nations film" by the commissioner of the film board in 2008, Obomsawin received the Governor General's Performing Arts Award for Lifetime Artistic Achievement that year.

One of her major works is *Kanehsatake: 270 Years of Resistance* (1993). It details a wrenching incident in 1990 that pitted native peoples against the government over lands about an hour west of Montréal that were slated to be turned into a golf course. The clash degenerated into a months-long armed standoff between Mohawks and authorities. "What the confrontation of 1990 showed is that this is a generation that is not going to put up with what happened in the past," says Obomsawin. Her movies are available through the National Film Board (www.nfb.ca).

Marker for the site of the Amerindian Horchelaga Settlement.

❷ Site of the Amerindian Hochelaga Settlement. On rue Sherbrooke, just to the left of the main gate of McGill University, a stone on the lawn marks the spot of the village of Hochelaga, a community of Iroquois who lived and farmed here before the first Europeans arrived. When French explorer Jacques Cartier stepped from his ship onto the land and visited Hochelaga in 1535, he noted that the village had 50 large homes, each housing several families. When the French returned in 1603, the village was empty. ⏲ *10 min. Near 845 rue Sherbrooke ouest. Métro: McGill.*

❸ ★★★ Pointe-à-Callière. Built on the very site where the original colony of Montréal was

The Pointe-à-Callière history museum sits on the exact location of the city's founding.

Just around the corner from Pointe-à-Callière, **4 Marché de la Villette** offers a traditional French snack or meal. It started life as an atmospheric boucherie and charcuterie market specializing in cheeses, meats, and breads, and started adding tables. The staff is flirty and welcoming to the locals and waves of tourists who settle in. We return regularly for the hearty cassoulet de maison, which is packed with duck confit, pork belly, homemade sausage, and silky smooth beans, all topped with crunchy bread crumbs. *324 rue St-Paul ouest. www.marche-villette.com* ☎ *514/807-8084. $$.*

established in 1642, this modern Museum of Archaeology and History provides details on the region's inhabitants, from Amerindians to French trappers to Scottish merchants. The 18-minute multimedia show "Yours Truly, Montréal" keeps the history slick and painless. ⏲ *1½ hr. See p 11, bullet* **4**.

5 Musée du Château Ramezay. Claude de Ramezay, the colony's 11th governor, built this château as his residence in 1705. It was home to the city's royal French governors for almost 4 decades, until Ramezay's heirs sold it to a trading company in 1745. Fifteen years later, British

Marguerite Bourgeoys

One of the "first women" of Montréal is Marguerite Bourgeoys (1620–1700), a teacher who traveled from France in the mid–17th century to join the nascent New France colony of 50 people. She was 33 when she arrived. She built schools for both the settlers and native children, and cofounded the Congregation of Notre-Dame, Canada's first nuns' order. The settlement prospered, contained until the 1800s in the area known today as Vieux-Montréal. Bourgeoys was canonized in 1982 as the Canadian church's first female saint.

The Musée Marguerite-Bourgeoys is devoted to relating Bourgeoys' life and work. It's housed in a restored 18th-century crypt in the Chapelle Notre-Dame-de-Bon-Secours (p 64, bullet **9**), in Vieux-Montréal. For the chapel's 350th birthday, Marguerite's remains were brought to the church and interred in the altar.

1759: Britain Takes Québec City from France

It can't be overstated how much the British and French struggle for dominance in the 1700s and 1800s for North America—the New World—continues to shape the character of the Québec province today. A bit of history is in order. In 1607, a group of British entrepreneurs under a charter from King James I sailed west and founded the British colony of Jamestown, in what would later become Virginia. French explorer Samuel de Champlain arrived in Québec City a year later, determined to establish a French colony on the North American continent as well.

By the 1750s, the constant struggle between Britain and France for dominance in the Canadian region had escalated. The French appointed General Louis Joseph, marquis de Montcalm, to command their forces in Québec City. The British sent an expedition of 4,500 men in a fleet under the command of General James Wolfe. The British troops surprised the French by coming up and over the cliffs of Québec City's Cap Diamant, and the ensuing skirmish, fought on September 13, 1759, lasted 18 to 25 minutes, depending on whose account you read. It resulted in 600 casualties, including both generals.

The battle had a significant impact on the future of North America. Britain was victorious, and as a result, the continent remained under English influence for more than a century. That authority carries on today: Queen Elizabeth II's face graces all Canadian currency.

The museum located under the Chapelle Notre-Dame-de-Bon-Secours offers visitors a glimpse into the life of Marguerite Bourgeoys.

conquerors took it over, and then in 1775 an army of American revolutionaries invaded Montréal and used the château as their headquarters. For 6 weeks in 1776, Benjamin Franklin spent his days here, trying to persuade the Québécois to rise with the American colonists against British rule (he failed). Exhibits about natives and the New World, the fur trade, and New France share space with old portraits, Amerindian artifacts, and other memorabilia related to the economic and social activities of the 18th and 19th centuries. ⏱ 1 hr. 280 rue Notre-Dame est. www.chateauramezay.qc.ca.

Musée du Château Ramezay explores recreations of the 18th century.

☎ 514/861-3708. Admission C$10 adults, with discounts for students, children, and seniors; free for children 4 and under. Free admission to governor's garden. June to mid-Oct daily 9:30am–6pm; mid-Oct to May Tues–Sun 10am–4:30pm. Métro: Champ-de-Mars.

The Language of Separatism

The defining dialectic of Canadian life is culture and language, and they're thorny issues that have long threatened to tear the country apart. Many Québécois have long believed that making their province a separate, independent state is the only way to maintain their rich French culture in the face of the Anglophone (English-speaking) ocean that surrounds them. Québec's role within the Canadian federation has been the most debated and volatile topic of conversation in Canadian politics for the past 50 years. The tension is long simmering: After France lost power in Québec to the British in the 18th century, a kind of linguistic exclusionism developed, with wealthy Scottish and English bankers and merchants denying French-Canadians access to upper levels of business and government. The bias continued well into the 20th century.

The separatist movement began in earnest when René Lévesque founded the Parti Québécois (PQ) in 1968. The PQ became the governing party in 1976, and in 1977 passed Bill 101, which all but banned the use of English on public signage. French remains the state language across the Québec province, and all signs are still required to be in French.

Cultural Montréal

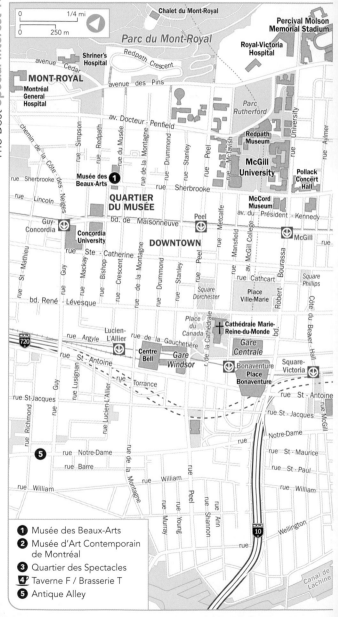

1 Musée des Beaux-Arts
2 Musée d'Art Contemporain de Montréal
3 Quartier des Spectacles
4 Taverne F / Brasserie T
5 Antique Alley

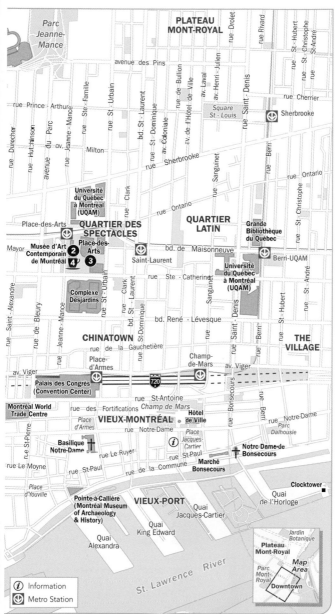

Parc
Jeanne-
Mance

PLATEAU
MONT-ROYAL

rue Rivard

rue St-Hubert

rue St-Christophe

rue St-André

rue Drolet

avenue des Pins

rue de Bullion

rue de l'Hôtel-de-Ville

av. Laval

av. Henri-Julien

rue Saint - Denis

rue Cherrier

rue Prince - Arthure

rue Ste-Famille

rue St-Urbain

bd. St-Laurent

rue St-Dominique

av. Coloniale

Square
St - Louis

Sherbrooke

rue Durocher

rue Hutchinson

avenue du Parc

av. Jeanne-Mance

Milton

rue Sherbrooke

rue Clark

Sanguinet

rue Ontario

rue St-Christophe

rue Berri

rue Ontario

Université
du Québec
à Montréal
(UQAM)

rue Ontario

QUARTIER DES
SPECTACLES

QUARTIER
LATIN

Grande
Bibliothèque
du Québec

Place-des-Arts

Musée d'Art
Contemporain
de Montréal

Place-des-
Arts ❸

❷ ❹

Mayor

Saint-Laurent

bd. de Maisonneuve

Berri-UQAM

rue Ste - Catherine

Université
du Québec
à Montréal
(UQAM)

rue St-Hubert

rue St-André

Complexe
Desjardins

rue Clark

bd. St-Laurent

rue St-Dominique

Sanguinet

Saint-Denis

rue Saint-Alexandre

rue de Bleury

rue Jeanne-Mance

St-Urbain

bd. René - Lévesque

rue Berri

THE
VILLAGE

CHINATOWN

rue de la Gauchetière

Place-
d'Armes

Champ-
de-Mars

av. Viger

av. Viger

rue Bonsecours

Palais des Congrès
(Convention Center)

720

rue St-Antoine

Montréal World
Trade Centre

rue des Fortifications

Champ de Mars

Hôtel
de Ville

rue Berri

rue Notre-Dame

Parc
Dalhousie

Place
d'Armes

VIEUX-MONTRÉAL

rue Notre-Dame

ⓘ

Place
Jacques-
Cartier

rue Le Moyne

rue St-Pierre

Basilique
Notre-Dame ✝

rue Le Ruyer

rue St-Paul

Notre Dame-de-
Bonsecours ✝

rue St-Paul

Marché
Bonsecours

rue de la Commune

Place
d'Youville

Pointe-à-Callière
(Montréal Museum
of Archaeology
& History)

VIEUX-PORT

Quai
Jacques-Cartier

Clocktower ∎

Quai
de l'Horloge

Quai
King Edward

Quai
Alexandra

St. Lawrence River

Plateau
Mont-Royal

Jardin
Botanique

Map
Area

Parc
Mont-
Royal

Downtown

ⓘ Information
🔽 Metro Station

With comprehensive museums, a rich artistic tradition that draws from the old and the very new, and a creative music community, Montréal is Canada's cultural mecca. At the destinations highlighted here, you can sample fine art from the Renaissance, musical masterpieces, and funky galleries where everything old is new again. START: **Métro: Guy-Concordia.**

❶ ★★★ Musée des Beaux-Arts. The best destination for art hounds is one of Canada's most comprehensive art repositories. Included are works by prominent French-Canadian landscape watercolorist Marc-Aurèle Fortin (1888–1970), and, in the ultramodern Moshe Safdie–designed Jean-Noël Desmarais Pavilion, works by Old European masters and modern paintings by Picasso and Miró. Special exhibitions are often dazzling. 🕐 *2 hr. See p 13, bullet* ❷.

❷ ★★ Musée d'Art Contemporain de Montréal. This museum revels in the eclectic. There are usually two or three exhibitions open and they most often include video installations, digital

The Musée des Beaux-Arts is known primarily for its European and Canadian paintings, but also houses an excellent collection of sculpture, including this Rodin.

robotic arts, and studio glass creations. An outdoor sculpture garden is open from May through October. The museum has a restaurant (lunch Tues–Fri, dinner Thurs–Sat) and an appealing boutique with many items handmade by Québec artisans. 🕐 *1 hr. 185 rue Ste-Catherine ouest. www.macm.org.* ☎ *514/847-6226. Admission C$14 adults, with discounts for students and seniors; free for children 12 and under; half-price admission Wed 5–9pm. Tues 11am–6pm; Wed–Fri 11am–9pm; Sat–Sun 10am–6pm (check website for frequent changes for holidays). Métro: Place des Arts.*

❸ ★★ Quartier des Spectacles. This newly vibrant neighborhood is home to the **Place des Arts** (a plaza with the city's large concert halls and restaurants) and the Musée d'Art Contemporain de Montréal, and is the city's cultural heart. This is where people flock for music concerts, opera, many of the popular indoor and outdoor festivals, digital art displays, and more. In summers, an interactive installation of swings that light up and play music, called 21 Balançoires ("21 Swings"), delights visitors of all ages. A project set for completion in 2018 will rework the esplanade into a giant outdoor stage and add two large pools with fountains. *175 rue Ste-Catherine ouest. www.quartierdes spectacles.com. Métro: Place des Arts.*

Directly on the sidewalk of Quartier des Spectacles are two restaurants housed in unique glass boxes: **4**

Taverne F, a trendy Portuguese restaurant specializing in petiscos (small plates to be shared among friends), and  **Brasserie T,** where you can make a creative meal out of just the appetizers, charcuteries, and tartares. At night in warm months, a pool of water alongside both and the length of a city block has a "dancing waters" lightshow. *Taverne F, 1485 Rue Jeanne-Mance. www.tavernef.com.* ☎ *514/289 4558. $$. Brasserie T, see p 98.*

The Musée d'Art Contemporain de Montréal is a sure bet for thought-provoking art.

⑤ Antique Alley. If you walk west from Vieux-Montréal on rue Notre-Dame, you'll find a decent strip of high-end antique shops. You'll pass under a tangle of highways, and then some of the city's newer (and then older) condominium complexes. About 20 minutes after you've started, just after rue Guy, the gentrified Antique Alley begins. Little shops on the next streets are chock-a-block with high- and low-end antiques, along with cafes, bars, and good restaurants. You'll eventually reach **Marché Atwater,** a major food and vegetable market (see p 35), and the Lionel-Groulx Métro stop. ⏱ *1½ hr. Rue Notre-Dame from about rue Guy to av. Atwater. Métro: Square Victoria to start, Lionel-Groulx to return.*

Inside the Place des Arts—Canada's top cultural complex.

Gastronomic Montréal

Map Area

Jardin Botanique

Plateau Mont-Royal

Downtown

Parc Mont-Royal

Metro Station

MILE END

Rosemont

Parc Père-Marquette

Parc Sir-Wilfrid-Laurier

Papineau

av. Laurier

bd. St - Joseph

Laurier

PLATEAU MONT-ROYAL

Mont - Royal

Parc du Mont-Royal

Parc Jeanne-Mance

Monument Sir-George-Étienne Cartier

Croix du Mont-Royal

Rachel

Duluth

Parc La Fontaine

av. des Pins

Sherbrooke

Sherbrooke

McGill University

McCord Museum

Place-des-Arts

St-Laurent

Berri-UQAM

QUARTIER LATIN

Ontario

THE VILLAGE

Peel

McGill

rue Ste - Catherine

bd. de Maisonneuve

Beaudry

Papineau

DOWNTOWN INTERNATIONAL QUARTER

Bonaventure

Square-Victoria

Palais des Congrès (Convention Center)

CHINATOWN

Champ-de-Mars

Place-d'Armes

bd. René - Lévesque

rue St - Antoine

rue Notre - Dame

VIEUX-MONTRÉAL

VIEUX-PORT

St. Lawrence River

Pont de la Concorde

0   1/4 mi
0   250 m

1 Marché Atwater
2 Toqué!
3 Ferreira Café
4 Au Pied de Cochon
5 Schwartz's
6A St-Viateur Bagels
6B Fairmont Bagels

Despite the prevalence of French and American influences on the local cuisine, the city's international flavor permeates the kitchens of its restaurants and the shelves of its gourmet groceries and markets. The result? Creation of many fusion foodstuffs that have become inextricable parts of the city's personality. Use every opportunity to sample the treats you find—go in with the idea that if you haven't tried it before, the time is now. START: **Métro: Lionel-Groulx.**

❶ ★ **Marché Atwater.** The Atwater market, west of Vieux-Montréal, is an indoor-outdoor farmer's market that's open daily year-round. French in flavor (of course), it features *boulangeries* and *fromageries*, fresh fruits, vegetables, chocolates, and flowers, as well as shops with food to go. Be sure to visit **Première Moisson** (p 102) for jewel-like pastries, artisan breads, and sublime terrines. You can walk here in about 45 minutes from Vieux-Montréal by heading west on rue Notre-Dame, or take the Métro. ⏱ *1 hr. 138 rue Atwater. Open daily. Métro: Lionel-Groulx.*

Artistry on a plate at the celebrated Toque! restaurant.

Marché Atwater, Montréal's best public market, sells a mouthwatering array of fresh produce and other delicacies.

❷ ★★★ **Toque!** When chef Normand Laprise opened this gem in 1993, the city's culinary reputation was virtually non-existent. Toque! changed all that, and more than 20 years later it's still the local standard-bearer. The menu is playful and is heavily influenced by local ingredients. Items change regularly, but you're likely to find perennial favorites such as a version of Magret duck and outstanding pasta dishes, such as squash cavatelli or rabbit-stuffed pasta with ricotta and rabbit *jus*. See p 104.

❸ ★★★ **Ferreira Café.** In a city where French food and its derivations rule, the lush orange and blue Mediterranean decor at this Portuguese restaurant and its big, fleshy mounds of grilled squid and black cod create an experience that is downright sexy. Another highlight: *Cataplana*, a fragrant stew of mussels, clams, potatoes, shrimp, *chouriço* sausage, and chunks of cod

Your table awaits at the Ferreira Café, a seafood haven.

and salmon. A late-night menu for C$24 is available from 10pm every night but Sunday. *See p 99.*

④ ★ Au Pied de Cochon. Packed to the walls 5 nights a week, this Plateau restaurant remains a cult favorite. The PDC's Cut, a slab of pork weighing in at more than a pound, is emblematic. Chef Martin Picard gets particularly

The legendary Schwartz's delicatessen, renowned for its smoked meat.

clever with foie gras, which comes in nine combinations. A goofy creation called Duck in a Can does, indeed, arrive with a can opener. When you feel like another bite will send you into a cholesterol-induced coma, sugar pie (tarte au sucre) is the only fitting finish. *See p 98.*

⑤ ★★★ Schwartz's. Housed in a long, narrow storefront, with a lunch counter and simple tables and chairs crammed impossibly close to each other, this is as nondescript a culinary landmark as you'll find. French-first language laws turned the official name of this old-time Jewish delicatessen into "Chez Schwartz Charcuterie Hébraïque de Montréal," but everyone calls it Schwartz's. There's usually a line to get in, and most people order sandwich plates that come heaped with its famed smoked meat (*viande fumée*—a kind of brisket) and piles of rye bread. There's a "fat" choice to make and most folks opt for medium or medium-fat. Take out is an option. *See p 103.*

A Tasty Mess

It's the national comfort food: French fries with gravy and cheese on top. Québécois say the beauty of their beloved *poutine* lies in the cheese: Real *poutine* uses cheese curds that don't melt completely. Legend has it that the dish's name originated in 1957 when restaurateur Fernand LaChance received a request from a customer for french fries and cheese in a bag. He responded, "Ca va faire une maudite poutine!" Roughly translated: "That's going to make a damn mess!" A mess it may have been, but it also was a bona fide culinary hit, made even more so when gravy was tacked onto the recipe a few years later. Today *poutine* is a fixture on the Québec dining scene, and a must-try when you're in town. It's available both in fast-food venues (such as the good **St-Hubert** chain, which specializes in chicken) and high-end restaurants. In between is **La Banquise,** at the northwest corner of Parc La Fontaine, where there are 25 variations on the menu. *See p 100.*

Poutine—french fries with cheese curds and gravy—is arguably the city's favorite fast food. Try it at La Banquise.

Fairmont Bagels serves up to nearly 20 varieties of Montréal's famous baked goods every day.

★★★ **⑥Ⓐ St-Viateur Bagels & ⑥Ⓑ Fairmont Bagels.** The unique texture and delicious, honey-tinged flavor of Montréal bagels warrant a pair of entries on this tour—the giants who battle it out every year for the title of Best Bagel in the City. St-Viateur uses wood-burning ovens and old-fashioned baking techniques brought from eastern Europe by founder Myer Lewkowicz. Fairmont, offers greater variety and is open 24 hours 7 days a week. Compare a classic sesame and be the ultimate arbiter yourself. *St-Viateur, 1127 av. du Mont-Royal est. www.stviateurbagel.com.* ☎ *514/528-6361. $. Fairmount, see p 99.*

Romantic Montréal

MONTRÉAL
Longueuil
Lachine
Lasalle
La Prairie

ch. de la Côte - Ste. - Catherine

MILE END

Rosemont

Parc Père-Marquette

rue St - Denis

av. Laurier
bd. St - Joseph

Parc Sir-Wilfrid-Laurier

Laurier

PLATEAU MONT-ROYAL

av. Papineau

Parc du Mont-Royal

av. du Parc

bd. St - Laurent

av. du Parc

Parc Jeanne-Mance

Mont. - Royal
Mont-Royal

■ Monument Sir-George-Étienne Cartier

rue Rachel

Parc La Fontaine

6 ■ Croix du Mont-Royal

av. Duluth

5

av. des Pins

Pins

rue St - Denis

Sherbrooke

McGill University

rue University

McCord Museum ■

Place-des-Arts

Sherbrooke

bd. St - Laurent

rue Amherst

QUARTIER LATIN

Ontario

av. Papineau

THE VILLAGE

← 2

Peel

McGill

rue

St-Laurent

Berri-UQAM

bd. de Maisonneuve

Papineau

rue Peel

DOWNTOWN

QUARTIER DES SPECTACLES

CHINATOWN

Ste. - Catherine

Beaudry

bd. René - Lévesque

Bonaventure

INTERNATIONAL QUARTER

Square-Victoria

Champ-de-Mars

rue St - Antoine

720

Palais des Congrès (Convention Center)

Place-d'Armes

rue Notre - Dame

VIEUX-MONTRÉAL

10

5

4

VIEUX-PORT

Île Sainte-Hélène

Parc Jean-Drapeau

3

Pont de la Concorde

■ La Biosphère

Jean-Drapeau

0   1/4 mi
0   250 m

Île Notre-Dame

🚇 Metro Station

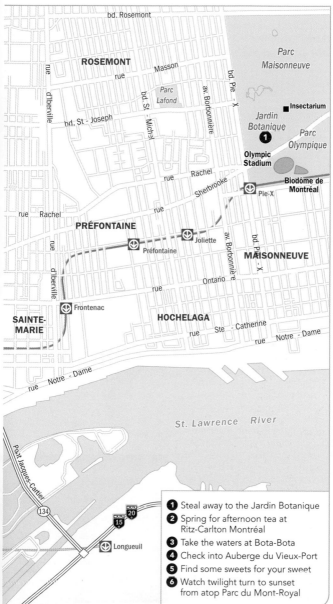

bd. Rosemont

ROSEMONT

Masson

rue

rue

Parc Lafond

bd. St - Joseph

bd. St - Michel

av. Borbonnière

bd. Pie - X

rue d'Iberville

Parc Maisonneuve

Insectarium

Jardin Botanique
❶

Parc Olympique

Olympic Stadium

rue Rachel

rue

Sherbrooke

Pie-X

Biodôme de Montréal

rue Rachel

PRÉFONTAINE

rue

Joliette

av. Borbonnière

bd. Pie - X

Préfontaine

MAISONNEUVE

rue d'Iberville

rue

Ontario

Frontenac

HOCHELAGA

Ste - Catherine

SAINTE-
MARIE

rue

rue

Notre - Dame

rue Notre - Dame

St. Lawrence River

Pont Jacques-Cartier

134

15
20

Longueuil

❶ Steal away to the Jardin Botanique
❷ Spring for afternoon tea at Ritz-Carlton Montréal
❸ Take the waters at Bota-Bota
❹ Check into Auberge du Vieux-Port
❺ Find some sweets for your sweet
❻ Watch twilight turn to sunset from atop Parc du Mont-Royal

Romance is in the eyes of the beholder, which makes this a tricky tour to propose. Sitting hand in hand on a quiet park bench might be all you need for a moment to be luminous—while your best friend might dream of having a partner drop C$300 on a luxurious dinner in a sky-high restaurant. Options here range from the modest to the opulent. START: **Métro: Pie-IX.**

Jardin Botanique's beautiful Chinese Garden is the perfect spot for a romantic stroll.

❶ Steal away to the Jardin Botanique. You'll be hard-pressed to find an area within the botanical gardens that isn't conducive to cuddling. The Japanese Garden has a serene Zen garden, while the butterfly house hosts hundreds of live butterflies who flit around and sometimes alight on visitors' shoulders. And the Chinese Garden has pavilions and inner courtyards to tuck into. ⏱ *1½ hr.* See p 21, bullet **❾**.

❷ Spring for afternoon tea at Ritz-Carlton Montréal. Tea is served at the Ritz from 1 to 4:30pm daily in its gilded Palm Court. The menu includes scones, finger sandwiches, and mini pastries, with champagne as an option (C$35 or C$45 with the bubbly). ⏱ *1½ hr.* See p 132.

❸ Take the waters at Bota Bota. Bath complexes are common throughout Scandinavia, but less so in North America. This all-season spa is housed in a

Tea for two—swanky and romantic—at the Ritz-Carlton Montréal.

converted boat docked on the far western end of Vieux Port. It offers a luxurious water circuit of dry saunas, steam rooms, and three Jacuzzis, two of which are outside and offer stunning northern views of the Old Port. Access to the boat's "water circuit" starts at C$35 (depending on time of day) for 3 hours in all the water facilities, lounges, and bistro. An extension—onto dry land—opened in 2015 and includes an infinity pool and gardens. ⏱ *2+ hr. The boat is docked in the water near the corner of rue de la Commune ouest and rue McGill. www.botabota.ca.* ☎ *855/284-0333 or 514/284-0333. Mon–Thurs 10am–10pm, Fri–Sun 9am–10pm. Métro: Square-Victoria.*

④ Check into Auberge du Vieux-Port. Exposed brick and stone walls, massive beams, and polished hardwood floors—all with

Taking in the waters at Bota Bota is a great way to unwind.

A cozy, charming double at Auberge du Vieux-Port.

modern fixtures and enveloping beds—define the hideaway bedrooms, many of which offer unobstructed views of Vieux-Port. *See p 127.*

⑤ Find some sweets for your sweet. Perhaps treats by local chocolatier **Les Chocolats de Chloé**, which spices up offerings with cardamom, lime zest, and Espelette pepper? The chocolates are sold out of a shop in the Plateau and at the Vieux-Montréal restaurant Olive + Gourmando. *546 rue Duluth est. www.leschocolats dechloe.com.* ☎ *514/849-5550. Olive + Gourmando see p 89.*

⑥ Watch twilight turn to sunset from atop Parc Mont-Royal. The lookouts along rue Camillien-Houde and the front terrace of the Chalet du Mont-Royal at the top of the small mountain called Mont-Royal offer the most popular panoramic view of Montréal and the St-Lawrence River. There is a web of options for trekking the small mountain (see our suggested walk in chapter 3), or you can take a cab, a bus, or your own car. *See p 80, bullet ⑨.*

High Design Montréal

1 Palais des Congrès (Convention Center)
2 Hotel Gault
3 Habitat 67
4 La Biosphère
5 Darling Foundry
6 Harricana

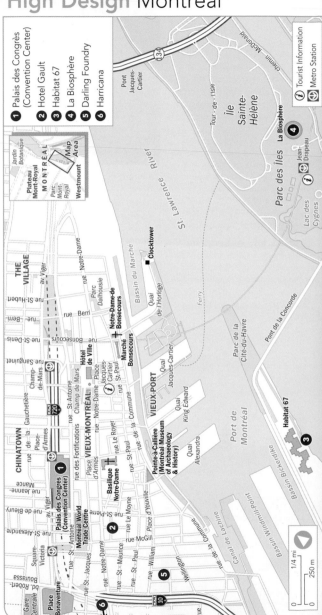

ⓘ Tourist Information
Ⓜ Metro Station

Jardin Botanique

MONTRÉAL

Map Area

Plateau Mont-Royal

Parc Mont-Royal

Westmount

M O N T R É A L

Pont Jacques-Cartier

Tour - de - l'Isle

chemin - McDonald

Île Sainte-Hélène

La Biosphère 4

Parc des Îles

Jean- Drapeau ⓘ

Lac des Cygnes

St. Lawrence River

Clocktower

Quai de l'Horloge

Bassin du Marché

Ferry

Pont de la Concorde

Parc de la Cité-du-Havre

av. Viger

THE VILLAGE

rue Notre-Dame

rue Viger

Parc Dalhousie

rue St-Hubert

rue - Berri

rue St-Denis

rue Bonsecours

rue Sanguinet

Notre-Dame-de Bonsecours

Hôtel de Ville

Champ-de-Mars

CHINATOWN

rue de la Gauchetière

20

St-Antoine

Champ de Mars

Place VIEUX-MONTRÉAL

Place Jacques-Cartier

ⓘ

Marché Bonsecours

VIEUX-PORT

Quai Jacques-Cartier

Quai King Edward

Port de Montréal

Bassin Bickerdike

Habitat 67 3

rue de la Place-d'Armes

rue des Fortifications

Place d'Armes

rue Notre-Dame

rue St-Paul

rue St-Paul

Place Cartier

rue Le Royer

rue St-Paul

rue de la Commune

Quai Alexandra

Bassin Windmill Point

rue Jeanne-Mance

Basilique Notre-Dame

Pointe-à-Callière (Montreal Museum of Archaeology & History)

av. de Bleury

rue St-Alexandre

Montreal World Trade Centre

Palais des Congrès (Convention Center) 1

rue St-Antoine

rue St-Pierre

rue Le Moyne

Place d'Youville

rue McGill

rue de la Commune

Canal de Lachine

Bassin de la Lachine

Square Victoria

bd. Robert-Bourassa

Gare Centrale

Place Bonaventure

rue St-Jacques

rue Notre-Dame

rue St-Maurice

rue St-Paul

rue St-Maurice

rue William

rue Wellington

5

6

10

0   1/4 mi
0   250 m

Montréal is one of North America's most stylish cities, and the municipality has worked in recent years to capitalize on that appeal to entice artists to create and art-minded travelers to visit. In 2006, it became the first North American city to be appointed a UNESCO City of Design. News and details on some of the city's key players is at www.designmontreal.com/en/news, a city-run website and organization that celebrates and initiates creative design throughout Montréal. Here are some highlights to take in, in and around Vieux-Montréal. START: **Métro: Place d'Armes.**

An interior view of the Palais des Congrès's patchwork glass walls.

❶ Palais des Congrès. A convention center as design triumph? As unlikely as that seems, yes. The center's transparent glass exterior walls are a crazy quilt of pink, yellow, blue, green, red, and purple rectangles. Step into the inside hallway for the full effect—when the sun streams in, it's like being inside a huge kaleidoscope. The walls went up from 2000 to 2002 as part of renovation and extension of the center and are the vision of Montréal architect Mario Saia. ⏱ *15*

min. *201 ave Viger ouest. www. congresmtl.com.* ☎ *514/871-8122. Métro: Place d'Armes.*

❷ ★★ Hôtel Gault. Vieux-Montréal's rich character derives from the careful reuse of industrial buildings. Why tear down beauty just to put up more of the same old, same old? For this hotel, which opened in 2002, interior designer Atelier YH2 and architect Paul Bernier left the monumental concrete walls of a 19th-century textile warehouse raw and added brushed-steel work surfaces for a chic, contemporary feel. As one journalist noted, "Hôtel Gault caters to exactly the sort of guest who might choose lodging based on the provenance of the furniture, and

Hôtel Gault merges stylish modern design with industrial architecture.

Montréal Fashion & Design Festival

Fashion simmers in this city, where innovative locals are making international names for themselves. Montréal's Fashion & Design Festival, held in August, is the best place to take it all in. There are runway shows, do-it-yourself panels, and pop up stores, with events at the Musée d'Art Contemporain de Montréal and throughout the Quartier des Spectacles. Festival details: www.festivalmodedesign.com. A city map of designer venues is online at www.modemontreal.tv/en.

exemplifies the ways in which Montréal has been, like other cities around the world, reinventing itself to attract a certain breed of urban sophisticate." The sleek lobby, with its massive arched windows, also functions as a bar/cafe/breakfast area, and the Gault Restaurant invites all to come and play. ① *30 min. See p 130.*

❸ **Habitat 67.** In 1967, Montréal hosted the World's Fair, which it called Expo 67. It was hugely successful—62 nations participated and over 50 million people visited—and overnight, Montréal was a star. Its avant-garde vision was on display, and it became a kind of prototype for a 20th-century city. One of the most exhilarating buildings built for display was Habitat 67, a 158-unit housing complex on the St. Lawrence River facing Vieux-Montréal. Designed by Montréal architect Moshe Safdie, it looks like a collection of module concrete blocks, all piled together and interconnected. The vision was to show what affordable, community housing could be. Today it's higher-end housing and not open to the public. But it can be seen from the western end of Vieux-Port, and photos and information can be found at Safdie's website,

www.msafdie.com. ① *30 min. View from corner of rue St-Pierre and rue de la Commune in Vieux-Port.*

❹ **La Biosphère.** Geodesic domes popped up across the world's landscape during the 20th century for industrial and even residential use. This building, located on Île Ste-Hélène near to Vieux-Montréal, was designed by American architect Buckminster Fuller to serve as the American Pavilion for

Built for the 1967 World's Fair, the modern Habitat 67 is now a private residence.

La Biosphère is home to a number of multimedia exhibitions on ecological issues.

Expo 67. A fire destroyed the sphere's acrylic skin in 1976, and for almost 20 years it served no purpose other than as a harbor landmark. In 1995, Environment Canada (www.ec.gc.ca) joined with the city of Montréal to convert the space, and it's now environment museum about "Spaceship Earth" and sustainable development. ◷ *2 hr. 160 chemin Tour-de-l'Isle (Île Ste-Hélène). www.ec.gc.ca/biosphere.* ☎ *855/773-8200 or 514/283-5000. Admission C$15 adults, C$12 seniors, C$10 students 18 and over, free for children 17 and under. Métro: Parc Jean-Drapeau.*

❺ **Darling Foundry.** For the last decade, artists and high-tech businesses have been moving into the loft-and-factory district west of avenue McGill, at the edge of Vieux-Montréal. Among the pioneers is the Darling Foundry, an avant-garde exhibition space in a vast, raw, former foundry. It showcases modern art and hosts occasional dance programs and multimedia installations, with the mission of supporting emerging artists living and working in the heart of the city. ◷ *30 min. 745 rue Ottawa. www.fonderie darling.org.* ☎ *514/392-1554. Métro: Square Victoria.*

❻ **Harricana.** One of Montréal's most prominent fashion designers takes a unique cue from the city's long history with the fur trade. Mariouche Gagné, who was born on Île d'Orléans near Québec City in 1971, recycles old fur into funky patchwork garments and uses the slogan "for the love of reinvention." A leader in the so-called ecoluxe movement, Gagné also recycles cashmere wool, turning it into scarfs. ◷ *30 min. See p 88.*

Millennial Montréal

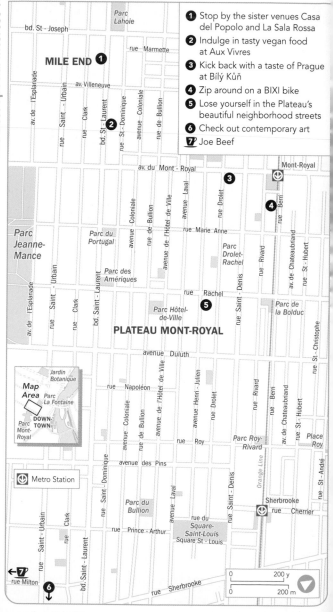

1 Stop by the sister venues Casa del Popolo and La Sala Rossa
2 Indulge in tasty vegan food at Aux Vivres
3 Kick back with a taste of Prague at Bílý Kůň
4 Zip around on a BIXI bike
5 Lose yourself in the Plateau's beautiful neighborhood streets
6 Check out contemporary art
7 Joe Beef

bd. St - Joseph

Parc Lahoie

rue Marmette

MILE END 1

av. Villeneuve

av. de l'Esplanade
rue Saint - Urbain
rue Clark
bd. St-Laurent
rue -St-Dominique
avenue Coloniale
rue de Bullion

2

av. du Mont - Royal

Mont-Royal

av. du Mont - Royal

avenue Laval
avenue de l'Hôtel de Ville
avenue Drolet

3

rue Berri

4

rue Marie - Anne

Coloniale
Bullion

Parc Jeanne-Mance

Parc du Portugal

Parc des Amériques

Parc Drolet-Rachel

rue - Rivard

av. de Chateaubriand
rue - St - Hubert

av. de l'Esplanade
rue Saint - Urbain
rue Clark
bd. Saint - Laurent

rue Rachel

rue Saint - Denis

Parc de la Bolduc

5

Parc Hôtel-de-Ville

rue St - Christophe

PLATEAU MONT-ROYAL

avenue Duluth

Map Area

Jardin Botanique
Parc La Fontaine
DOWN-TOWN
Parc Mont-Royal

rue Napoléon

avenue de l'Hôtel de Ville
avenue Henri - Julien
rue Drolet

rue - Rivard
rue Berri
av. de Chateaubriand
rue - St - Hubert

avenue Coloniale
rue de Bullion

rue Roy

Parc Roy-Rivard

Place Roy

avenue des Pins

rue Saint - Dominique

Orange Line

rue Saint - Denis

rue St - André

🔽 Metro Station

avenue Laval

Sherbrooke
rue Cherrier

rue Saint - Urbain
rue Clark
rue Saint - Laurent

Parc du Bullion

rue Prince - Arthur

rue du Square-Saint-Louis
Square St - Louis

7

rue Milton

6

rue Sherbrooke

| 0 | | 200 y |
| 0 | | 200 m |

Visitors in their 20s and 30s may want to head to the northern reaches of Plateau Mont-Royal and into Mile End, the neighborhood a little more north still. Here is where you'll find some of the most creative and innovative people in the city. Here's a sample day, starting at one of the most important venues for the independent music scene in the city. START: **Métro: Laurier.**

❶ Stop by the sister venues Casa del Popolo and La Sala Rosa. Spanish for "The House of the People," the cozy Casa del Popolo is set in a scruffy storefront and serves vegetarian food, operates a laid-back bar, and has a small first-floor stage. For many it's a refuge from the trendier, more expensive venues farther south on boulevard St-Laurent. Across the street, sister performance space La Sala Rosa is a terrific music venue with a full calendar of interesting offerings from around the city and beyond. ⏲ *30 min. See p 113 and 114.*

❷ Indulge in tasty vegan food at Aux Vivres. This is a long-time Frommer's favorite. Aux

Renting a BIXI bike is a popular Montréal pastime.

Vivres has been humming and busy since moving into its current location in 2006. The restaurant is bright and cheery, and it operates a juice bar off to one side and a back terrace. All foods are vegan, all vegetables are organic, and all tofu and tempeh are local. ⏲ *1 hr. See p 59.*

❸ Kick back with a taste of Prague at Bílý Kůň. Exuding a relaxed cool, Bílý Kůň brings in students and professionals who sit elbow to elbow at small tables. The room is lit by candles at night, and in summer twirling ceiling fans and picture windows open to the street. Decor is quirky (hello, mounted ostrich heads) and there are several absinthe drink options. Open daily

Quirky and hip, Bílý Kůň is a great place to grab a drink after exploring the surrounding shops.

A pleasant park setting where Plateau Mont-Royal meets Mile End.

from 3pm to 3am. If you're visiting in the day, build time to stop by the little shops along the same street. There's lots of used clothing and kitschy stuff, and Aime Com Moi, at 150 av. Mont-Royal est, features fabulously funky dresses by Québécois designers. ◷ *2 hr. See p 110.*

④ Zip around on a BIXI bike. The city's popular self-service bicycle rental program is called BIXI, an abbreviated combination of the words *bicyclette* and *taxi*. It's similar to programs in Berlin, Paris, and Boston. After registering (and putting a deposit down via credit card), users pick up BIXI bikes from designated stands throughout the city and drop them off at any other stand, for a small fee. Some 5,200 bikes are in operation and available at 460 stations in Montréal's central boroughs. ◷ *1 hr. Stands are located throughout the city, including at Métro Mont-Royal. See p 161.*

⑤ Lose yourself in the Plateau's beautiful neighborhood streets. Just walk with no agenda?

Naturellement! Whether its tree-lined streets are littered with gold and scarlet leaves in the fall or fresh snow in the winter, this neighborhood is perfect for a leisurely stroll. Sit tête-à-tête at a cafe on rue St-Denis or head to the boutiques and bars on avenue du Mont-Royal or make it up as you go along—a destination-free stroll is the best way to get into the neighborhood's flow. ◷ *2 hr. Area bordered by rues St-Urbain and Papineau and rues Sherbrooke to Laurier. Métro: Mont-Royal.*

⑥ Check out contemporary art. The Musée d'Art Contemporain de Montréal started a new concept in 2016 for its long-popular Friday Nocturnes: Four times a year it now stays open past midnight. The events feature live music, bar service, and tours of the exhibition galleries. If the timing isn't right, the museum always has temporary exhibitions up during its regular hours. ◷ *2 hr. See p 32.*

Cycling in the Plateau, one of Montréal's most picturesque and romantic neighborhoods.

Venison carpaccio at Joe Beef.

If you're sporting sleeve tattoos, cute little vintage clothes, or a C$200 haircut designed to look like you just fell out of bed, head south and west to **7 Joe Beef.** Foodies will have heard of the glutton-inducing restaurant—think boisterous diner with adventurous food—which has been profiled everywhere since its 2005 opening. Many guests start with oysters or the Foie Gras Double Down: two slabs of deep-fried foie sandwiching bacon, cheddar, and maple syrup. The menu often includes chicken, grits, and crayfish; cornflake sturgeon nuggets; and saucisse de lapin (rabbit and pork sausage). The restaurant describes itself as "a drunken crawl away from the Historic Atwater market." *2491 rue Notre-Dame ouest. www.joebeef. ca.* ☎ *514/935-6504. Main courses C$19–C$50. Tues–Sat 6pm–close. Métro: Lionel-Groulx. $$.*

Montréal's Parks

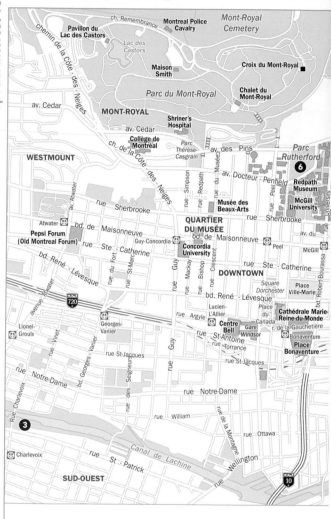

1. Poke around Vieux-Port
2. Bike or blade the Lachine Canal bike path
3. Get in the water
4. Take in the Tam Tams

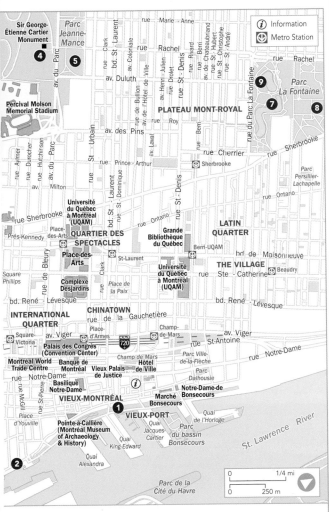

5 Leap onto the beach volleyball courts
6 Find some pick-up Frisbee
7 Relax at a waterside café
8 Hit the tennis courts
9 Plan a night at Théâtre de Verdure

Shopping, eating, spending, drinking—sometimes all that consuming gets to be just a little much. When you're looking to simply hang out in some green space, or hit the water, or go for a bike ride, make like a Montréaler. Here are three great parks and some popular ways to take them in.

Vieux-Port & Lachine Canal

Montréal's Old Port—called Vieux-Port in French—was transformed in 1992 from a dreary commercial wharf area into a promenade and public park with bicycle paths, exhibition halls, and a variety of family activities. It stretches along the waterfront parallel to rue de la Commune from rue Berri in the east to rue McGill in the west. The Lachine Canal bike path starts right at rue McGill.

❶ Poke around Vieux-Port. The port area really isn't that big—2km (1¼-mile) long, and 53 hectares (131 acres) in all. A fun summer option is to rent a **quadricycle** bike-buggy that can hold two to six people. The rental booth is in the heart of the waterfront area, next to the **Centre des Sciences de Montréal,** and the cost is C$22 for a three-seater and C$44 for a

six-seater. See www.oldportof montreal.com. At the same spot, you can hop onboard the open-sided **mini electric train.** (C$4 per person). At the port's far eastern end, in the last of the old warehouses, the 1922 clock tower, **La Tour de l'Horloge,** can be climbed for free. It has 192 steps that lead past exposed clockworks to observation decks overlooking the St. Lawrence River.

❷ Bike or blade the Lachine Canal bike path. ÇaRoule/Montréal on Wheels (27 rue de la Commune est; www.caroulemontreal. com; ☎ 877/866-0633 or 514/866-0633), on the waterfront road bordering Vieux-Port, rents bicycles and rollerblades from March to November. Rentals are C$30 on weekdays and C$35 on weekends. The staff can set you up with a map (also downloadable from their

Strolling along Vieux-Port.

Enjoy the Outdoors, Come Snow or Come Shine

Starting with the first thaw, locals pour outside to get sun and warm air at every possible opportunity. Even if you arrive without your regular outdoor gear, it's easy to join in.

In warm weather, biking and rollerblading are hugely popular (see "Tap Your Own Pedal Power," p 161). Hikers and joggers take to Parc Mont-Royal and the city streets. And getting onto the water is big. In addition to kayaking on the Lachine Canal (see above), a popular option is taking a cruise on the St. Lawrence River. Trips are available from mid-May to mid-October, with companies such as **Le Bateau-Mouche** (www.bateau-mouche.com; ☎ 800/361-9952 or 514/849-9952) and **Croisières AML Cruises** (www.croisieres aml.com; ☎ 800/563-4643 or 514/842-3871) offering 60-minute, 90-minute, and evening trips. Adult fares start at C$25, and the boats leave from the piers in Vieux-Port.

There's plenty to do when there's snow on the ground, too. In winter, cross-country skiers take advantage of the extensive course at Parc Mont-Royal (although you have to bring your own equipment). Outdoor skating rinks are set up in Vieux-Port and at Lac des Castors (Beaver Lake) in Parc Mont-Royal, with skate rentals available at both locales.

website) and point you toward the peaceful Lachine Canal, a nearly flat 11km (6.8-mile) bicycle path that travels alongside locks and over small bridges. The path is open year-round and maintained by Parks Canada from mid-April to the end of October.

The bike shop also offers a variety of bike tours including a **4-hour bicycling tour** that goes from Vieux-Port through the Quartier Latin up to Parc La Fontaine, the Plateau, Mile End, and Parc Mont-Royal. The cost is C$69. Reservations required.

❸ Don't just look at the water—get in it. Rent kayaks, large Rabaska canoes, pedal boats, or small eco-friendly electric boats about 4km (2½ miles) down the

Cycling the Lachine Canal Bike Path is one of Montréal's best outdoor experiences.

canal. **H2O Adventures** (www. h2oadventures.com; ☎ 514/842-1306) won a Grand Prix du tourisme Québécois award for its operation. Rentals include kayaks, canoes, pedal boats, and small electric boats. If you don't want to bike or walk there, take the Métro to Lionel-Groulx and head south to the canal. You'll pass the **Marché Atwater,** one of the city's premiere markets, where you can pick up food from the *boulangerie* and *fromagerie* or from any of the many prepared food shops.

Parc du Mont-Royal

Take a look at the map and suggested walk of Parc Mont-Royal on p 76. That will give you your bearings on how to get into and around the 200-hectare (494-acre) park and a feel for some of the walking highlights. Here are some additional ways to enjoy the park and its environs.

❹ **Take in the Tam Tams.** If you have a Sunday to spare from early May to late September, try out this enormous gathering of musicians, vendors, and fantasy combatants. Tam Tams attracts a few hundred drummers who congregate late in the morning around the statue of Sir George-Etienne Cartier near avenue du Parc at the corner rue Rachel, on the park's far eastern side. Anyone is free to watch or join in. As the mass of random percussionists builds around the steps of the statue, the rest of the park fills with sunbathers and picnickers who turn the impromptu concert into a festive social event. You'll also find vendors hawking homemade jewelry and art, and kooky LARPers (Live Action Role Players) putting on whimsical faux battles with foam weapons in a grove of trees to the north. *Inside Parc Mont-Royal at av. du Parc and rue Rachel.*

❺ **Leap onto the beach volleyball courts or the ice rink at Parc Jeanne-Mance.** If you'd rather break a sweat, check out the park across from avenue du Parc, near where the Tam Tams set up. You'll find a baseball field, tennis courts, a football/soccer field and, best of all, beach volleyball courts. When the weather is acceptable, these giant sandboxes are full of shirtless men and bikini-clad women setting and spiking. Cold weather brings an excellent ice rink that's popular among hockey players who do without full padding and play just with gloves, skates, and sticks. Even when it's –40°C (–40°F) you can still find die-hards at it. *Inside Parc Jeanne-Mance at av. du Parc and rue Duluth.*

❻ **Find some pick-up Frisbee in Parc Rutherford.** Just south of where the walking tour of Park Mont-Royal (p 76) begins is Parc Rutherford, an enormous expanse of grass known to locals simply as as McTavish or the Réservoir. Adjacent to McGill, it's where students come to study on warm days. It's also one of the best spots for

Every Sunday in summer, Montréalers gather in Parc Mont-Royal for the Tam Tam drum sessions.

Ice skating in Parc La Fontaine.

finding an ultimate Frisbee game: The university's club team practices and plays here, but you'll likely find pick-up games on other days. *Rue McTavish and av. des Pins.*

Parc La Fontaine
Many locals come to this green oasis to play in its two lakes. A popular open amphitheater, the **Théâtre de Verdure,** is set to reopen in 2017 in time for the city's 375th birthday celebrations. Many people also come simply to find some quiet among the flower beds that bloom bright: Some of the landscaping is done in a formal French manner, and some in a more casual English style.

⑦ Relax at a waterside café. Espace La Fontaine, just adjacent to the two man-made lakes set in the middle of Parc La Fontaine, is a bistro offering light meals, local beers, an outdoor patio, and an exhibition and entertainment space.

⑧ Hit the tennis courts. The 14 courts here are in decent condition and are the most convenient option in downtown Montréal for tennis enthusiasts. They're lit and stay open until 10pm, and can sometimes get crowded, but try to score an evening session if you can. With the often-oppressive summer humidity, playing is far more comfortable in the cooler Montréal nights. Reservations aren't required, but to make sure you get the slot you want you'll either have to sign up at the courts in person or call ahead of time. ☎ 514/872-3626. *East side of Parc La Fontaine, 3500 ave. Émile-Duployé.*

⑨ Plan a night at Théâtre de Verdure. Sunset does not send park visitors heading for the exits. Instead, many stay after dark because of this excellent, open-air theater—long one of the best places to see a show in all of Montréal. The venue was closed for the 2014–16 seasons after falling into disrepair, but by 2017 it will have reopened after undergoing major renovations and upgrading. In the past it has offered free outdoor theater, music, and tango dancing. Presumably, you will still be able to pack a bottle of rosé and a picnic basket and have a wonderfully relaxing dinner as you take it all in under the night sky. Call the city's Infotouriste Centre for updates. ☎ 877/266-5687 or 514/873-2015. *West end of Parc La Fontaine.*

Summertime pleasures in Parc La Fontaine.

Montréal with Kids

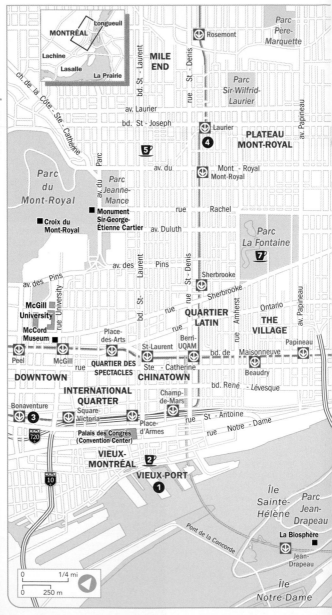

MONTRÉAL

Longueuil

Lachine

Lasalle   La Prairie

ch. de la Côte - Ste - Catherine

Parc
Père-
Marquette

�֎ Rosemont

MILE
END

bd. St - Laurent

St - Denis

Parc
Sir-Wilfrid-
Laurier

av. Laurier

bd. St - Joseph

rue

🔵 Laurier

4

PLATEAU
MONT-ROYAL

av. Papineau

5

Parc
du
Mont-Royal

av. du

av. du

Parc
Jeanne-
Mance

■ Monument
Sir-George-
Étienne Cartier

🔵 Mont - Royal
Mont-Royal

rue   Rachel

■ Croix du
Mont-Royal

av. Duluth

Parc
La Fontaine

7

av. des - Pins

av. des   Pins

Laurent

St - Denis

🔵 Sherbrooke

St -

🔵

McGill
University

McCord
Museum ■

rue   University

rue   St -

bd. St -

rue

rue

Sherbrooke

QUARTIER
LATIN

Amherst

Ontario

THE
VILLAGE

av. Papineau

Place-
des-Arts

🔵

🔵

🔵   St-Laurent

Berri-
UQAM

🔵 bd. de   Maisonneuve

Papineau

🔵

Peel   McGill

rue

DOWNTOWN

QUARTIER DES
SPECTACLES

Ste - Catherine

CHINATOWN

🔵
Beaudry

INTERNATIONAL
QUARTER

Champ-
de-Mars

bd. René - Lévesque

Bonaventure

🔵 3

Square-
Victoria

🔵

🔵   Place-
d'Armes

rue   St - Antoine

720

Palais des Congrès
(Convention Center)

rue   Notre - Dame

10

VIEUX-
MONTRÉAL

2

VIEUX-PORT

1

Île
Sainte-
Hélène

Parc
Jean-
Drapeau

■ La Biosphère

🔵
Jean-
Drapeau

Pont de la Concorde

Île
Notre-Dame

0   1/4 mi
0   250 m

57

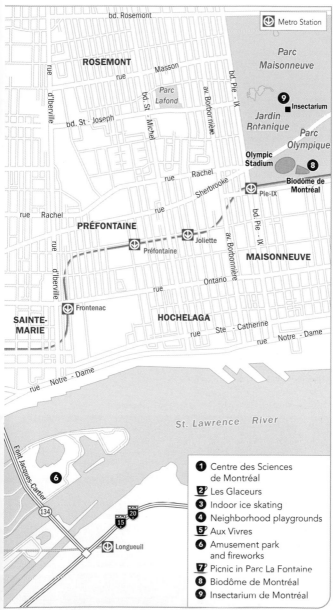

1 Centre des Sciences de Montréal
2 Les Glaceurs
3 Indoor ice skating
4 Neighborhood playgrounds
5 Aux Vivres
6 Amusement park and fireworks
7 Picnic in Parc La Fontaine
8 Biodôme de Montréal
9 Insectarium de Montréal

Montréal is as much a playground for children as it is for adults. A good number of the city's museums and attractions, including those listed below, are tailored to the tiniest sightseers. There are also good expanses of grass for running around on in the city's big parks (see p 50), the Jardin Botanique (p 21), and on the main campus of McGill University (enter at 845 rue Sherbrooke ouest). START: Métro: Place d'Armes or Champs-de-Mars.

1 ★★ **Centre des Sciences de Montréal.** The Montréal Science Centre is a family-friendly complex that approaches science and technology in a hands-on way. Some of its programming is geared toward children and young teens (a show about sex was extremely straightforward and popular), while other exhibits will tap the inner kid in all visitors, such as the recent show that revisited the history of video games and included 100 games and consoles. The permanent exhibition "Clic!" is really just a play space for younger children; the museum says it's for 4 to 7 year olds, but 2 to 3 year olds will love it, too. Also onsite is an **IMAX** theater and a small gift shop. An international food court is next door. ⏱ 2 hr. 2 rue de la Commune ouest, on Quai King Edward (Vieux-Port). www.montrealsciencecentre.com.

☎ 877/496-4724 or 514/496-4724. Admission C$21 adults, C$18 ages 13–17 and 60+; C$12 ages 4–12; free for children 3 and under; C$58 family package. Admission to just the permanent exhibitions C$4–C$6 less per ticket. Daily at least 10am–4pm; check website for extended hours, which change. Métro: Place d'Armes or Champ-de-Mars.

The rise in cupcake shops was one of the great phenomena of the early 21st century, and it's in full bloom at **2** **Les Glaceurs.** This cheery café across the street from the grand Basilique Notre-Dame sells cupcakes in flavors including red velvet, coconut rum, and praline, which features caramelized hazelnut frosting. You can also pick up sandwiches and ice cream made by Montréal favorite Bilboquet. It is

Kids love the hands-on exhibits at the Centre des Sciences de Montréal.

Skaters flock to the ice rink at Atrium Le 1000.

open daily from 11am to 6pm. *453 rue St-Sulpice. www.lesglaceurs.ca. ☎ 514/504-1469. $.*

❸ ★ Indoor ice skating.

Escape the city's stifling heat or freezing cold at **Atrium Le 1000,** a year-round facility in a downtown office building. The cozy rink is surrounded by plenty of eateries and has skate rentals on-site. It attracts a full mix of patrons: groups of giggling teenage girls, middle-aged friends chatting and skating side by side, and young children teetering in helmets. **Tiny Tots Time,** typically Saturday and Sunday from 11:00am to 12:30pm, is reserved for children 12 and younger and their parents. ⏱ *1 hr. 1000 rue de la Gauchetiere ouest. www.le1000.com. ☎ 514/395-0555. Admission C$8 adults, with discounts for children and seniors. Skate rental C$7. Open daily; check website for schedules. Métro: Bonaventure.*

❹ Neighborhood playgrounds.

If you've traveling with toddlers who simply want to run on a playground on a warm day, head to the less-touristy neighborhoods such as Plateau Mont-Royal, Mile End, and Outremont, the neighborhood west of Mile End. Parks are well maintained and many include playgrounds. One option: Take the Métro to Laurier, a pretty residential neighborhood where the Plateau meets Mile End. Walk south on rue Berri one block to **Parc Albert-Saint-Martin.** This compact urban playground includes a play area for 18 months to 5 year olds and another for 5 to 12 year olds. The park is also a 10-minute walk from our favorite doll store, **Raplapla,** p 85, and a favorite kid-friendly restaurant, **Aux Vivres,** below. ⏱ *1½ hr. Parc Albert-Saint-Martin is at the corner of rue Berri and rue de Bienville. Métro: Laurier.*

Kids will love the wraps, burgers, and juice concoctions at ❺ **Aux Vivres,** a bright and cheery vegan restaurant. A large selection of foods are also available to-go, including lunch boxes, nori rolls, salads, and homemade desserts. *See p 98.*

❻ ★ Amusement park and fireworks.

Located on Parc Jean-Drapeau, which sits in the St. Lawrence River near Vieux-Port's waterfront, is **La Ronde Amusement Park.** It's part of the American-owned Six Flags theme-park empire and has roller coasters galore, a Ferris wheel, and 12 kid rides such as a carousel and a small Tchou Tchou Train. For 8 evenings in the summer, the park is host to a **huge fireworks competition** called L'International des Feux Loto-Québec. Although the fireworks can be enjoyed for free from almost anywhere in the city overlooking the river, tickets can be purchased to watch from an open-air theater at La Ronde. Fireworks tickets include entrance to the park.

22 chemin Macdonald, Parc Jean-Drapeau on Île Ste-Hélène. www.laronde.com. ☎ 514/397-2000. Admission C$62 adults, C$45 children 1.37m (54 in.) or shorter and seniors, free for children 2 and under. Parking C$20–C$27. Check website for hours. Métro: Papineau, then bus no. 769; or Parc Jean-Drapeau, then bus no. 767.

Pack up gourmet cheeses and baguettes for the adults and whatever the kids will need for a **7** **picnic in Parc La Fontaine.** The Plateau's gorgeous green space has scenic ponds on the quaint English (west) half and dreamy garden paths in the distinctly French (east) side. The park is a microcosm of Montréal, from its bilingual nature to its laid-back atmosphere. ⏱ *1 hr. Rue Sherbrooke and av. du Parc La Fontaine. Métro: Sherbrooke.*

8 ★★★ **Biodôme de Montréal.** Great fun for all ages, from young kids to teens to adults. Four ecosystems are re-created in this unusual attraction, and all have accurate temperatures, flora, and fauna. The rainforest and polar environments are the biggest hits with the littlest ones, with macaws

Four ecosystems are re-created at the Biodôme de Montréal.

and penguins mesmerizing young visitors. Once the kids have gotten tired of watching the animals, they can try out Naturalia, a hands-on activity room. ⏱ *2 hr. See p 21.*

9 **Insectarium de Montréal.** The Insectarium is part of the **Jardin Botanique** (p 21) and admission is included in the (rather steep) joint ticket price for the gardens. If you are already planning a trip to the gardens, this is worth taking in; otherwise, it's probably too small to justify a trip and a ticket on its own. That said, it's the place to be if bugs and spiders make you squirm with delight. There are live exhibits of insects from scorpions and tarantulas to ants and hissing cockroaches. Alongside the crawly little creatures are thousands of mounted ones, including butterflies and beetles. An outdoor playground is well designed for children 12 and under. ⏱ *1 hr. 4581 rue Sherbrooke est. www.espace pourlavie.ca/en/insectarium. ☎ 514/872-1400. Tickets may only be purchased in a package with the Jardin Botanique. Check the website for hours, which change seasonally. Métro: Pie-IX.* ●

Flying high at La Ronde amusement park.

Vieux-Montréal

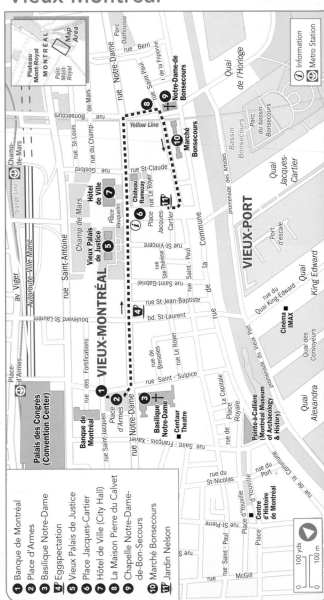

1 Banque de Montréal
2 Place d'Armes
3 Basilique Notre-Dame
4 Eggspectation
5 Vieux Palais de Justice
6 Place Jacques-Cartier
7 Hôtel de Ville (City Hall)
8 La Maison Pierre du Calvet
9 Chapelle Notre-Dame-de-Bon-Secours
10 Marché Bonsecours
11 Jardin Nelson

ⓘ Information
Ⓜ Metro Station

Previous page: A stroll along Place Jacques-Cartier in Vieux-Montréal.

M any cities are best explored on foot, and Montréal is one of North America's most pedestrian-friendly. There's much to see in the concentrated districts—especially cobblestoned Vieux-Montréal, where the city was born. Its architectural heritage has been substantially preserved, and restored 18th- and 19th-century structures now house shops, boutique hotels, galleries, cafes, bars, and apartments. Take this tour to get the lay of the land: You'll pass many of the neighborhood's highlights. START: **Métro: Place d'Armes.**

Stanford White's commanding Banque de Montréal.

❶ **Banque de Montréal.** Montréal's oldest bank building dates from 1847. From 1901 to 1905, American architect Stanford White (1853–1906) extended the original building, and in this enlarged space, he created a vast chamber with green-marble columns topped with golden capitals. The public is welcome to stop in for a look. Besides being lavishly appointed inside and out, the bank also houses a small and quirky banking museum, which illustrates early operations. It's just off the main lobby to the left, and admission is free. ⏱ *15 min. 129 rue St-Jacques.* ☎ *514/877-6810. Museum open Mon–Fri 10am–4pm.*

❷ **Place d'Armes.** The architecture of the buildings that surround this outdoor plaza is representative of Montréal's growth: the Sulpician

residence of the 17th century, the Banque de Montréal and Basilique Notre-Dame of the 19th century, and the Art Deco Edifice Aldred of the 20th century. (If the 23-story Aldred looks familiar, there's a reason; built in 1931, it clearly resembles New York's Empire State Building, which was completed the same year.) The centerpiece of this square is a monument to city founder Paul de Chomedey, Sieur de Maisonneuve (1612–76). These five statues mark the spot where settlers defeated Iroquois warriors in bloody hand-to-hand fighting, with de Maisonneuve himself locked in combat with the Iroquois chief. De Maisonneuve won and lived here another 23 years. Note the dog depicted here—his bark alerted the settlers to the impending invasion. *Intersection of rues Notre-Dame and St-Sulpice.*

❸ ★★★ **Basilique Notre-Dame de Montréal.** American architect James O'Donnell bucked a trend toward neoclassicism when he designed this Gothic Revival masterpiece. The exterior is somewhat reminiscent of the cathedral in Paris that it shares its name with, but this basilica's stunning interior sets it apart. The magnificent altar (carved from rare linden wood), the vaulted ceiling (studded with 24-karat gold stars), the 12-ton bell (among the largest in North America), and the Limoges stained-glass windows (depicting moments from the city's history) are just some of the highlights. *See p 11.*

4 **Eggspectation.** Don't be put off by the goofy name. This breakfast-centric restaurant delivers. Food is fresh and comes out fast. The menu has 10 versions of eggs benedict as well as non-breakfast foods. *12 rue Notre-Dame est. See p 99.*

5 **Vieux Palais de Justice.** Court sessions ceased here for good in 1978 when the newer Palais de Justice was erected next door, but the Old Court House continues to serve the city as a civic office building. Though the building was completed in 1856, the dome and the top floor were added in 1891. Take a close look and you'll be able to spot the differences. A more modern landmark is also on display near here: Looking east on rue Notre-Dame, you should be able to see the Molson beer factory in the distance. *155 rue Notre-Dame est.*

6 **Place Jacques-Cartier.** Opened in 1804 as a marketplace, this central plaza is a magnet for locals and visitors year-round. In summer, performers fill the air with music, outdoor cafes serve as perches for people-watchers, and artists try to convince tourists to serve as their subjects. As you stroll past the 17th-century houses that line the promenade, observe the steeply pitched roofs, which were designed to shed heavy winter snows, and the small windows with double casements that let in light while keeping out wintry breezes. *Btw. rues Notre-Dame and de la Commune.*

7 **Hôtel de Ville (City Hall).** This ornate building has been Montréal's official City Hall since 1878,

Montréal's lovely plaza, Place d'Armes, is surrounded by architecture from 3 centuries.

and it was here, in 1967, that French president Charles de Gaulle delighted Québec separatists by shouting from the balcony, "Vive le Québec libre!" (Long live free Québec!) *275 rue Notre-Dame est.*

8 **La Maison Pierre du Calvet.** Built in the 18th century and sumptuously restored in the 1960s, this house was inhabited by a well-to-do family in its first years. Pierre du Calvet, believed to be the original owner, was a French Huguenot who supported the American Revolution and met here with Benjamin Franklin in 1775. (Calvet was later imprisoned for supplying money to the radicals south of the border.) With a characteristic sloped roof and raised end walls that serve as firebreaks, the building is constructed of Montréal gray stone. It is now a *hostellerie* and restaurant. *See p 128.*

9 ★ **Chapelle Notre-Dame-de-Bon-Secours.** Called the Sailors' Church because so many seamen made pilgrimages here to give thanks for being saved at sea, this chapel was founded by Marguerite Bourgeoys, a nun and teacher who was canonized in 1982. Excavations have unearthed foundations of her original 1675 church—although the building has been much altered, and the present facade was built in the late 18th century. A museum tells the story of Bourgeoys's life and incorporates the archaeological

site. Climb up to the tower for a view of the port and Old Town.
🕐 15 min. 400 rue St-Paul est (at the foot of rue Bonsecours). www.marguerite-bourgeoys.com. ☎ 514/282-8670. Free admission to chapel. Museum (includes archaeological site) C$10 adults, C$7 seniors and students, C$5 kids ages 6–12, free for children 5 and under. C$20 families. May to mid-Oct Tues–Sun 10am–5:30pm; mid-Oct to mid-Jan and Mar–Apr 11am–3:30pm. Closed mid-Jan to Feb. Métro: Champ-de-Mars.

🔟 **Marché Bonsecours.** Like so many landmark buildings in Montréal, the Bonsecours market has been used for a variety of purposes. Completed in 1847, it first was home to the Parliament of United Canada, then served as Montréal's City Hall, and eventually housed the municipality's housing and planning offices. It's now a retail center with art shops, clothing boutiques, and sidewalk cafes. It's most renowned, however, for its massive dome, which served as a landmark for seafarers sailing into the harbor. Today the dome is lit at night. The building also offers public restrooms. 350 rue St-Paul est (at the foot of rue St-Claude). www.marchebonsecours.qc.ca. ☎ 514/872-7730. Free admission. Fall–spring

Inside the glorious Chapelle Notre-Dame-de-Bon-Secours.

daily 10am–6pm; summer daily 10am–9pm. Métro: Champ-de-Mars.

For a good cafe to kick back in and just take in Vieux-Montréal, head to 1️⃣1️⃣ **Jardin Nelson.** It has a porch adjacent to the plaza and a tree-shaded garden court where live jazz is presented every afternoon and evening. Pizzas and crepes dominate, with crepe options both sweet and savory (including lobster). When the weather's nice, it's open until 2am. It is closed November through mid-April. 407 Place Jacques-Cartier. www.jardinnelson.com. ☎ 514/861-5731. $$.

Marché Bonsecours and City Hall by night.

Downtown Montréal

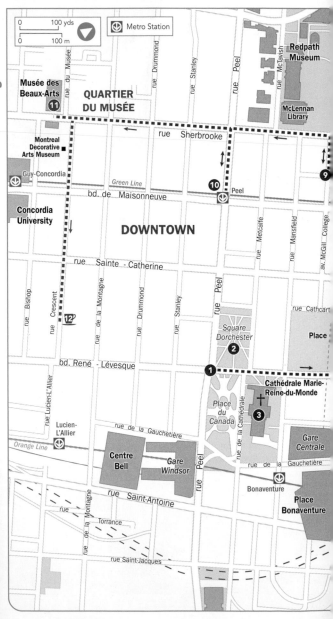

0   100 yds
0   100 m

🔽 Metro Station

Redpath Museum

rue du Musée

rue Drummond

rue Stanley

rue Peel

rue McTavish

Musée des Beaux-Arts ⑪

QUARTIER DU MUSÉE

McLennan Library

rue Sherbrooke

Montreal Decorative Arts Museum ■

🔽 Guy-Concordia

Green Line

⑩ Peel 🔽

⑨

bd. de Maisonneuve

Concordia University

DOWNTOWN

rue Metcalfe

rue Mansfield

av. McGill College

rue Sainte - Catherine

rue Bishop

rue Crescent

rue de la Montagne

rue Drummond

rue Stanley

rue Peel

rue Cathcart

⑫

Square Dorchester ②

Place

bd. René - Lévesque

①

Cathédrale Marie-Reine-du-Monde ✝ ③

rue Lucien-L'Allier

🔽 Lucien-L'Allier

Orange Line

rue de la Gauchetière

Place du Canada

rue de la Cathédrale

Gare Centrale

Centre Bell

Gare Windsor

rue Peel

rue de la Gauchetière

🔽 Bonaventure

Place Bonaventure

rue Saint-Antoine

rue de la Montagne

rue Torrance

rue Saint-Jacques

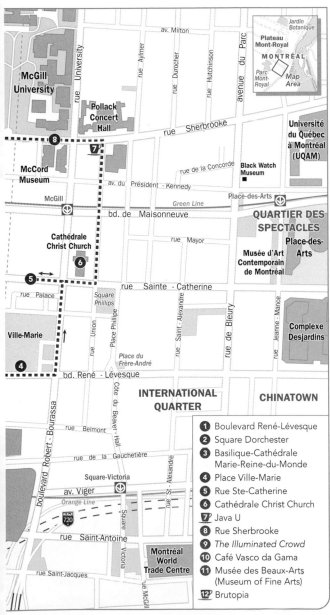

av. Milton

rue Aylmer
rue Durocher
rue Hutchinson
avenue du Parc

McGill University

rue University

Pollack Concert Hall

rue Sherbrooke

Université du Québec à Montréal (UQAM)

rue de la Concorde

Black Watch Museum

McCord Museum

av. du Président - Kennedy

Place-des-Arts

McGill

Green Line

bd. de Maisonneuve

QUARTIER DES SPECTACLES

rue Mayor

Place-des-Arts

Cathédrale Christ Church

Musée d'Art Contemporain de Montréal

rue Sainte - Catherine

rue Palace

Square Phillips

rue Saint - Alexandre

rue de Bleury

rue Jeanne - Mance

Complexe Desjardins

Ville-Marie

rue Union

Place Phillips

Place du Frère-André

bd. René - Lévesque

INTERNATIONAL QUARTER

CHINATOWN

boulevard Robert - Bourassa

Côte du Beaver - Hall

rue Belmont

rue de la Gauchetière

Square-Victoria

av. Viger

Orange Line

720

rue Saint-Antoine

rue St-Alexandre

rue Square

rue Victoria

rue McGill

Montréal World Trade Centre

rue Saint-Jacques

1 Boulevard René-Lévesque
2 Square Dorchester
3 Basilique-Cathédrale Marie-Reine-du-Monde
4 Place Ville-Marie
5 Rue Ste-Catherine
6 Cathédrale Christ Church
7 Java U
8 Rue Sherbrooke
9 *The Illuminated Crowd*
10 Café Vasco da Gama
11 Musée des Beaux-Arts (Museum of Fine Arts)
12 Brutopia

MONTRÉAL

Plateau Mont-Royal

Jardin Botanique

Parc Mont-Royal

Map Area

The core of downtown Montréal isn't as densely packed as those of other major cities in North America, but it's deceptively large. For that reason, it will probably take at least a half-day to make this tour into the city's commercial heart. START: **Métro: Bonaventure.**

1 Boulevard René-Lévesque. Formerly Dorchester Boulevard, this street was renamed in 1988 following the death of René Lévesque, the Parti Québécois leader who led the movement for Québec independence and the province's use of the French language. Boulevard René-Lévesque is the city's broadest downtown thoroughfare. Start at the corner of boulevard René-Lévesque and rue Peel.

2 Square Dorchester. This is one of downtown's central locations. It's a gathering point for tour buses and horse-drawn calèches, and the square's trees and benches invite lunchtime brown-baggers. This used to be called Dominion Square, but it was renamed for Baron Dorchester, an early English governor, when the adjacent street, once named for Dorchester, was changed to boulevard René-Lévesque. Montréal's central tourist office is at the northern end of the park, at 1255 rue Peel, and is open daily. Visitors can ask questions of the bilingual attendants, purchase tour tickets, make hotel reservations, or arrange a car rental.

3 Basilique-Cathédrale Marie-Reine-du-Monde. Suddenly get the feeling you're in Rome? This cathedral is a copy of St. Peter's Basilica in Vatican City, albeit roughly one-quarter of the size. It was built between 1875 and 1894 as the headquarters for Montréal's Roman Catholic bishop. The statue in front is of Bishop Ignace Bourget (1799–1885), the force behind the construction. Most impressive is the 76m-high (249-ft.) dome, about a third of the size of the Rome original. The statues standing on the roofline represent patron saints of the Québec region, providing a local touch. *1085 rue de la Cathédrale. www.cathedralecatholiquede montreal.org.* ☎ *514/866-1661. Free admission, donations welcome. Mon–Fri 7am–5pm; Sat–Sun 7:30am–5pm. Métro: Bonaventure.*

Centrally located Dorchester Square is popular at lunchtime.

A beautiful nighttime view of the Basilique-Cathédrale Marie-Reine-du-Monde and 1000 de La Gauchetière.

④ Place Ville-Marie. One thing to keep in mind is that the French word place, or plaza, sometimes means an outdoor square, such as Place Jacques-Cartier in Vieux-Montréal. Other times, it refers to a building or complex that includes stores and offices. Place Ville-Marie is in this category. Known as PVM, the glass building was considered a gem of the 1960s urban redevelopment efforts. Its architect was I.M. Pei, who also designed the glass pyramid at the Louvre in Paris. Pei gave the skyscraper a cross-shaped footprint, recalling the cross atop Mont Royal. The underground houses a large shopping mall (www.placevillemarie.com). In 2016, a rooftop observatory and all-season terrasse opened to the public. *See p 91.*

⑤ Rue Ste-Catherine. This is one of the city's prime shopping streets, with name brands, local businesses, and department stores. Among them is La Baie—or "the Bay"—successor to the famous fur-trapping firm Hudson's Bay Co., founded in the 17th century. Also here is Henry Birks et Fils, a preeminent jeweler since 1879 (the company is now known as Maison Birks, but the original name remains on the building.) Its Birks Café is a decidedly posh spot to enjoy lunch, high tea, or buy super-premium chocolates or macarons. Ste-Catherine has a smattering of adult strip clubs and sex shops right alongside the family-friendly fare; the street's mixed use is a Montréal signature.

⑥ Cathédrale Christ Church. Built from 1856 to 1859, this neo-Gothic building stands in glorious contrast to the city's downtown skyscrapers and is the seat of the Anglican bishop of Montréal. The church garden is modeled on a medieval European cloister. It offers a Sunday 10am Sung Eucharist and 4pm Choral Evensong, and weekday services at 8:15am, 12:15pm, and 5:15pm. *635 rue Ste-Catherine ouest.*

Place Ville-Marie, designed by I. M. Pei, is one of downtown's most important architectural landmarks.

Rue Ste-Catherine is one of the city's prime thoroughfares for shopping.

At the corner of rues Union and Sherbrooke, you'll find an outpost of the jovial **7** **Java U,** a local food chain. This friendly, laid-back spot serves quiches, salads, wraps, and cake. *626 rue Sherbrooke. www. java-u.com.* ☎ *514/286-1991. $.*

8 **Rue Sherbrooke.** This is the city's grand boulevard, still rich with former mansions, ritzy hotels, high-end boutiques, and special museums that give it its personality. The main campus of Canada's most prestigious school, McGill University, is here. The university was founded after a bequest from a Scottish-born fur trader, James McGill. The central campus mixes modern concrete and glass structures alongside older stone buildings and is the focal point for the school's 39,000 students. The McCord Museum maintains an eccentric collection of photographs, paintings, and First Nations folk art. Its special exhibits make it especially worth a visit. *See p 13.*

9 ***The Illuminated Crowd.*** This is an eggnog-colored work in polyester resin (1985) by sculptor Raymond Mason. The piece captures

The neo-Gothic Cathédrale Christ Church.

Montréal's most important museum, the Musée des Beaux-Arts de Montréal (Museum of Fine Arts).

the faces of a life-size crowd of figures in a slew of emotional states: hope, irritation, fear, and "the flow of man's emotion through space" as it says on the descriptive plaque. The work is outdoors near the intersection of avenue McGill College and avenue du President Kennedy. Mason was born in England but moved to Paris early in his career—giving his own life the mixture of British and French influences that is emblematic of Montréal. *1981 av. McGill College.*

Downtown is full of restaurants both fancy and casual, and right in between is 10 **Café Vasco Da Gama,** a sleek, high-ceilinged eatery with a Portuguese feel—the owners also run the esteemed Ferreira Café (p 35) on the same block. It's a great place for big breakfasts, pastries, sandwiches, and tapas. *1472 rue Peel.* www.vascodagama.ca. ☎ 514/286-2688. $.

11 **Musée des Beaux-Arts de Montréal (Museum of Fine Arts).** This is Montréal's most prominent museum. The modern annex on the south side of rue Sherbrooke was added in 1991 and is connected to the original stately Beaux-Arts building (1912) on the north side by an underground tunnel that doubles as a gallery. A new four-level pavilion devoted to the Old Masters is in the works and is slated to open by 2017, to coincide with Montréal's 375th anniversary celebrations. *See p 13.*

Lively spots for food and drink are abundant along rue Crescent. Thursday's and Sir Winston Churchill, at nos. 1449 and 1459, both have large, festive balconies that overlook the street. 12 **Brutopia,** at no. 1219, pulls endless pints of its own microbrews. With several rooms on three levels, a terrace in back, and its own street-side balcony, Brutopia draws students with laptops and old friends just hanging out. Bands perform, too, with an open-mic night on Sunday. *See p 111.*

Plateau Mont-Royal

① St-Viateur Bagel & Café
② Boutique window-shopping along rue St-Denis
③ Kanuk
④ La Banquise
⑤ Parc La Fontaine
⑥ Rue Duluth
⑦ Boulevard St-Laurent
⑧ Schwartz's
⑨ Rue Prince-Arthur

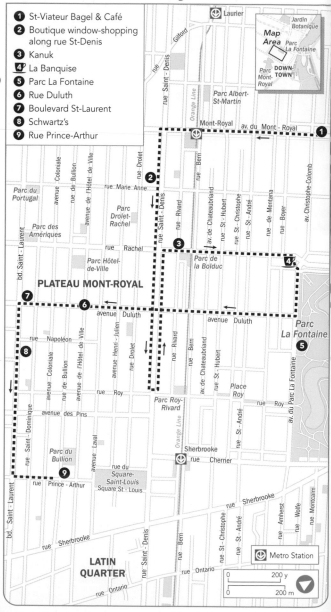

This is essentially a browsing and grazing tour, designed to provide a sampling of the sea of ethnicities that make up Plateau Mont-Royal. The largely Francophone (French-speaking) neighborhood flourishes with restaurants, cafes, clubs, and shops, and the residential side streets are filled with row houses that are home to students, young professionals, and immigrants old and new. It's bounded more or less by rue Sherbrooke on the south, boulevard St-Joseph on the north, boulevard St-Laurent on the west, and avenue Papineau on the east. START: **Métro: Mont-Royal.**

The famed St-Viateur Bagel & Café.

❶ St-Viateur Bagel & Café.
Start with fortifications from St-Viateur. Myer Lewkowicz brought his bagel recipe from Eastern Europe in 1957, with a process that includes shaping each bagel by hand, dressing with seeds or spices, and baking in a wood-fired oven (there's a great photo spread on the website). You can get bagels and coffee to go or eat in and choose from sandwiches, salads, soups, and even wine or beer. *1127 ave du Mont-Royal est. www.stviateurbagel.com.* ☎ *514/528-6361.*

❷ Boutique window-shopping along St-Denis.
From avenue du Mont-Royal in the north to rue Roy (and farther) to the south, this main drag is thick with great places to poke around. Renaud-Bray, at no. 4380, is a large bookstore with mostly French stock as well as CDs, magazines, and newspapers from around the world. Zone, at no. 4246, is part of a small Montréal-based chain that specializes in

contemporary housewares, sleekly monochromatic and brightly hued. Kaliyana, at 4107, is another Canadian clothing company, offering natural-fiber outfits that are flowing and angular—think Asian-influenced Eileen Fisher. (A reminder: Only cross streets at the corners; jaywalking is illegal and police regularly issue tickets.)

❸ Kanuk.
One of Canada's top manufacturers of high-end winter coats and accessory designs, sews and sells its wares right here. Like EMS or L.L.Bean in the U.S., Kanuk first sold its heavy parkas primarily to outdoor enthusiasts. Back then, the company wryly notes on its website, customers had a choice of royal blue or royal blue. Today, its jackets come in 38 colors and 70 models. The showroom's fluorescent lighting and mile-high racks of coats does

Rue St-Denis is busy night and day.

The landmark La Banquise serves up 30 kinds of poutine.

not suggest luxury, although a parka can set you back C$600 to C$900. They're an extremely popular practical necessity—and a status symbol. *See p 88.*

If you haven't yet tried *poutine*, the national comfort food, by all means hop into **4** **La Banquise.** The restaurant is practically a city landmark with its 25 variations of the french fries with cheese curds. The funky little restaurant is open 24 hours a day, every day. *See p 100.*

5 Parc La Fontaine. Strolling this grand park, particularly on a warm day, is an enormously satisfying way to see Montréal at play. This northwestern end of La Fontaine is well used by people and puppies of all ages. In the warm months, see if anything's happening at the park's Théâtre de Verdure, an open-air theater performance space, which, at press time, was set to reopen in 2017 after major renovations. *See p 20 and p 55.*

6 Rue Duluth. This somewhat drab street is dotted with an ever-changing collection of Greek, Portuguese, Italian, North African, Malaysian, and Vietnamese eateries. Many of the restaurants state that you can *apportez votre vin* (bring your own wine). There are also several small antiques shops here. *Rue Duluth btw. the parc and bd. St-Laurent.*

7 Boulevard St-Laurent. St-Laurent is the north-south thoroughfare that divides Montréal into its east and west sides. It's so prominent in Montréal's cultural history that it's known to Anglophones (English speakers), Francophones (French speakers), and Allophones (people whose primary language is neither English nor French) simply as "the Main." Traditionally a beachhead for immigrants to the city, St-Laurent has become a street of bistros and clubs. The late-night section runs for several miles, roughly from rue Laurier in the north down to rue Sherbrooke in the south. The boom in entertainment venues was fueled by low rent prices and the large number of industrial lofts in this area, a legacy of St-Laurent's heyday as a garment-manufacturing center. Today, these cavernous spaces are places for the city's students, professionals, artists, and guests to eat and play.

8 Schwartz's. The language police insisted on the exterior sign with the French mouthful SCHWARZ CHARCUTERIE HEBRAIQUE DE MONTRÉAL, but everyone just calls it Schwartz's. This narrow, no-frills Hebrew deli might appear completely unassuming, but it serves the smoked meat against which all other smoked meats are measured. *See p 103.*

9 Rue Prince-Arthur. Named after Queen Victoria's third son, who was governor-general of

Pedestrianized Rue Prince-Arthur is lined with bars and restaurants.

Jewish Montréal

At the turn of the 20th century, Montréal was home to more Jews than any other Canadian city, attracting an especially large Yiddish-speaking population from Eastern Europe. Today Toronto has nearly twice as many Jewish residents, but vestiges of the community's history and ongoing practices remain here.

The Bagg Street Shul, at the corner of rue Clark (1 block west of bd. St-Laurent) and rue Bagg (1 block south of rue Duluth), began as a two-family residence and was converted to a synagogue in 1920 and 1921. It has been in continuous use ever since. Other synagogues dot the neighborhood but have transitioned as the Jewish community dispersed—one became a French college, another an evangelical church (though it still houses 10 murals of the history of Jews in Montréal).

Kosher edibles abound. One could start the day with a bagel from either **St-Viateur Bagel & Café** (1127 av. Mont-Royal est), or **Fairmont Bagel** (74 av. Fairmont ouest), a few blocks farther north, and then travel back in time for lunch with an old-school fountain soda from **Wilensky Light Lunch** (34 rue Fairmount ouest). For dinner, there's always **Schwartz's** (p 103) or steaks at the posh **Moishes** (3961 bd. St-Laurent).

The Snowden neighborhood in western Montréal is home to the city's contemporary Jewish organizations. The **Jewish Public Library** (www.jewishpubliclibrary.org; ☎ 514/345-2627) boasts the largest circulating collection of Judaica in North America and hosts lectures, cultural events, and concerts. Its archive of minutes, correspondence, flyers, posters, manuscripts, and artifacts includes more than 30,000 photos related to Montréal's Jewish history. The library shares a building at 5151 Côte-Ste-Catherine with the **Montréal Holocaust Memorial Centre** (www.mhmc.ca; ☎ 514/345-2605) and two dozen other Jewish community service agencies. The memorial center features exhibits to commemorate lives lost in the Holocaust. Just across the street is the **Segal Centre for Performing Arts** (p 122), which presents plays in Yiddish.

Canada from 1911 to 1916, this pedestrian street is filled with bars and restaurants which add more to the area's liveliness than to the city's gastronomic reputation. The older establishments go by such names as La Cabane Grecque, La Caverne Grec, Casa Grecque—no doubt you will discern an emerging theme—but the Greek stalwarts are being challenged by Latino and Asian newcomers. Their owners vie constantly with gimmicks to haul in passersby, including two-for-one drinks and dueling tables d'hôte. Tables and chairs are set out along the sides of the street, and in warm weather, street performers, vendors, and caricaturists also compete for tourist dollars.

Parc du Mont-Royal

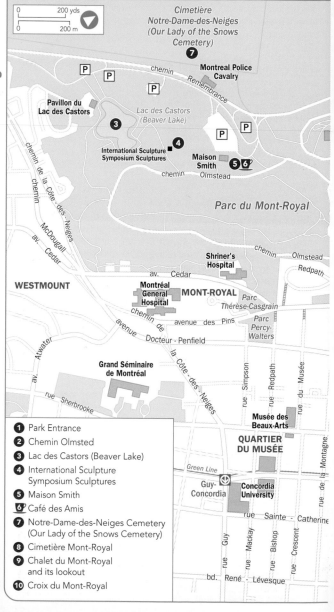

1 Park Entrance
2 Chemin Olmsted
3 Lac des Castors (Beaver Lake)
4 International Sculpture Symposium Sculptures
5 Maison Smith
6 Café des Amis
7 Notre-Dame-des-Neiges Cemetery (Our Lady of the Snows Cemetery)
8 Cimetière Mont-Royal
9 Chalet du Mont-Royal and its lookout
10 Croix du Mont-Royal

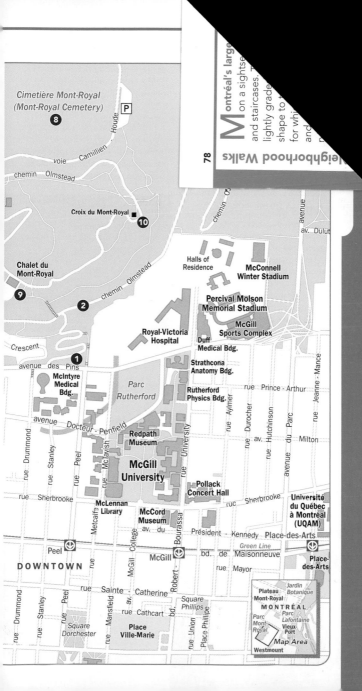

Montréal's large
on a sightse
and staircases.
lightly grade
shape to t
for whi
and

Cimetière Mont-Royal
(Mont-Royal Cemetery) **8** P

Houde

voie Camillien

chemin Olmstead

Croix du Mont-Royal ■ **10**

chemin O

avenue

av. Dulut

Halls of
Residence

**McConnell
Winter Stadium**

**Chalet du
Mont-Royal**

9

2 chemin Olmstead

**Percival Molson
Memorial Stadium**

**Royal-Victoria
Hospital**

**McGill
Sports Complex**

Crescent

1

**Duff
Medical Bdg.**

avenue des Pins

**Strathcona
Anatomy Bdg.**

**McIntyre
Medical
Bdg.**

*Parc
Rutherford*

rue Prince - Arthur

avenue Docteur - Penfield

**Rutherford
Physics Bdg.**

rue Aylmer

rue Durocher

rue Hutchinson

avenue du Parc

rue Jeanne - Mance

rue Drummond

rue Stanley

rue Peel

rue McTavish

**Redpath
Museum**

rue University

Milton

rue Sherbrooke

**McGill
University**

**Pollack
Concert Hall**

rue Sherbrooke

**Université
du Québec
à Montréal
(UQAM)**

**McLennan
Library**

Metcalfe

rue McGill College

**McCord
Museum**

av. du

rue Bourassa

Président - Kennedy Place-des-Arts

Peel

McGill

Green Line

bd. de Maisonneuve

Place-
des-Arts

DOWNTOWN

rue Robert -

rue Mayor

rue Drummond

rue Stanley

rue Peel

rue Sainte - Catherine

av. Union

bd.

rue Cathcart

Square
Phillips

**Place
Ville-Marie**

rue Mansfield

Place Phillip

Square
Dorchester

Plateau
Mont-Royal

*Jardin
Botanique*

MONTRÉAL

Parc
Mont-
Royal

Parc
Lafontaine

Vieux-
Port

Map Area

Westmount

st green space may also be the most taxing ...er's legs, given the park's occasionally steep hills ...hat said, there are options for staying on a broad, ...bridle path, so you need only be in reasonably good ...ackle the 200-hectare (494-acre) park. The small mountain ...ch Montréal is named is a popular place for walkers, runners, ...anyone seeking out broad panoramas of the city. If you're car-...ing a phone with Internet access, you can pull up a terrific interactive map at www.lemontroyal.qc.ca/carte/en/index.sn. You can also download podcasts for guided audio-video walks from the same website. START: **Corner of rue Peel and avenue des Pins.**

1 Park Entrance. After years of construction, this entrance is finally a thing of beauty, with broad steps and beautiful plantings. (Note that if you're heading up with a stroller—as we recently did—there's another entrance about 30 meters to the left that doesn't have steps.) From either entrance, it's possible to reach the top of this small mountain by a variety of routes. Hearty souls can choose the quickest and most strenuous approach—taking the steepest sets of stairs at every opportunity, which go directly to the Chalet du Mont-Royal and its lookout at the top (see no. 9). Those who prefer to take their time and gain altitude slowly can use the switchback bridle path. Or mix and match the options

Notre-Dame-des-Neiges Cemetery, Montréal's largest cemetery.

as you go along. Don't be too worried about getting lost; the park is small enough that it's easy enough to regain your sense of direction no matter which way you head. *Corner of rue Peel and av. des Pins.*

2 ★ Chemin Olmsted. The broad path that loops through the park was named for the park's designer, American landscape architect Frederick Law Olmsted (1802–1903), who also designed Central Park in New York City. It's actually the only part of Olmsted's design that became a reality as the rest of the park wasn't completed to his scheme. Walkers, joggers, mountain bikers, and mounted policemen all cross paths here. The road is closed to vehicular traffic, making it a joy for those looking for peace and quiet from the city.

Montréal's angel: Monument George-Étienne-Cartier.

A skyline view from Mont-Royal.

❸ ★ **Lac des Castors (Beaver Lake).** This lake's name refers to the once-profitable fur industry, not to the actual presence of the long-gone animals. In summer, the lake is surrounded by sunbathers and picnickers, and you can rent a paddleboat. In the winter, there's a nearby skating rink (the lake cannot support skaters), with skates, cross-country skis, and snowshoes available to rent at Maison Smith (see ❺).

❹ **International Sculpture Symposium sculptures.** On the grassy rise to the east of Beaver Lake sit several stone and metal structures. These sculptures were erected in 1964 as part of the International Sculpture Symposium in Montréal. A collection of artists was given marble, granite, or metal to shape their abstract visions, and a limited amount of time to complete

At play in Parc Mont-Royal.

their work. The representation of four priestesses, made in Italian marble by Yerassimos Sklavos (1927–67), is one of the most striking pieces. Not far from the sculptures, see if you can find two granite plaques (out of a total of five such plaques spread around the park) that have poetic phrases or humorous quips by Montréaler Gilbert Boyer chiseled into the rock. *Near Beaver Lake.*

❺ ★ **Maison Smith.** The park's year-round information center has restrooms, a gift shop, and a set of educational displays that describe the history, flora, and fauna of Mont-Royal. Café des Amis, a terrace restaurant, has food and refreshments. There's a parking lot here if you choose to drive to the park instead of walk. *1260 chemin Remembrance. www.lemontroyal.qc.ca.*

❻ **Café des Amis.** Inside Maison Smith is a cafe that from mid-May through mid-October also spills out onto a lovely terrace. It offers sandwiches, homemade soups, sweets (try the pineapple-carrot cake if they have it), and beverages including beer, wine, and fair-trade Camino hot chocolate. ☎ 514/843-8240.

❼ **Notre-Dame-des-Neiges Cemetery (Our Lady of the Snows Cemetery).** Many famous Montréalers have been laid to rest in the city's largest, and mostly Catholic, cemetery. Included are the Molson crypts, where members of the influential Canadian brewing family are buried. Other prominent residents include statesman Sir George-Etienne Cartier, poet Emile Nelligan, architect Ernest Cormier, and hockey star Maurice "The Rocket" Richard. The cemetery's website offers a search function to

Extreme Weather in Montréal

For the most part, Montréal lives in either winter or summer—the spring and fall seasons are sweet but short-lived. Winter lasts from November until late March, and summer lasts from June through September. The cold months often include snow blizzards, freezing rain, and ice storms. Summers often include stifling humidity during July and August. Luckily, there's an Underground City below much of downtown, with miles of shops, restaurants, movie theaters, and connections to the subway (see p 91 for highlights).

An autumn scene in Parc Mont-Royal.

locate specific graves. *4601 chemin Côte-des-Neiges. www.cimetierend dn.org.* ☎ *514/735-1361.*

❽ Cimetière Mont-Royal. Smaller than its Catholic neighbor to the west, Mont Royal Cemetery was founded in 1852 by a group of Christian (but non-Catholic) denominations. The beautifully terraced cemetery was designed to resemble a garden and makes for peaceful strolling. Among those interred here is Anna Leonowens, the British governess who was the real-life inspiration for the musical comedy *The King and I. 1297 chemin de la Fôret. www.mountroyalcem.com.* ☎ *514/279-7358.*

❾ ★ Chalet du Mont-Royal and its lookout. The front terrace here offers the most popular panoramic view of the city and the river.

The chalet itself was constructed from 1931 to 1932 and has been used over the years for receptions, concerts, and various other events. Inside the chalet, take a look at the 17 paintings hanging just below the ceiling. They relate the region's history and the story of the French explorations of North America.

❿ Croix du Mont-Royal. Legend has it that Paul de Chomedey, Sieur de Maisonneuve, erected a wooden cross here in 1643 after the young colony survived a flood threat. The present incarnation, installed in 1924, is made of steel and is 31.4 m (103 ft.) tall. It is lit at night and visible from all over the city. Beside the cross is a plaque marking where a time capsule was interred in August 1992, during Montréal's 350th-birthday celebration. Some 12,000 children ages 6 to 12 filled the capsule with messages and drawings depicting their visions for the city in the year 2142, when Montréal will be 500 years old and the capsule will be opened. *To return to downtown Montréal, go back along the path toward the chalet terrace. On the left, just before the terrace, is a path to a staircase that descends to where the tour began. The walk down by this route takes about 15 minutes. Or, the no. 11 bus travels along chemin de la Remembrance.* ●

Shopping in Montréal

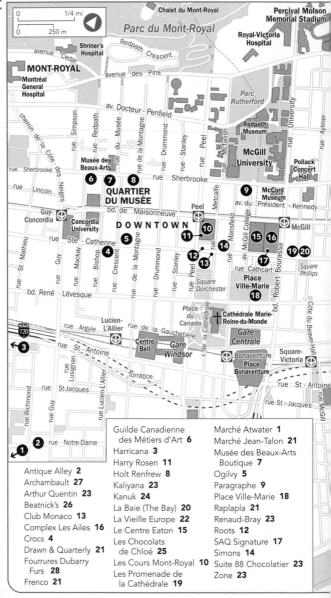

Antique Alley 2
Archambault 27
Arthur Quentin 23
Beatnick's 26
Club Monaco 13
Complex Les Ailes 16
Crocs 4
Drawn & Quarterly 21
Fourrures Dubarry
  Furs 28
Frenco 21

Guilde Canadienne
  des Métiers d'Art 6
Harricana 3
Harry Rosen 11
Holt Renfrew 8
Kaliyana 23
Kanuk 24
La Baie (The Bay) 20
La Vieille Europe 22
Le Centre Eaton 15
Les Chocolats
  de Chloé 25
Les Cours Mont-Royal 10
Les Promenade de
  la Cathédrale 19

Marché Atwater 1
Marché Jean-Talon 21
Musée des Beaux-Arts
  Boutique 7
Ogilvy 5
Paragraphe 9
Place Ville-Marie 18
Raplapla 21
Renaud-Bray 23
Roots 12
SAQ Signature 17
Simons 14
Suite 88 Chocolatier 23
Zone 23

Previous page: Fancy, delicious chocolates at Suite 88 Chocolatier.

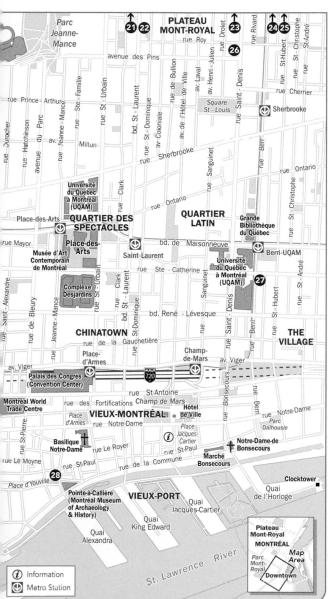

Parc
Jeanne-
Mance

㉑ ㉒ PLATEAU
MONT-ROYAL
rue Roy
㉓ ㉔ ㉕
㉖

rue Rivard
rue Drolet
rue St-Hubert
rue St-Christophe
rue St-André

avenue des Pins

rue Prince-Arthur

rue Durocher
rue Hutchison
avenue du Parc
avenue Jeanne-Mance
rue Ste-Famille
rue St-Urbain
bd. St-Laurent
rue St-Dominique
av. Coloniale
av. de l'Hôtel-de-Ville
av. Laval
av. Henri-Julien
rue Saint-Denis

rue de Bullion

Square
St-Louis

rue Cherrier

🔵 Sherbrooke

Milton

rue Clark

rue Sherbrooke

rue Sanguinet
rue Berri
rue Ontario
rue St-Christophe

Université
du Québec
à Montréal
(UQAM)

rue Ontario

Place-des-Arts
🔵 QUARTIER DES
SPECTACLES

QUARTIER
LATIN

Grande
Bibliothèque
du Québec

rue St-André

rue Mayor

Place-des-
Arts
🔵

Saint-Laurent
🔵

bd. de Maisonneuve

🔵 Berri-UQAM

Musée d'Art
Contemporain
de Montréal

rue Ste-Catherine

Université
du Québec
à Montréal
(UQAM)
㉗

rue St-Hubert

rue Saint-Alexandre
rue de Bleury
rue Jeanne-Mance

Complexe
Desjardins

rue Clark
bd. St-Laurent
rue St-Dominique

bd. René-Lévesque

rue Saint-Denis
rue Berri

THE
VILLAGE

CHINATOWN
rue de la Gauchetière
Place-
d'Armes
🔵

Champ-
de-Mars
🔵

av. Viger
rue Bonsecours

Palais des Congrès
(Convention Center)
🔵

720

rue St-Antoine

Montréal World
Trade Centre

rue des Fortifications Champ de Mars

rue Notre-Dame

rue St-Pierre

Place
d'Armes

VIEUX-MONTRÉAL

Hôtel
de Ville

Parc
Dalhousie

rue Le Moyne

Basilique
Notre-Dame

rue Notre-Dame
rue Le Royer
rue St-Paul

Place
Jacques-
Cartier
ⓘ
rue St-Paul
Marché
Bonsecours

Notre-Dame-de-
Bonsecours

rue de la Commune

Place d'Youville
㉘

Pointe-à-Callière
(Montréal Museum
of Archaeology
& History)

VIEUX-PORT

Quai
Jacques-Cartier

Clocktower

Quai
de l'Horloge

Quai
King Edward

Quai
Alexandra

St. Lawrence River

Plateau
Mont-Royal
MONTRÉAL
Parc
Mont-
Royal
Downtown
Map
Area

ⓘ Information
🔵 Metro Station

Shopping Best Bets

Best Street for Parisian & Québécois Fashion
Avenue Laurier has boutiques for shopping and restaurants for relaxing, *Avenue Laurier, between bd. St-Laurent and ave. de l'Epée* (p 87)

Best Store for Warding-Off-Winter Fashion
★ Kanuk, *485 rue Rachel est* (p 88)

Best Department Store for High Fashion
★ Holt Renfrew, *1300 rue Sherbrooke ouest* (p 86)

Best Adorable, Handmade Dolls
★ Raplapla, *69 rue Villeneuve ouest* (p 85)

Best Department Store for Teen Fashion
Simons, *977 rue Ste-Catherine ouest* (p 87)

Best High-End Inuit Sculpture
★ Guilde Canadienne des Métiers d'Art, *1460 rue Sherbrooke ouest* (p 85)

Best Wool Blanket
★ La Baie (The Bay), *585 Ste-Catherine ouest* (p 86)

Best Store for Seeing a Bagpiper
★★ Ogilvy, *1307 Ste-Catherine ouest* (p 86)

Best Antiques
★ Antique Alley, *rue Notre-Dame ouest* (p 85)

Best Destination Food Market
★★ Marché Atwater, *138 rue Atwater* (p 89) and Marché Jean-Talon, *7070 av. Henri-Julien* (p 89)

Best Chocolate Shop
It's a tie: ★ Les Chocolats de Chloé, *546 rue Duluth est* (p 89); and Suite 88 Chocolatier, *3957 rue St-Denis* (p 90)

Best Wine Shop
SAQ Signature, *677 rue Ste-Catherine ouest* (p 89)

Best Shop for Tracking Down Rare Records
Beatnick's, *3770 rue St-Denis* (p 90)

Best Snazzy Housewares
Arthur Quentin, *3960 rue St-Denis* (p 90)

Best Museum Shop
Musée des Beaux-Arts Boutique, *1390 rue Sherbrooke ouest* (p 90)

Best Mall to Start Exploring the Underground City
Place Ville-Marie, *1 Place Ville Marie* (p 91)

Best Avant-Garde Clothing for Women
Kaliyana, *4107 rue St-Denis* (p 88)

The Canadian Guild of Crafts offers fine crafts at many price points.

Shopping **A to Z**

Antiques, Arts & Crafts & Galleries

★ **Antique Alley** VIEUX-MONTREAL Some of the city's quirkier antiques shops have disappeared in recent years—thanks a lot, eBay. But there are still tempting shops along Antique Alley, as it's nicknamed, a strip of rue Notre-Dame west of Vieux Montréal. *Rue Notre-Dame ouest, especially btw. rue Guy and av. Atwater. Métro: Lionel-Groulx.*

★ **Guilde Canadienne des Métiers d'Art** DOWNTOWN In English, it's called the Canadian Guild of Crafts. A well-curated collection of items is displayed in a meticulously arranged gallery setting, including blown glass, tapestries, and wooden bowls. The store is particularly strong in avant-garde jewelry and Inuk sculpture. A small carving might be had for C$100 to C$300, while larger, more important pieces go for thousands. *1460 rue Sherbrooke ouest. www.canadian guild.com.* ☎ *866/477-6091. Métro: Guy-Concordia.*

Books & Toys

★ **Drawn & Quarterly** PLATEAU This Mile End bookstore is a cultural hub, with book launch parties, a graphic novel book club, and food writing workshops. It specializes in graphic novels, including those from its own publishing company, but also has children's books, quirky notecards, and fine arts books. *211 rue Bernard ouest. http://211blog.drawnandquarterly. com.* ☎ *514/279-2224. Métro: Rosemont or Outremont.*

Paragraphe DOWNTOWN Though it caters to university students seeking course materials, this store's many shelves are also

Mile End's Drawn & Quarterly is a true community bookstore.

stocked with a decent selection of novels and classics. Once in a while the shop's couches are cleared out for in-store author appearances and small-scale musical performances. *2220 av. McGill College. www.paragraphbooks.com.* ☎ *514/845-5811. Métro: McGill.*

★ **kids Raplapla** PLATEAU Sweet dolls for infants and young children made from organic cotton are the specialty of this local company and sold directly from this studio-boutique. Look for the rectangular-shaped Monsieur Tsé-Tsé doll, which is soft and adorable and our favorite icon for the Montréal handcraft movement. *69 rue Villeneuve ouest. www.raplapla.com.* ☎ *514/563-1209. Métro: Mont-Royal.*

kids Renaud-Bray PLATEAU MONT-ROYAL For those who know French or want to brush up, this two-level bookstore with a primarily French-language stock is a valuable resource. It also sells DVDs/Blu-Rays, CDs, and newspapers and magazines from all over the world. Most English-language books are on the upper floor. There's a large children's section, too. *4380 rue St-Denis.*

Montréal's Underground City

Montréal's harsh winters and sticky summers were the motivating force behind the construction of a series of underground tunnels that has created a network of subterranean shops, cafes, and entrances to hotels and Métro stations. This monumental achievement in urban planning stretches for nearly 33km (21 miles) and typically sees 500,000 people passing through each day. You can buy a new outfit, take in some art, or even catch a movie—all without ever venturing outdoors. To head *souterrain* from street level, look for blue signs with a white arrow pointing down or signs marked "RESO." You can also enter at the many malls that operate both above and below ground. For more information see "Exploring the Underground City," later in this chapter.

www.renaud-bray.com. ☎ 514/844-2587. Métro: Mont-Royal.

Department Stores
Also see "Exploring the Underground City," later in this chapter, for some of the city's larger shopping complexes.

★ Holt Renfrew DOWNTOWN
After starting life as a hat shop in 1837, Holt Renfrew has evolved into a store for clothes shoppers with big budgets and big taste. Hermès, Armani, Prada, and Stella McCartney are just a few of the designer labels you'll find. *1300 rue Sherbrooke ouest. www.holtrenfrew.com.* ☎ 514/842-5111. Métro: Peel.

★ La Baie (The Bay) DOWNTOWN
No retailer has an older or more celebrated pedigree than the Hudson's Bay Company, whose name was shortened to "The Bay" and then transformed into "La Baie" by Québec language laws. The company was incorporated in Canada in 1670 but is now under a corporate umbrella with Lord & Taylor, Saks Fifth Avenue, and other brands. You'll find clothing and housewares and La Baie's

famous Hudson's Bay "point blanket." A "learning centre" online is devoted to the history of the fur trade. *585 Ste-Catherine ouest. www.hbc.com.* ☎ 514/281-4422. Métro: McGill.

★★ Ogilvy DOWNTOWN
This most vibrant example of a classy breed of department store that appears to be fading from the scene was established in 1866 and has been at this location since 1912, however a merger with Holt Renfrew may keep it partially under

Holt Renfrew is the place for designer duds.

construction through 2017. A bag-piper still announces the noon hour (a favorite sight for tourists). Ogilvy has always had a reputation for quality merchandise and now contains more than 60 boutiques, including Louis Vuitton, Tiffany & Co., and Burberry. Its Christmas windows are eagerly awaited each season. *1307 rue Ste-Catherine ouest. www.ogilvycanada.com.* ☎ *855/842-7711 or 514/842-7711. Métro: Peel.*

Simons DOWNTOWN This branch was the first expansion for Québec City's long-established family-owned department store. The in-house Twik label is a must for teens while other labels for work, sleep, and play are geared toward women and men. A few cutting-edge designers are thrown in for good measure. *977 rue Ste-Catherine ouest. www.simons.ca.* ☎ *514/282-1840. Métro: Peel.*

Fashion

A trip to the shops in the bohemian Plateau and adjacent Mile End neighborhoods should send you home with a dash of local style. For ritzier offerings, go further north: Avenue Laurier, between boulevard St-Laurent and avenue de l'Epée, is home to Parisian boutiques and products from the ateliers of young Québécois designers. Montréal's Fashion & Design Festival, held in August, features runway shows and pop-up stores, with events throughout the Quartier des Spectacles and on avenue de McGill College. Festival details: www.festivalmodedesign.com. There's a plus-sized fashion weekend in May; details are at www.montrealplusfashionweek.com.

Club Monaco DOWNTOWN A trendier version of Banana Republic, and cheaper than Prada, this Canadian-gone-global chain (and now owned by Ralph Lauren) has a refined edge, using simple, bold

Montréal's well-loved Ogilvy department store was established in 1866.

colors in clothes for both sexes. *1000 rue Ste-Catherine ouest. www.clubmonaco.com.* ☎ *514/871-9841. Métro: Peel.*

kids Crocs DOWNTOWN Fun fact: The marshmallowy, brightly colored clog originated in Québec and was originally manufactured in the province—who knew? It was acquired by the American Crocs company in 2004. The product is named after the crocodile, because it can be worn on land or in water. The company has branched into more normal-looking (read: less childlike) footwear and has a store in the heart of downtown. *1384 rue Ste-Catherine ouest. www.crocs.com.* ☎ *514/750-9796. Métro. Guy-Concordia.*

Fourrures Dubarry Furs VIEUX-MONTREAL A nod back to the city's history in fur trading. Coats and capes in fur, shearling, cashmere, and leather, along with hats, earmuffs, purses, and scarves, are all on display at the family-run, high-end Dubarry Furs. *206 rue St-Paul ouest. www.dubarryfurs.com.* ☎ *514/844-7483. Métro: Place d'Armes.*

★ **Harricana** DOWNTOWN
Designer Mariouche Gagné takes her unique cue from the city's long history with the fur trade, recycling old fur into funky patchwork garments. A leader in the so-called ecoluxe movement, Gagné's workshop-boutique is close to the Marché Atwater (below). *3000 rue St-Antoine ouest. www.harricana. qc.ca. ☎ 877/894-9919 or 514/287-6517. Métro: Lionel-Groulx.*

★ **Harry Rosen** DOWNTOWN
For more than 60 years, this well-known retailer of designer suits and accessories has been making men look good in Armani, Dolce & Gabbana, and its own made-to-measure suits. *1455 rue Peel. www.harryrosen. com. ☎ 514/284-3315. Métro: Peel.*

Kaliyana PLATEAU Vaguely Japanese and certainly minimalist, the free-flowing garments sold here are largely asymmetrical separates. Made by a Canadian designer, they come in muted tones of solid colors. Components of "the anti-suit" (C\$687)—a getaway jacket, an oversize white shirt, and palazzo pants—are meant to transcend travel and spiff up any fashion situation. Simple complementary necklaces and comfy but übercool shoes are available, too. *4107 rue St-Denis. www. kaliyana.com. ☎ 514/844-0633. Métro: Mont-Royal.*

Kaliyana's clothing offers a minimalist vibe.

Fourrures Dubarry Furs is a reminder of Montréal's fur-trading past.

★ **Kanuk** PLATEAU One of the top Canadian manufacturers of high-end winter jackets makes its clothes right in Montréal and has a warehouse-like factory store in the heart of Plateau Mont-Royal. Like L.L. Bean in the U.S., the first customers for Kanuk's heavy parkas were outdoor enthusiasts. Today, clientele includes the general public. Heavy-duty winter coats cost nearly C\$1000, but they're extremely popular. More modestly priced winter caps make nice (and cozy) souvenirs. Look, too, for end-of-season sales. *485 rue Rachel est. www.kanuk.com. ☎ 877/284-4494 or 514/284-4494. Métro: Mont-Royal.*

Roots DOWNTOWN This Canadian company has churned out stylish casual wear for the masses since 1973. Along with clothing, this three-floor store sells leather bags, briefcases, and home accessories. *1025 rue Ste-Catherine ouest. www.roots. com. ☎ 514/845-7995. Métro: Peel.*

Edibles
Frenco PLATEAU Your body will rejoice at this small health-food grocery. Whole grains, oats, wheat germ, and all sorts of fiber-rich foodstuffs are dispensed from plastic towers, and the organic and natural medicines behind the counter might ease the effects of a night of *poutine* or smoked meat. *3985 bd. St-Laurent. www.frenco.ca. ☎ 514/ 285-1319. Métro: St-Laurent.*

La Vieille Europe PLATEAU
Create the mother of all picnic lunches with the wide selection of delectable cheeses and salty cold cuts found here. The gourmet fare is imported mostly from France, England, and Germany. *3855 bd. St-Laurent. www.facebook.com/ LaVieilleEurope.* ☎ *514/842-5773. Métro: St-Laurent.*

★ **Les Chocolats de Chloé**
PLATEAU If you approach chocolate the way certain aficionados approach wine or cheese—that is, on the lookout for the best of the best—then this teeny shop will bring great delight. Perhaps a cardamom bonbon? Or a pop of "pâte de pistache" enrobed in milk chocolate? *546 rue Duluth est. www. leschocolatsdechloe.com.* ☎ *514/ 849-5550. Métro: Mont-Royal.*

★★ **Marché Atwater** DOWN-TOWN Atwater market, a 45-minute walk west of Old Montréal, is an indoor-outdoor farmer's market that's open daily. A long interior shed is bordered by stalls stocked with gleaming produce and flowers. The two-story center section is devoted to vintners, butchers, bakeries, and cheese stores. La Fromagerie Atwater (☎ 514/932-4653) lays out more than 750 local and international cheeses—with hundreds from Québec alone—as well as pâtés and charcuterie. Première Moisson (p 102) is filled with the tantalizing aromas of breads and pastries, and has a seating area at which to nibble baguettes or sip a bowl of café au lait. Satay Brothers (☎ 514/933-3507), a Singaporean and Malaysian food stall, is also popular. *138 av. Atwater. www. marche-atwater.com.* ☎ *514/937-7754. Métro: Lionel-Groulx.*

★★ **Marché Jean-Talon** MILE END As with the Marché Atwater, above, Marché Jean-Talon is a must-visit for food fans looking for a fun destination. Stalls, some permanent and some seasonal, sell smoked seafood, cured meat, fresh flowers, local wine and cheese, and delicacies such as sprays of fresh lavender and trays of pastel-hued macarons. There's a counter (La Boite aux Huitres; www.laboiteaux huitres.ca; ☎ 514/277-7575) that shucks oysters while you wait, C$30 per dozen. Aqua Mare (☎ 514/ 277-7575), just adjacent, sells fish 'n' chips, fried calamari, shrimp, and éperlans (smelt). On our most recent visit, we were taken in by the maple butter chocolate and golden madeleines—petite, traditional butter cakes of France—from Chocolats Privilège (☎ 514/276-7070). It's an easy ride on the Métro—just head north to the Jean-Talon stop. *7070 av. Henri-Julien, north of Mile End. www.marche-jean-talon.com. Métro:Jean-Talon.*

SAQ Signature DOWNTOWN
Wine and spirits (although not beer) are heavily regulated by the provincial government and sold in SAQ outlets. The Express outlets offer the most popular libations and are open until 10pm, while the Signature shops have the rarest and most expensive bottles. Consider Québec's unique ice cider

Fresh, colorful produce at Marché Atwater.

(cidre de glace), which is made from apples left on trees after the first frost. Domaine Pinnacle (www.icecider.com), based about an hour and a half from the city, is a regular gold medalist in international competitions. *677 rue Ste-Catherine ouest. www.saq.com.* ☎ *514/282-9445. Métro: McGill.*

Suite 88 Chocolatier DOWNTOWN More fancy chocolates. These are displayed in cases like fine jewelry, with flavors that include lychee and ginger, gianduja, and praline and Rice Krispies. Small boxes (one dozen domes) run about C$40. On cold days be sure to try the hot chocolate—it's made with cayenne. *1225 de Maisonneuve ouest. www.suite88.com.* ☎ *514/284-3488. Métro: Peel.*

Housewares
Arthur Quentin PLATEAU Doling out household products of quiet taste and discernment since 1975, this St-Denis stalwart sells chic tableware, leather goods, kitchen gadgets, and home decor. That means Le Jacquard Francais French linens, Limoges china, cast iron casseroles, and dainty tea trays. *3960 rue St-Denis. www.arthurquentin.com.* ☎ *514/843-7513. Métro: Sherbrooke.*

★ kids **Musée des Beaux-Arts Boutique** DOWNTOWN This unusually large and impressive shop sells everything from folk art to furniture. The expected art-related

postcards and prints are on hand, along with ties, watches, scarves, address books, toys, jewelry, and Inuit crafts, with special focus on work by Québec artisans. *1390 rue Sherbrooke ouest. www.mbam.qc.ca.* ☎ *514/285-1600. Métro: Peel.*

Zone PLATEAU A Québec company with a half dozen locations, this housewares store features colorful bowls and plates, clocks and frames, furnishings, and more. Think clean lines of Ikea products, but a step up in style and flair. *4246 rue St-Denis. www.zonemaison.com.* ☎ *514/845-3530. Métro: Mont-Royal.*

Music
Archambault DOWNTOWN There's a huge selection of English and French CDs and a good variety of Québécois albums that you won't find outside of the province. This chain calls itself Québec's largest music store and this outlet sells sheet music, instruments, and even repairs guitars. *500 rue Ste-Catherine est. www.archambault.ca.* ☎ *514/849-6201. Métro: Berri-UQAM.*

Beatnick's PLATEAU The storefront at this everyman's record store hasn't changed much in the last decade, and its faithful customers return again and again. Selection is varied and you might be able to score that highly sought-after '60s release you've always wanted. *3770 rue St-Denis. www.beatnickmusic.com.* ☎ *514/842-0664. Métro: Sherbrooke.*

Marché Jean-Talon is a must-do for visiting foodies.

Exploring the **Underground City**

If you'd like to visit Montréal's Underground City (a network of subterranean shops, cafes, and entrances to hotels and Métro stations), but you're intimidated about where to start, here's a mini-tour that hits five of the anchors. Keep in mind that no singular entity manages the network, which means that sections open and close according to hours set by the businesses, and maps, signage, and even the numbering of levels can differ from one section to the next. Persons using wheelchairs or strollers may face navigational challenges.

Downtown's huge Le Centre Eaton mall.

Place Ville-Marie. There is no prettier way to enter the underground than through one of I. M. Pei's glass pyramids in front of his famous crucifix-shaped office building, known locally as PVM. Built in 1962 to cover an unsightly railway trench north of Gare Central, the now-famous 41-story building became not just home to the city's first subterranean shopping mall but a cornerstone of the Underground City as well. Take the escalator down. You'll find a food court and shops, and several exits into the network. Look for the tunnel to Eaton Centre. *1 Place Ville-Marie. www.placevillemarie.com.* ☎ 514/866-6666.

Le Centre Eaton. You'll know you're in Eaton Centre when you arrive at a courtyard and can look up at four floors of stores and restaurants and a scrape of sky through the glass-peaked roof. Eaton is the largest commercial space downtown and one of the most popular places in the pedestrian network. One local clothier described Eaton's ongoing appeal as "happy, happy, happy." Maybe it's that peep of sky? *705 rue Ste-Catherine ouest. www.centre eatondemontreal.com.* ☎ 514/288-3708.

Les Cours Mont-Royal. From Eaton's courtyard, follow the signs to boulevard de Maisonneuve or to the Métro (you must go up from "level one tunnel" to "level two Métro"). You'll walk the equivalent of 3 short city blocks. Les Cours Mont-Royal has a distinct personality: Many of its shops are independently owned, so cutting-edge fashion and trendy styles reign supreme. Some shops cater to the young, moneyed, clubbing crowd while others to the chic, personal tailor audience. There's a beautiful central chandelier (and some smaller ones in the food court) and six metal birdlike sculptures in permanent flight above the atrium made by First Nations artist David Ruben Piqtoukun. *1455 rue Peel. www.lcmr.ca.* ☎ *514/842-7777.*

Complex Les Ailes. Follow the signs from the Eaton Centre to the tri-level Complex Les Ailes, home to some of the city's most recognizable boutiques—Forever 21, Sephora, and Swarovski, to name a few. The anchor store, Le Grand Magasin Ailes de la Mode, closed in 2016, throwing the future of this mall somewhat into question. The landmark building in which the complex resides was built in 1927 for the now-departed Eaton's department store. *677 rue Ste-Catherine ouest. www.complexe lesailes.com.* ☎ *514/288-3759.*

Les Promenade de la Cathédrale. From Complex Les Ailes, follow the signs to Les Promenade de la Cathédrale to the site of one of Montréal's most unique architectural endeavors. The Cathédrale Christ Church (p 69), which sits above, was "floated" on supports as the arcades below were built. More than 8,200 tons (18 million lbs.) had to be stabilized for the duration of construction, and architects, historians, and artisans dismantled the cathedral's presbytery stone by stone then reconstructed it exactly as before. Look for photographs depicting the process in the halls of this mall. *625 rue Ste-Catherine. www. promenadescathedrale.com.* ☎ *514/ 845-8230.* ●

Dining Best Bets

Best **Restaurant in a Glass Box**
★★★ Brasserie T $$ *1425 rue Jeanne-Mance (p 98)*

Best **Fancy White Tablecloth Experience**
★★★ Europea $$$ *1227 rue de la Montagne (p 99)*

Best **Parisian-Style Bistro**
★ L'Express $$ *3927 rue St-Denis (p 101)*

Best **Contemporary Québécois**
★★★ Le Club Chasse et Pêche $$$ *423 rue St-Claude (p 101)*

Best **Cocktails**
★★ Hôtel Herman $$ *5171 blvd. St-Laurent (p 100)*

Best **Seafood**
★★★ Ferreira Café $$$ *1446 rue Peel (p 99)*

Best **Modern Italian**
★★★ Graziella $$$ *116 rue McGill (p 100)*

Best **Slabs of Pork**
★ Au Pied de Cochon $$$ *536 rue Duluth (p 98)*

Best **Vegetarian Buffet**
★ Resto Vego $$ *1204 av. McGill College (p 103)*

Best **Vegan**
★ Aux Vivres $ *4631 bd. St-Laurent (p 98)*

Best **Bakery**
★ Première Moisson $ *1490 rue Sherbrooke ouest (p 102)*

Best **Creative Cuisine**
★★★ Toque! $$$ *900 Place Jean-Paul-Riopelle (p 104)*

Best **Modern British**
★★★ Lawrence $$ *5201 blvd. St. Laurent (p 100)*

Prepare for a culinary adventure at Brasserie T.

Best **Indian**
★ Gandhi $$ *230 rue St-Paul ouest (p 100)*

Best **Polish**
★ Stash Café $$ *200 rue St-Paul ouest (p 104)*

Best **24-Hour Poutine**
★ La Banquise $ *994 rue Rachel est (p 100)*

Best **Smoked Meat**
★ Schwartz's $ *3895 bd. St-Laurent (p 103)*

Best **Dependable Breakfast**
Eggspectation $ *1313 de Maisonneuve ouest. (p 99)*

Best **Hearty Sandwich**
★★★ Olive + Gourmando $ *351 rue St-Paul est (p 102)*

Best **Old-Time Diner**
★★ Beauty's Luncheonette $ *93 av. du Mont-Royal ouest (p 98)*

Best **Bagel**
★★★ Fairmount Bagel $ *74 av. Fairmont ouest (p 99)*

Best **Pizza**
★ Magpie Pizzeria $ *16 rue Maguire (p 102)*

Previous page: Mouthwatering baked goods at Olive + Gourmando in Vieux-Montréal.

Dining in the Plateau & Mile End

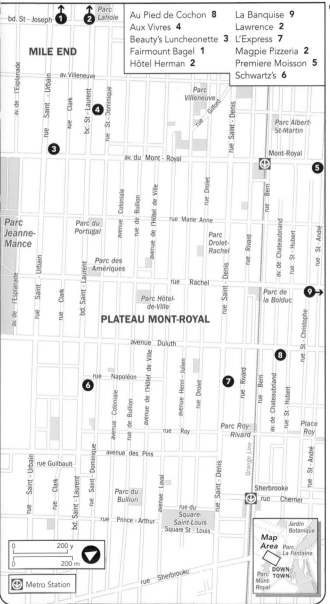

Au Pied de Cochon **8**	La Banquise **9**
Aux Vivres **4**	Lawrence **2**
Beauty's Luncheonette **3**	L'Express **7**
Fairmount Bagel **1**	Magpie Pizzeria **2**
Hôtel Herman **2**	Premiere Moisson **5**
	Schwartz's **6**

MILE END

bd. St - Joseph

Parc Lahaie

av. Villeneuve

av. de l'Esplanade

rue Saint - Urbain

rue Clark

bd. St - Laurent

rue St-Dominique

Parc Villeneuve

rue Gilford

rue Saint - Denis

Parc Albert-St-Martin

Mont-Royal

av. du Mont - Royal

rue Drolet

rue Berri

rue St-Hubert

rue St - André

Parc Jeanne-Mance

Parc du Portugal

avenue Coloniale

rue de Bullion

avenue de l'Hôtel - de - Ville

rue Marie - Anne

Parc Drolet-Rachel

rue Rivard

av. de Chateaubriand

Parc des Amériques

av. de l'Esplanade

rue Saint - Urbain

rue Clark

bd. Saint - Laurent

rue Rachel

rue Saint - Denis

Parc de la Bolduc

rue St - Christophe

Parc Hôtel-de-Ville

PLATEAU MONT-ROYAL

avenue Duluth

rue Napoléon

avenue Coloniale

rue de Bullion

avenue de l'Hôtel - de - Ville

avenue Henri - Julien

rue Drolet

rue Roy

Parc Roy-Rivard

rue Rivard

rue Berri

av. de Chateaubriand

rue St - Hubert

Place Roy

rue St - André

Orange Line

rue Saint - Urbain

rue Guilbault

rue Clark

bd. Saint - Laurent

rue Saint - Dominique

avenue des Pins

avenue Laval

Parc du Bullion

rue Saint - Denis

Sherbrooke

rue Cherrier

rue Prince - Arthur

rue du Square-Saint-Louis

Square St - Louis

rue Sherbrooke

Jardin Botanique

Map Area

Parc La Fontaine

DOWN-TOWN

Parc Mont-Royal

0   200 y

0   200 m

Metro Station

Dining in Downtown & Vieux-Montréal

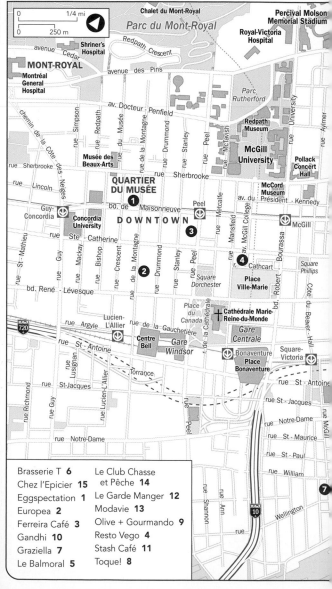

Brasserie T **6**
Chez l'Epicier **15**
Eggspectation **1**
Europea **2**
Ferreira Café **3**
Gandhi **10**
Graziella **7**
Le Balmoral **5**
Le Club Chasse et Pêche **14**
Le Garde Manger **12**
Modavie **13**
Olive + Gourmando **9**
Resto Vego **4**
Stash Café **11**
Toqué! **8**

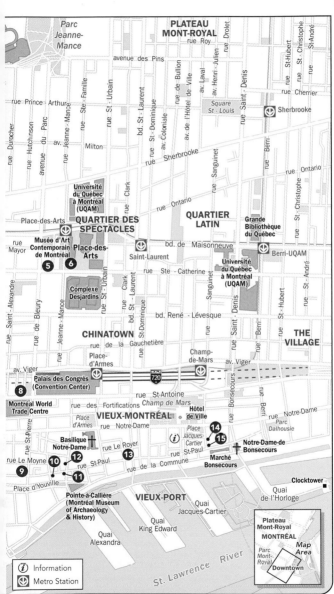

Restaurants **A to Z**

★ **Au Pied de Cochon** PLATEAU
CONTEMPORARY QUEBECOIS
Some of the best meals at "the
Pig's Foot," a low-key, upscale,
always packed restaurant, unsur-
prisingly feature cuts of pork—
though massive amounts of beef,
chicken, lamb, duck, and foie gras
are also used to create inventive
dishes. An elaborate raw bar is on
view and includes oysters, lobster,
and local catch. Celebrity chef Martin Picard runs a seasonal *cabane à
sucre* **(sugar shack)** 45 minutes
outside the city as well. Reservations at both restaurants are recommended. *536 rue Duluth. www.
restaurantaupieddecochon.ca.*
☎ *514/281-1114. Main courses
C$15–C$51. Dinner Wed–Sun. Métro:
Sherbrooke. Map p 95.*

★ kids **Aux Vivres** MILE END
VEGAN This cheery diner-style
restaurant offers flavors from every
continent: gyro with souvlaki-style
seitan, baked-to-order chapati with
vegelox, a BLT with bacon made
from coconut. There are also salads, rice bowls, and a daily chef's
special. A high-octane juice bar
runs all year, and a patio out back
is seasonal. Next door, the restaurant operates a vegan market and
express to-go counter. *4631 bd.
St-Laurent. www.auxvivres.com.*
☎ *514/842-3479. Most items under
C$15. Cash only. Lunch and dinner
daily. Map p 95.*

★★ kids **Beauty's Luncheonette** PLATEAU *LIGHT FARE* At
this iconic diner with banquette
seating, you'd be right to deduce
that a long line means good food,
as it has since 1942. Loyalists
debate which of the two signature
dishes is more quintessentially
Montréal: the Mish-Mash omelet
with hot dog, salami, fried onion,

and green pepper, or Beauty's Special, a bagel sandwich with lox,
cream cheese, sliced tomato, and
onion. *93 av. du Mont-Royal ouest.
www.beautys.ca.* ☎ *514/849-8883.
Most items cost less than C$13.
Breakfast and lunch daily. Métro:
Mont Royal. Map p 95.*

★★★ **Brasserie T** DOWNTOWN
BRASSERIE This restaurant comes
from chef Normand Laprise, of the
city's top restaurant, **Toqué!** (p 104).
It's fun, flirty, and adventurous.
Housed in a unique all-glass box
perched on a sidewalk in the city's
newly renovated fine-arts neighborhood, the Quartier des Spectacles,
it overlooks the **Musée d'Art Contemporain de Montréal** (p 32). The
hamburger is arguably the best in
the city, and we were smitten with
the garlic sea snails and the pan-
seared foie gras sprinkled with can-
died fennel, strawberries, and
popcorn. At night in warm months,
a pool of water alongside the restaurant has a "dancing waters"
lightshow. *1425 rue Jeanne-Mance.
www.brasserie-t.com.* ☎ *514/282-
0808. Main courses C$18–C$25.
Lunch and dinner daily. Métro:
Place-des-Arts. Map p 96.*

★ **Chez l'Epicier** VIEUX-
MONTREAL *CONTEMPORARY
QUEBECOIS* Chef Laurent God-
bout's inspiring haute cuisine menu
provides a perfect example of
modern gastronomy in Montréal.
The ever-changing menu features
playfully crafted food with a focus
on local ingredients and a global
feel. Inventive options have included
duck charcuterie with cauliflower-
miso puree and sea scallops with
sea urchin roe and carrot cream.
The many windows provide an airy
feeling throughout, with stone and
exposed brick walls punctuated by

a long, robin's egg blue wall with chalkboards displaying the evening's specials. *331 rue St-Paul est. www.chezlepicier.com.* ☎ *514/878-2232. Main courses C$31–C$40; 7-course tasting menu C$85. Dinner daily. Métro: Champ-de-Mars. Map p 96.*

kids Eggspectation DOWNTOWN *BREAKFAST/LIGHT FARE* The atmosphere is funky and creative, and prices are fair for the large portions. What's more, the kitchen knows how to deal with volume and turns out good meals quickly, even on packed weekend mornings. There are 10 variations of eggs benedict alone ("Montréal Style" comes with smoked meat) as well as burgers and club sandwiches. Other central outposts of this small chain include 190 Ste-Catherine ouest at the Quartier des Spectacles and 12 rue Notre Dame est in Vieux-Montréal. *1313 de Maisonneuve ouest. www. eggspectation.com.* ☎ *514/842-3447. Most items cost less than C$12. Breakfast and lunch daily. Métro: Peel. Map p 96.*

★★★ Europea DOWNTOWN *CONTEMPORARY FRENCH* Montréal has a handful of celebrity chefs, and Europea's Jérôme Ferrer is justifiably one of them. While many upscale white tablecloth restaurants have fallen by the wayside, this venue remains one of the special celebration spots in the city. For the full treatment, order the extravagant *menu dégustation*, which starts with a lobster cream "cappuccino" with truffle puree and goes on to include maple bark stewed foie gras and "cornish hen encapsulated in breakable clay." At lunch, there's a three-course option for C$35. *1227 rue de la Montagne. www.europea.ca.* ☎ *514/398-9229. Reservations recommended. Main courses C$43–C$58; menu dégustation C$120. Lunch Tues–Fri, dinner daily. Métro: Peel. Map p 96.*

★★★ kids Fairmount Bagel MILE END *BAKERY* Montréal's bagels have a justifiable renown for their dense, sweet dough. Bakers hand-roll each bagel, which are then dropped in boiling water sweetened with a touch of honey and baked in big wood-fired ovens. Fairmount's poppyseed is its original flavor, though sesame may be the most popular. Founded in 1919, this shop is small and to-go only, but absolutely worth visiting to see the bakers in action. It's open 24 hours a day, 7 days a week—even on Jewish holidays. *74 av. Fairmount ouest. www.fairmountbagel.com.* ☎ *514/272-0667. Most bagels under C$1. Cash only. Daily 24 hr. Métro: Laurier. Map p 95.*

★★★ Ferreira Café DOWNTOWN *SEAFOOD/PORTUGUESE* Ferreira exudes a warm, festive, Mediterranean grace, and you can't go wrong with its take on Portuguese classics, including oysters (*huîtres à la portugaise*), salted cod (*morue salée rôtie en croûte*), and

Fairmount Bagels can often be enjoyed right out of the wood-fired oven.

The Best Dining

bouillabaisse. A smaller, late-night menu is also available. For lighter fare, Ferreira's sister venue, **Café Vasco de Gama,** on the same block (at 1472 rue Peel), offers big breakfasts, a variety of salads, and delectable desserts indoors—as well as sidewalk tables in warm months (open daily into the early evening). *1446 rue Peel. www. ferreiracafe.com.* ☎ *514/848-0988. Main courses C$28–C$45. Lunch Mon–Fri, dinner daily. Métro: Peel. Map p 96.*

Count on amiable service at Ferreira Café, known for its Mediterranean dishes and seafood.

★ **kids Gandhi** VIEUX-MONTREAL *INDIAN* The always busy Gandhi won't disappoint with its usual Indian fare (chicken tandoori, *tikka,* and so on) and offers over a dozen vegetarian options, including the chickpea dish *chana masala* and *matter panir,* a homemade cheese with green peas. *230 rue St-Paul ouest. www.restaurantgandhi.com.* ☎ *514/845-5866. Entrees C$13–C$24 Lunch Mon–Fri, dinner daily. Métro: Place d'Armes. Map p 96.*

★★★ **Graziella** VIEUX-MONTREAL *ITALIAN* Chef-owner Graziella Battista and her staff prepare modern Italian dishes served in understated yet beautiful presentations, like little works of art. Our top recommendations are the fall-off-the-bone *osso buco* and the homemade pasta dishes—like capon-filled tortelli with speck and a buttery sauce infused with sage. Reservations recommended. *116 rue McGill. www.restaurantgraziella. ca.* ☎ *514/876-0116. Main courses C$26–C$45. Lunch Mon–Fri, dinner Mon–Sat. Métro: Square Victoria. Map p 96.*

★★ **Hôtel Herman** MILE END *CONTEMPORARY QUEBE-COIS* Impeccably cool environs with menu listings that border on spare and predictably Québécois ("duck from the Goulu farm, sweet onions, black chanterelles"), but

one bite in and, wow. Plates range from small to mid-size and you'll want to order at least two per person. The restaurant is intense about cocktails, too, down to the glassware. Reservations recommended. *5171 blvd. St-Laurent. www.hotel herman.com.* ☎ *514/278-7000. Small plates C$9–C$21. Dinner Wed–Mon. Métro: Laurier. Map p 95.*

★ **kids La Banquise** PLATEAU *LIGHT FARE* Open 24 hours a day, this friendly, hippy-meets-hipster diner is a city landmark for its *poutine,* with 30 variations on the standard french fries with gravy and cheese curds. Add-ons range from hot peppers to smoked meat, and there are vegetarian and vegan options, too. Despite *poutine*'s reputation for being a post–2am binge food, La Banquise is kid-friendly. It's located on the north end of the Plateau's pretty **Parc La Fontaine** (p 20), where the whole family can stretch their legs after a meal. *994 rue Rachel est. www.labanquise.com.* ☎ *514/525-2415. Poutine plates C$7–C$16; most other items less than C$10. Cash only. Daily 24 hr. Map p 95.*

★★★ **Lawrence** MILE END *BIS-TRO* Emblematic of everything that's exciting about the Mile End dining scene, Lawrence takes modern British cuisine to a new level. Its hugely popular English breakfast and brunch are what most people rave about, but the lunch and dinner menus are equally outstanding. They include masterful turns of pub standards like bubble and squeak, kedgeree, and suet dumplings (served with succulent braised oxtail). Breakfast and brunch stay true to British culinary tradition while lunch and dinner gets a touch of classic French technique. *5201 blvd. St. Laurent. www.lawrence restaurant.com.* ☎ *514/503-1070. Brunch main courses C$12–C$16. Dinner main courses C$27–C$30. Lunch Tues–Fri, dinner Tues–Sat, brunch Sat–Sun. Métro: Laurier. Map p 95.*

★★ **Le Balmoral** DOWNTOWN *BISTRO* Top-notch bistro fare, with a particular affinity for beef, from burgers to a French-Japanese fusion of beef tataki with maple vinaigrette. Sandwiches, salads, and lighter fare are available at lunch. Le Balmoral is a sharp-looking room that overlooks Quartier des Spectacles, and its proceeds help fund the **Festival International de Jazz de Montréal** (p 113). Thursday through Saturday evenings the restaurant becomes a jazz club featuring local and national musical acts. *305 rue Ste-Catherine ouest. www. bistrobalmoral.ca.* ☎ *514/288-5992. Main courses C$18–C$26. Lunch*

Kids love the poutine—french fries with gravy—at La Banquise, open 24 hours a day.

Hôtel Herman brings contemporary Québécois flair to a menu that favors fish and game.

Mon–Fri, dinner Tues–Sat. Métro: Place des Arts. Map p 96.

★★★ **Le Club Chasse et Pêche** VIEUX-MONTRÉAL *CONTEMPORARY QUEBECOIS* One of the top restaurants in Montréal. Chef Claude Pelletier's menu changes frequently, but certain favorites are always on the menu, including braised piglet risotto with fois gras shavings. The stone and brick dining room is dark and masculine, with leather chairs and waterfowl-themed light fixtures, and there is a 15-page wine list. The nondescript entrance is easily missed, marked only by a small sign with a crest on it. *423 rue St-Claude. www.leclubchasseetpeche.com.* ☎ *514/861-1112. Main courses C$34–C$39. Dinner Tues–Sat. Métro: Champ-de-Mars. Map p 96.*

★ **kids L'Express** PLATEAU *BISTRO* No obvious sign announces L'Express, perhaps because all Montréal knows exactly where this most classic of Parisian-style bistros is. Eternally busy and open until at least 2am, the bistro's atmosphere hits all the right notes: checkered floor, high ceiling, mirrored walls, *soupe de poisson, croque-monsieur.* The maple syrup pie is outstanding. Walk-ins can often find a seat at the zinc-topped bar. *3927 rue St-Denis. www.restaurant lexpress.com.* ☎ *514/845-5333. Main courses C$12–C$27. Breakfast, lunch, and dinner daily. Métro: Sherbrooke. Map p 95.*

★★ **Le Garde Manger** VIEUX-MONTREAL *SEAFOOD* From the dark roadhouse decor to the rowdy slip of a bar, this giddy supper club is a smack down to its more proper Vieux-Montréal neighbors. The interior decor is half hunting lodge, half antique shop, and chefs pump out top-notch grub along the lines of lobster *poutine*, devilled eggs with bacon-wrapped oysters, and pork liver sausage paired with octopus and cheese grits. Expect a packed house, loud music, and copious tattoos. There is no signage other than a dimly lit neon pink square out front. Reservations recommended. *408 rue St-François-Xavier. www.gardemanger.ca.* ☎ *514/ 678-5044. Main courses C$28–C$50. Dinner Tues–Sun. Métro: Place d'Armes. Map p 96.*

★ **kids** **Magpie Pizzeria** MILE END *PIZZA* We love the wood-fired pizza here as much as the rustically hip atmosphere of schoolhouse-style chairs, thick pine tables, and industrial lighting. Mouth-watering toppings include caramelized onions and ricotta. And unlike most pizza joints, this one is serious about dessert, with offerings such as a *tarte tatin* with lemon *crème anglaise* over almond shortbread. It's fine to bring kids, although service, while friendly, can be slow. Reservations recommended. *16 rue Maguire. www.pizzeriamagpie.com.* ☎ *514/507-2900. Pizzas C$13–C$19. Lunch Tues–Fri, dinner Tues–Sun. Métro: Laurier. Map p 95.*

★ **Modavie** VIEUX-MONTREAL *MEDITERRANEAN* Featuring a combination of French bistro

Lawrence serves an exceptional brunch, lunch, and dinner.

classics and Italian-influenced pasta dishes, Modavie is loud and convivial. Steak frites are always excellent, and an entire section of the menu is dedicated to lamb. There is live jazz every evening in the upstairs lounge (no cover). *1 rue St-Paul ouest. www.modavie.com.* ☎ *514/287-9582. Main courses C$17–C$38. Lunch and dinner daily. Métro: Place d'Armes. Map p 96.*

★★★ **kids** **Olive + Gourmando** VIEUX-MONTREAL *BAKERY/LIGHT FARE* A local favorite. It started out as an earthy bakery, added table service, and transformed into a full-fledged cafe. Croissants, scones, biscuits, and creative sandwiches are all good. Options always available include the Cuban sandwich and a deliriously yummy truffle mac 'n' cheese with caramelized onions. *351 rue St-Paul ouest. www.oliveetgourmando. com.* ☎ *514/350-1083. Most items under C$15. Cash only. Breakfast and lunch until 5pm Tues–Sat. Métro: Square-Victoria. Map p 96.*

★ **kids** **Première Moisson** PLATEAU *BAKERY* Arguably Montréal's best bakery (certainly its best chain: there are multiple branches throughout the city). Première Moisson got its reputation by crafting over 45 varieties of breads and baguettes along with mind-bogglingly beautiful pastries. *860 av. du Mont-Royal est. www.premiere moisson.com.* ☎ *514/523-2751. Most items under C$12. Breakfast, lunch, and early dinner daily. Métro: Mont-Royal. Map p 95.*

Bargain Hunters: Look for the *Table d'Hôte*

Always consider the *table d'hôte* meals at restaurants. Ubiquitous in Montréal, they are fixed-price menus with three or four courses, and they usually cost just a little more than the price of a single a la carte main course. Restaurants at all price ranges offer them, and they represent the best value around. *Table d'hôte* meals are often offered not just at dinner but at lunch, too, when they are even less expensive. Having your main meal midday instead of in the evening is the most economical way to sample many of the top establishments.

★ **kids** **Resto Vego** DOWN-TOWN *VEGETARIAN* Located on a second floor with floor to ceiling glass windows overlooking the always bustling rue Ste-Catherine and avenue McGill, Resto Vego was formerly known as Le Commensal. The owners re-branded after a disastrous attempt to incorporate chicken and fish into the menu. Now completely vegetarian again, food is served buffet-style, and you pay by the weight. Options can include vegetable lasagna, quesa-dillas, ginger tofu, and puff pastry with asparagus and mushrooms.

The baked goods taste as good as they look at Olive + Gourmando.

There's also an outpost in the Quartier Latin, at 1720 rue St-Denis. *1204 av. McGill College. www. restovego.ca.* ☎ *514/871-1480. Pay by the weight: C$2.35 per 100 g, or about C$12 for a dinner portion. Fixed price of C$8 for children 10 and under. Lunch and dinner daily. Métro: McGill. Map p 96.*

★ **Schwartz's** PLATEAU *DELI* Many are convinced that this legendary Montréal eatery is the only place to indulge in the guilty treat of *viande fumée*—a brisket that's called, simply, smoked meat. Most guests also order sides of fries and mammoth garlicky pickles. It's one of many city landmarks created by a Jewish immigrant, in this case by Reuben Schwartz in 1928, making it Canada's oldest deli. Tables are communal and packed tight so come prepared to rub elbows with strangers. Take-out is an option, as is a midnight snack: Schwartz's is open until 12:30am during the week, later on week-ends. *3895 bd. St-Laurent. www. schwartzsdeli.com.* ☎ *514/842-4813. Sandwiches and meat plates C$7– C$22. Cash only. Lunch and dinner daily, plus breakfast take-out. Métro: Sherbrooke. Map p 95.*

Say Cheese, Please

The cheeses of Québec are renowned for their rich flavors and textures, and many can only be sampled in Canada because they are often unpasteurized—made of *lait cru* (raw milk)—and therefore subject to strict export law. When dining in Montréal, do try some as a final course. Choices include the buttery St-Basil de Port Neuf; Le Chèvre Noire, a sharp goat's-milk variety that's covered in black wax; and the creamy Blue Ermite, made by monks at the Abbaye de Saint-Benoît-du-Lac, 2 hours west of the city.

Cheeses with the *fromages de pays* label are made in Québec with no modified milk ingredients. The label represents solidarity among artisanal producers and is supported by Solidarité Rurale du Québec, a group devoted to revitalizing rural communities. It's also supported by Slow Food Québec, which promotes sustainable agriculture and local production. Information is available at www.fromageduquebec.qc.ca.

Schwartz's Deli has been serving sought-after smoked meat sandwiches since 1928.

★ **kids Stash Café** VIEUX-MONTRÉAL *POLISH* Alongside Vieux-Montréal's many French restaurants and steakhouses sits this old-fashioned gem serving traditional Polish cuisine at affordable prices—main courses are almost all in the C\$15 range, a rarity in this part of town. We recommend the *golabki* (cabbage leaves stuffed with pork and rice in a savory tomato sauce) and the *pierogis* (dumplings filled with meat, cheese and potato, or mushrooms and cabbage). There's also a variety of classic soups and game meats, including roast boar and duck—a nod to Poland's traditional game-hunting culture. A pianist plays nightly, starting at 6pm. *200 rue St-Paul ouest. www.stashcafe.com.* ☎ *514/845-6611. Main courses C\$12–C\$19. Lunch and dinner daily. Métro: Place d'Armes. Map p 96.*

★★★ **Toque!** DOWNTOWN *CONTEMPORARY FRENCH* The celebrated Toque! overwhelms with unparalleled service and dazzling cuisine. Items change regularly, but perennial favorites include a version of Magret duck and outstanding pasta dishes, such as squash cavatelli and rabbit-stuffed pasta with ricotta and rabbit *jus*. Adventurous eaters should try the seven-course tasting menu (C\$120) to fully sample the famed kitchen's amazing creations. Reservations recommended. *900 Place Jean-Paul-Riopelle. www.restaurant-toque.com.* ☎ *514/499-2084. Main courses C\$42–C\$52. Lunch Tues–Fri, dinner Tues–Sat. Métro: Square-Victoria. Map p 96.* ●

Nightlife Best Bets

Best **Bar in Old Fur Warehouse**
★★ Bar Furco, 425 rue Mayor (p 110)

Best **Downtown Wine Bar**
★★ Pullman, 3424 av. du Parc (p 112)

Best **Upscale Cocktails**
★ Bar Henrietta, 115 av. Laurier ouest (p 110)

Best **Mysterious Night Club**
★ Velvet, 426 rue St-Gabriel (p 112)

Best **Low-Key Jazz Venue**
★ Upstairs Jazz Bar & Grill, 1254 rue Mackay (p 114)

Best **Bar for a Huge Group**
★ Brasserie Harricana, 95 rue Jean-Talon ouest. (p 110)

Best **Gay Night Out**
★ Sky Club & Pub, 1474 rue Ste-Catherine est (p 113)

Best **Fans During Habs Games**
La Cage Brasserie Sportive, 1212 av. des Canadiens du Montréal (p 111)

Best **Craft Beers**
★★★ Dieu du Ciel, 29 av. Laurier ouest (p 111)

Best **Late-Night Menu in Sexy Setting**
★★★ Ferreira Café, 1446 rue Peel (p 99)

Best **Hipster Bar**
★★ Bílý Kůň, 354 av. Mont-Royal est (p 110)

Best **Oyster Bar**
★ Philémon, 111 rue St-Paul ouest (p 112)

Best **People-Watching**
★ Sir Winston Churchill Pub, 1459 rue Crescent (p 112)

The super cool Bar Furco serves vintage cocktails in a converted fur warehouse.

Best **Bar for 20-Somethings**
Biftek, 3702 bd. St-Laurent (p 110)

Best **Live Celtic Music**
Hurley's Irish Pub, 1225 rue Crescent (p 114)

Best **Rock Scene**
Club Soda, 1225 bd. St-Laurent (p 113)

Best **Drag Club**
★ Cabaret Mado, 1115 rue Ste-Catherine est (p 113)

Best **Beer Garden**
★ Vices & Versa, 6631 bd. St-Laurent (p 113)

Best **Paris-Style Bistro Open Until 3am**
★ L'Express, 3927 rue St-Denis (p 101)

Previous page: Musicians play at Montréal's famed International Festival of Jazz.

Nightlife in Plateau Mont-Royal & the Village

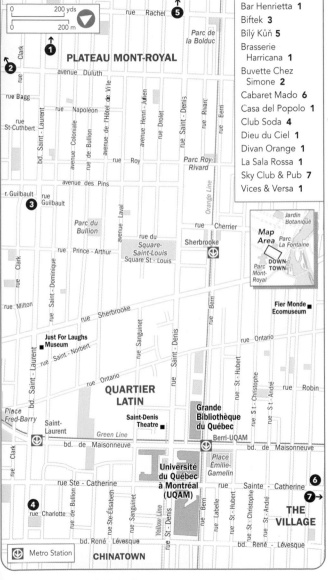

Bar Henrietta **1**
Biftek **3**
Bílý Kůň **5**
Brasserie Harricana **1**
Buvette Chez Simone **2**
Cabaret Mado **6**
Casa del Popolo **1**
Club Soda **4**
Dieu du Ciel **1**
Divan Orange **1**
La Sala Rossa **1**
Sky Club & Pub **7**
Vices & Versa **1**

Nightlife in Downtown Montréal

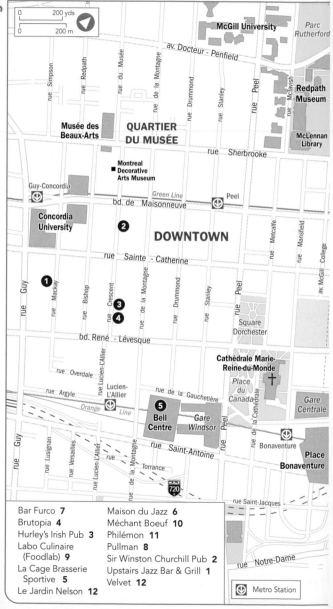

Bar Furco **7**
Brutopia **4**
Hurley's Irish Pub **3**
Labo Culinaire (Foodlab) **9**
La Cage Brasserie Sportive **5**
Le Jardin Nelson **12**
Maison du Jazz **6**
Méchant Boeuf **10**
Philémon **11**
Pullman **8**
Sir Winston Churchill Pub **2**
Upstairs Jazz Bar & Grill **1**
Velvet **12**

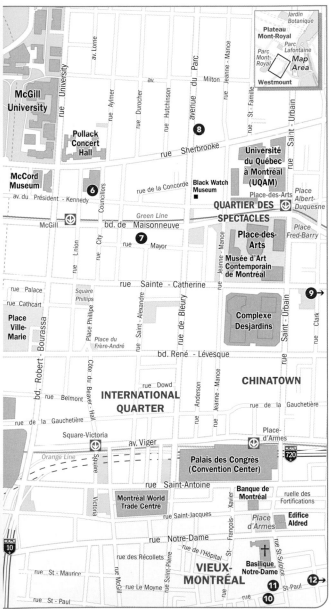

Jardin Botanique
Plateau Mont-Royal
Parc Lafontaine
Parc Mont-Royal
Map Area
Westmount

av. Lorne

avenue du Parc

rue Jeanne - Mance

Milton

rue University

rue Aylmer

rue Durocher

rue Hutchinson

av.

rue St - Famille

rue Saint - Urbain

McGill University

Pollack Concert Hall

rue Sherbrooke

8

Université du Québec à Montréal (UQAM)

Place-des-Arts

Place Albert-Duquesne

McCord Museum

rue de la Concorde

Black Watch Museum

QUARTIER DES SPECTACLES

av. du Président - Kennedy

6

Councillors

Green Line

Place Fred-Barry

McGill

bd. de Maisonneuve

7

Mayor

Place-des-Arts

rue U-nion

rue City

Musée d'Art Contemporain de Montréal

rue Sainte - Catherine

rue Palace

Square Phillips

rue Saint - Alexandre

rue de Bleury

rue Jeanne - Mance

9

rue Cathcart

Complexe Desjardins

rue Saint - Urbain

rue Clark

Place Ville-Marie

bd. Robert - Bourassa

Place Phillipe

Place du Frère-André

bd. René - Lévesque

Côte du Beaver - Hall

rue Dowd

CHINATOWN

rue Belmont

INTERNATIONAL QUARTER

Anderson

rue Jeanne - Mance

rue de la Gauchetière

rue de la Gauchetière

Place-d'Armes

Square-Victoria

av. Viger

720

Orange Line

Square

Palais des Congrès (Convention Center)

rue Saint-Antoine

Banque de Montréal

ruelle des Fortifications

Montréal World Trade Centre

Victoria

rue Saint-Jacques

Xavier

Place d'Armes

Edifice Aldred

rue Notre-Dame

rue de l'Hôpital

St- François-

rue St-Sulpice

10

rue des Récollets

VIEUX-MONTRÉAL

Basilique Notre-Dame

12

rue St - Maurice

rue McGill

rue Saint-Pierre

rue Le Moyne

St-Paul

11

10

rue St - Paul

Nightlife A to Z

Bars

★★ Bar Furco DOWNTOWN
Industrial-chic Berlin meets an old
Montréal fur warehouse. That's the
inspiration for this downtown
hotspot for cocktails and wine (the
food menu kicks in after 5pm).
Attractive 20- and 30-somethings
gather after work and will even wait
in line to soak up Furco's vintage-
mod vibe. (near Quartier des Spectacles). *425 rue Mayor. www.barfurco.
com.* ☎ *514/764-3588. Métro: Place-
des-Arts or McGill. Map p 108.*

★ Bar Henrietta PLATEAU
The split-level space of this newfan-
gled oyster bar attracts more of a
young professional than starv-
ing-artist crowd (even though
there's house red or white for just
C$5 a glass). This is the place to try
a fancy cocktail like the "Llita," with
Chartreuse, gin, cucumber, and
prosecco. *115 av. Laurier ouest.
www.barhenrietta.com.* ☎ *514/276-
4282. Métro: Laurier. Map p 107.*

Biftek PLATEAU A grungy crowd
aging from barely legal to early 30s
holds court at this perennially popular bar. The kind of place that tops
"get drunk cheap" lists. Play a
game of pool or just kick back listening to the city's best rotation of
indie and classic rock. *3702 bd.
St-Laurent.* ☎ *514/844-6211. Métro:
Sherbrooke. Map p 107.*

★★ Bílý Kůň PLATEAU Pronounced "Billy Coon," this is a bit
of Prague right in Montréal. Decor
is avant-garde and drink options
include Czech beers and martini
specials such as Absinthe Aux Pom-
mes. Students and professionals
jam in for the relaxed candlelit
atmosphere. There's live jazz from 6
to 8pm nightly and DJs spin upbeat
pop most evenings from 8pm to
3am. *354 av. Mont-Royal est. www.
bilykun.com.* ☎ *514/845-5392.
Métro: Mont-Royal. Map p 107.*

★ Brasserie Harricana PLATEAU
This massive brewpub is right near
Marché Jean-Talon (p 89) and the
Mile-Ex and Little Italy neighborhoods. It boasts some 40 beers on
taps, with about ten house labels
and the rest from throughout Québec. There are also rums, bourbons,
and ciders on tap and a lunch and
dinner food menu that includes a
so-called "poutine bun": fries,
cheese curds, and gravy in a hot
dog bun. Reservations are available
for large groups (15 or more). *95 rue
Jean-Talon ouest. www.brasserie
harricana.com.* ☎ *514/667-0006.
Métro: Jean-Talon. Map p 107.*

Bar Henrietta is a slim, upscale bar on swanky Avenue Laurier.

Celebrate warm weather on the rooftop terrace at Labo Culinaire (Foodlab).

★ **Brutopia** DOWNTOWN   Beer aficionados will love Brutopia's own homebrewed beer and its collection of Québec microbrews. Unlike other spots on rue Crescent, where the sound levels can be deafening, here you can actually have a conversation. It boasts Montreal's longest-running open mic, held every Sunday night. Bands perform most other evenings starting at 10pm. *1219 rue Crescent. www.brutopia. net.* ☎ *514/393-9277. Métro: Lucien-L'Allier. Map p 108.*

★ **Buvette Chez Simone** PLATEAU   Simone is one of a group of friends who own this popular bar. The terrace (framed by greenery in summer) is a coveted spot in sunny weather. Stripped-down industrial chic in the interior envelops a central, oval-shaped bar. The menu has a satisfying selection of small eats, including charcuterie and cheeses, as well as a strong selection of wines by the glass. *4869 av. du Parc. www.buvettechezsimone.com.* ☎ *514/750-6577. Métro: Mont Royal or Laurier. Map p 107.*

★★★ **Dieu du Ciel** PLATEAU   There are about 20 microbreweries in Montréal, and this is our favorite. This neighborhood hangout offers an alternating selection of some dozen beers, including house brews and exotic imports. Dieu du Ciel beers are also bottled and sold throughout the province. *29 av.*

Laurier ouest. www.dieuduciel.com. ☎ *514/490-9555. Métro: Laurier. Map p 107.*

★ **Labo Culinaire (Foodlab)** QUARTIER DES SPECTACLES   On the top floor of the Société Des Arts Technologiques, this venue hosts parties and business events, but it's also open Monday through Friday from 5pm for drinks and food. In warm weather, come for the terrasse and the art-world creatives. *1201 bd. St-Laurent. www.sat.qc.ca/foodlab.* ☎ *514/ 884-2033. Métro: Saint-Laurent. Map p 108.*

La Cage Brasserie Sportive DOWNTOWN   Part of a national chain, this upgraded outpost (now a brasserie with a chef!) is located in the Bell Centre and attracts some of the most devoted Canadiens fans around. During the hockey season, you'll find yourself surrounded by a sea of red, white, and blue jerseys. That is, if you can find a seat. *1212 av. des Canadiens du Montréal. www. cage.ca.* ☎ *514/925-2255. Métro: Lucien-L'Allier. Map p 108.*

★★ **Le Jardin Nelson** VIEUX-MONTREAL   In the summer, the outdoor dining options that line Place Jacques Cartier are tempting but touristy. Le Jardin Nelson has a people-watching porch adjacent to the plaza, but you're better off tucking into its large tree-shaded garden court, which sits behind a stone building dating from 1812. It's still touristy, but a pleasant hour or two can be spent listening to live jazz, played every afternoon and evening. Food takes second place, but the kitchen does well with its pizzas and crêpes. When the weather's nice, it's open as late as 1am; but it's closed November through mid-April. *407 Place Jacques-Cartier. www.jardinnelson.com.* ☎ *514/861-5731. Métro: Place d'Armes or Champ-de-Mars. Map p 108.*

★ **Méchant Boeuf** VIEUX-MON-TREAL Here, a young, stylish crowd piles into the bar of this brasserie during happy hour and doesn't seem to leave (a DJ keeps things moving with nonstop techno-pop). The menu has a large selection of shareable appetizers such as fried calamari and chicken wings, but the real focus is on beef. There's an array of well-crafted burgers and AAA-grade cuts of such as New York strip and bone-in filet mignon that will delight any carnivore. The well-stocked raw bar is popular, and a late night bar menu is available after 11pm. Reservations recommended on weekends. *124 rue St-Paul ouest. www.mechantboeuf.com.* ☎ *514/788-4020. Métro: Champs-de-Mars. Map p 108.*

★ **Philémon** VIEUX-MONTREAL The look here is chalet-chic, while the crowd is urban single professional. As one blogger put it, "you can always count on its strong quick 'n' dirty drinks, relaxed vibe, fashionable and good-looking 20-to-40 year old crowd . . . Oh, and being hit on." The oysters are good and there's a great charcuterie platter. *111 rue St-Paul ouest. www.philemonbar.com.* ☎ *514/289-3777. Métro: Place d'Armes. Map p 108.*

★★ **Pullman** DOWNTOWN This sleek wine bar offers either 2- or 4-ounce pours, so there is room for adventure. A competent tapas menu with standards like grilled cheese bedazzled with port and charcuterie are prepared with the precision of a sushi chef. The multi-level space creates pockets of ambience, from cozy corners to tables drenched in natural light. *3424 av. du Parc. www.pullman-mtl.com.* ☎ *514/288-7779. Métro: Place des Arts. Map p 108.*

★ **Sir Winston Churchill Pub** DOWNTOWN This gigantic rue Crescent landmark, and its New Orleans–style terraces (open in warm months), make perfect vantage points from which to check out the pedestrian traffic. With three floors geared toward three different crowds (wine bar, British pub, and contemporary bar) there's something for everyone. *1459 rue Crescent. www.swcpc.com.* ☎ *514/288-3814. Métro: Guy-Concordia. Map p 108.*

★ **Velvet** VIEUX-MONTREAL This cavernous nightclub cultivates the feel of an underground speakeasy, courtesy of its virtually nonexistent signage and its tunnel entrance through the bar of Auberge St-Gabriel. Even the website is hard to decipher. Some of the bartenders here are models and many of the patrons have deep pockets, so, yes, come dressed to impress. Music ranges from house,

A late-night menu at Méchant Boeuf bar-brasserie kicks in at 11pm.

Bring your friends to the enormous Sir Winston Churchill Pub, where each level has a different vibe.

hip-hop to electro. *426 rue St-Gabriel. Enter through the hotel bar.* www.velvetspeakeasy.ca. ☎ 514/995-8754. Metro: Place d'Armes. Map p 108.

★ **Vices & Versa** PLATEAU
This bistro au terroir has featured microbrews on draft and in cask as well as regional chow since 2004. It's a low-key, local joint with occasional musical acts and a lovely backyard beer garden. *6631 bd. St-Laurent. www.vicesetversa.com.* ☎ 514/272-2498. Métro: Beaubien. Map p 107.

Dance Clubs
★ **Sky Club & Pub** THE VILLAGE
This is a complex that includes drag performances in the cabaret room, a pub serving dinner daily, a hip-hop room, a spacious dance floor that's often set to house music, and a popular roof terrace. Sky is thought by many to be the city's top spot for the gay, young, and fabulous. *1474 rue Ste-Catherine est.* ☎ 514/529-6969. www.complexesky.com. Métro: Beaudry. Map p 107.

Music Venues
The **Festival International de Jazz de Montréal** is one of the monster events on the city's calendar. It costs serious money to hear big stars such as Erykah Badu, Tony Bennett, or Diana Krall and tickets sell out months in advance.

Fortunately, 450 free outdoor performances also take place during the 11-day July party, many right on downtown's streets and plazas. Visit www.montrealjazzfest.com or call ☎ 855/299-3378 or 514/871-1881 for information.

★ **Cabaret Mado** THE VILLAGE
The glint of the sequins can be blinding! Inspired by 1920s cabaret, this drag theater has a dance floor, performances most nights, and is considered a premiere venue. Look for the pink-haired drag queen on the retro marquee. *1115 rue Ste-Catherine est. www.mado.qc.ca.* ☎ 514/525-7566. Cover around C$10. Métro: Beaudry. Map p 107.

Casa del Popolo PLATEAU   Set in a scruffy storefront, Casa del Popolo serves vegetarian food, operates a laid-back bar, and has a small first-floor stage. Across the street is a larger, sister performance space, La Sala Rossa (see below). The two venues constitute the heart of the Montréal indie music scene. *4873 bd. St-Laurent. www.casadelpopolo.com.* ☎ 514/284-3804. Cover C$5–C$15. Métro: Laurier. Map p 107.

Club Soda QUARTIER LATIN
The long-established rock club in the old Red Light District of the Latin Quarter (and on the edge of

The Montréal Jazz Festival unifies the city's residents and visitors.

Looking for live rock? Start with Club Soda in the Latin Quarter.

the hotter Quartier des Spectacles) hosts national and international acts, cover bands, fashion shows, and parts of the city's music and comedy festivals. Occasionally they'll show pay-per-view sporting events too. *1225 bd. St-Laurent. www.clubsoda.ca.* ☎ *514/286-1010. Tickets from C$17. Métro: St-Laurent. Map p 107.*

Divan Orange PLATEAU A hopping club with a good, hipster vibe. Bands and combos here include indie rock, jazz, country, and traditional North African. *4234 bd. St-Laurent. www.divanorange.org.* ☎ *514/840-9090. Cover C$5–C$10. Métro: Mont-Royal. Map p 107.*

Hurley's Irish Pub DOWNTOWN In front is a street-level terrace, and in back are several semi-subterranean rooms. Celtic instrumentalists perform nightly, usually starting around 9:30pm. There are 19 beers on tap and more than 50 single-malt whiskeys to choose from. *1225 rue Crescent. www.hurleysirishpub.com.* ☎ *514/861-4111. Métro: Guy-Concordia. Map p 108.*

★ **La Sala Rossa** PLATEAU A bigger venue than its sister space Casa del Popolo (see above), La

Sala Rossa offers a calendar of interesting rock, experimental, and jazz music. The attached Sala Rosa restaurant has live flamenco music every Thursday with dancing and singing. *4848 bd. St-Laurent. www.casadelpopolo.com.* ☎ *514/844-4227. Cover C$5–C$30. Métro: Laurier. Map p 107.*

Maison du Jazz DOWNTOWN This New Orleans–style jazz venue has been on the scene for decades. Live music starts around 8pm most evenings. The ribs are OK, and the jazz is of the swinging mainstream variety. Popular bands can sell out the venue, so we recommend making reservations. *2060 rue Aylmer. www.houseofjazz.ca.* ☎ *514/842-8656. Cover C$10. Métro: McGill. Map p 108.*

★ **Upstairs Jazz Bar & Grill** DOWNTOWN Big names are infrequent at the Upstairs bar (which you have to walk downstairs to enter), but the groups are more than competent. Sets begin as early as 7:30pm. *1254 rue Mackay. www.upstairsjazz.com.* ☎ *514/931-6808. Cover C$5–C$30. Métro: Guy-Concordia. Map p 108.* ●

Houston Person on sax at Upstairs Jazz.

Arts & Entertainment Best Bets

Best **Circus**
★★★ Cirque du Soleil and Montréal Complètement Cirque festival, in July (p 117 and p 157)

Best **Opportunity to Hear French** *Chanson*
Les FrancoFolies de Montréal festival, held in June (p 156)

Best **Old-Time Jazz & Dinner Club**
Maison du Jazz, *2060 rue Aylmer* (p 114)

Best **Refined Evening Entertainment**
★★ L'Orchestre Symphonique de Montréal, *Place des Arts, 1600 rue St-Urban* (p 120)

Best **English-Speaking Theater**
★ Centaur Theatre, *453 rue St-Francois-Xavier* (p 122)

Best **Comedy Spot**
The Comedy Nest, *2313 Ste-Catherine ouest* (p 120)

Best **Drag Club**
★ Cabaret Mado, *1115 rue Ste-Catherine est* (p 113)

Best **Music Festival**
Festival International de Jazz de Montréal, held in June and July (p 156)

Best **Venue for Sports & Big-Name Concerts**
Centre Bell, *1909 av. des Canadiens-de-Montréal* (p 121)

Best **Humungous Movie Screen**
IMAX Theatre, *in the Centre des Sciences de Montréal, Quai King Edward* (p 121)

Best **Destination for Games of Chance**
Casino de Montréal, *Parc Jean-Drapeau* (p 117)

Best **Yiddish-Speaker Theater**
Segal Centre for Performing Arts at the Saidye, *5170 Côte-Ste-Catherine* (p 122)

Best **Small Venue for Indie Rock**
★ La Sala Rossa, *4848 bd. St-Laurent* (p 114)

Best **Free Classical Music**
Pollack Concert Hall, *555 rue Sherbrooke ouest* (p 120)

Best **Deafening Sports Venue**
Percival-Molson Memorial Stadium, *Top of rue University, on McGill campus* (p 122)

Previous page: L'Orchestre Symphonique tickets are specially priced for people 34 and under, 25 and under, and 17 and under.
Below: The Casino de Montréal.

Arts & Entertainment
A to Z

Montréal is home to the captivating Cirque du Soleil.

In addition to the venues and production companies listed here, additional listings for performing arts can be found in chapter 6, "The Best Nightlife," and "Festivals & Special Events" on p 156.

Casino
Casino de Montréal PARC JEAN-DRAPEAU   The province's original casino is housed in a complex recycled from the French and Québec pavilions from the 1967 World's Fair, Expo 67. Asymmetrical and groovy, the buildings provide a dramatic setting for games of chance, which include varieties of poker, roulette, blackjack, baccarat, and. More than 3,000 slot machines create a mind-numbing din. Visitors must be at least 18. *Parc Jean-Drapeau. www. casinosduquebec.com.* ☎ *800/665-2274 or 514/392-2746. Free admission. Métro: Parc Jean-Drapeau. Map p 118.*

Circus
★★★ Cirque du Soleil   The circus company Cirque du Soleil, now a global powerhouse, is based in Montréal. Each show is a celebration of pure skill with acrobats, trapeze artists, and performers costumed to look like creatures not of this world—iguanas crossed with goblins, peacocks born of trolls. Although there isn't a permanent show in Montréal, the troupe usually comes through the city at least once a year and often performs in an outdoor amphitheater in Vieux Montréal's Old Port. *www.cirque dusoleil.com.* ☎ *877/924-7783. Tickets from C$44. Map p 118.*

Classical Music
★ L'Opera de Montréal
QUARTIER DES SPECTACLES   Founded in 1980, this outstanding opera company mounts five productions per year in Montréal, with artists from Québec and abroad participating in such shows as Gershwin's "Porgy and Bess" and Puccini's "Madama Butterfly." Video translations are provided from the original languages into French and English. Performances are held from September through May. *Place des Arts, Salle Wilfrid-Pelletier. 175 rue Ste-Catherine ouest,*

The Orchestre Métropolitain du Grand Montréal performs at Place des Arts.

Arts & Entertainment in Montréal

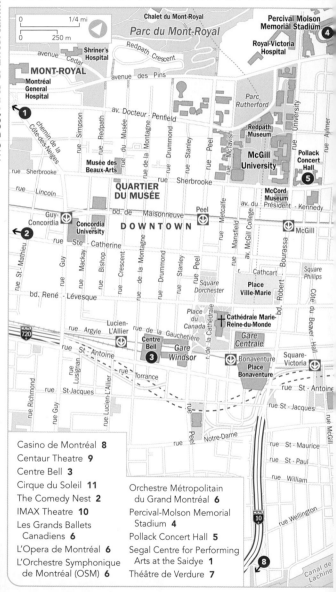

Chalet du Mont-Royal

Parc du Mont-Royal

Percival Molson
Memorial Stadium 4

Royal-Victoria
Hospital

Shriner's
Hospital

avenue Cedar

Redpath Crescent

MONT-ROYAL

Montréal
General
Hospital

avenue des Pins

Parc
Rutherford

av. Docteur - Penfield

Redpath
Museum

Musée des
Beaux-Arts

rue Sherbrooke

rue Lincoln

QUARTIER
DU MUSÉE

McGill
University

Pollack
Concert
Hall 5

rue Sherbrooke

McCord
Museum

bd. de   Maisonneuve

av. du Président - Kennedy

Guy-
Concordia

Peel

Concordia
University

DOWNTOWN

McGill

rue Ste - Catherine

bd. René - Lévesque

Square
Dorchester

Square
Phillips

Place
Ville-Marie

Place
du
Canada

Cathédrale Marie-
Reine-du-Monde

Gare
Centrale

Lucien-
L'Allier

rue de la Gauchetière

720

rue Argyle

Centre
Bell 3

Gare
Windsor

Bonaventure
Place
Bonaventure

Square-
Victoria

rue St - Antoine

rue St-Antoine

Torrance

rue St - Jacques

rue Richmond

rue St-Jacques

rue Notre-Dame

rue St - Maurice

rue St - Paul

rue William

rue Wellington

10

Canal de
Lachine

8

Casino de Montréal 8

Centaur Theatre 9

Centre Bell 3

Cirque du Soleil 11

The Comedy Nest 2

IMAX Theatre 10

Les Grands Ballets
  Canadiens 6

L'Opera de Montréal 6

L'Orchestre Symphonique
  de Montréal (OSM) 6

Orchestre Métropolitain
du Grand Montréal 6

Percival-Molson Memorial
Stadium 4

Pollack Concert Hall 5

Segal Centre for Performing
Arts at the Saidye 1

Théâtre de Verdure 7

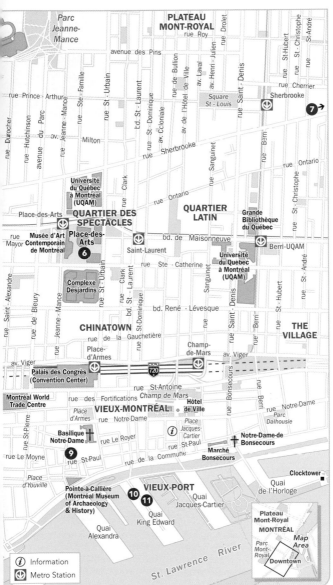

Parc Jeanne-Mance

PLATEAU MONT-ROYAL
rue Roy

avenue des Pins

rue Prince - Arthur

rue Durocher
rue Hutchinson
avenue du Parc
av. Jeanne-Mance
rue Ste-Famille
rue St-Urbain

Milton

 bd. St-Laurent
rue St-Dominique
av. de l'Hôtel-de-Ville
rue de Bullion
av. Laval
av. Henri - Julien
rue Saint - Denis

rue Roy

rue Cherrier

Sherbrooke

Square St - Louis

rue St-Hubert
rue St-Christophe
rue St-André

7 →

rue Sherbrooke

rue Coloniale
rue Clark

rue Ontario

Université du Québec à Montréal (UQAM)

Place-des-Arts

QUARTIER DES SPECTACLES

rue Mayor
Musée d'Art Contemporain de Montréal
6

Place-des-Arts

QUARTIER LATIN

Grande Bibliothèque du Québec

rue Ontario

rue Sanguinet
rue Berri
rue St-Christophe
rue St-André

Saint-Laurent
bd. de Maisonneuve
Berri-UQAM

rue Saint-Alexandre
rue de Bleury
av. Jeanne-Mance
rue St-Urbain
rue Clark
bd. St - Laurent
rue St-Dominique

rue Ste - Catherine

Complexe Desjardins

Université du Québec à Montréal (UQAM)

bd. René - Lévesque

CHINATOWN
rue de la Gauchetière

Place-d'Armes

Champ-de-Mars

av. Viger

rue Saint - Denis
rue Saint - Hubert
rue Berri

THE VILLAGE

av. Viger

Palais des Congrès (Convention Center)
720

Montréal World Trade Centre

rue St-Pierre
rue St-Antoine
rue des Fortifications Champ de Mars
Place d'Armes rue Notre-Dame

VIEUX-MONTRÉAL
Hôtel de Ville

rue Bonsecours
rue Berri
rue Notre-Dame
Parc Dalhousie

rue St-Paul
Basilique Notre-Dame
9
rue Le Royer
Place Jacques-Cartier
(i)

Notre-Dame-de-Bonsecours

rue Le Moyne
rue St-Paul
rue de la Commune
Marché Bonsecours

Place d'Youville

Pointe-à-Callière (Montréal Museum of Archaeology & History)
10 **11**

VIEUX-PORT

Quai Jacques-Cartier

Clocktower

Quai de l'Horloge

Quai King Edward

Quai Alexandra

St. Lawrence River

Plateau Mont-Royal
MONTRÉAL
Parc Mont-Royal
Map Area
Downtown

(i) Information
Ⓜ Metro Station

www.operademontreal.com. ☎ 877/385-2222 or 514/985-2222. Tickets from C$21. Métro: Place-des-Arts. Map p 118.

★★ L'Orchestre Symphonique de Montréal (OSM) QUARTIER DES SPECTACLES

The orchestra's home is designed "shoebox" style, with seats on multiple balcony levels surrounding the performers. Music director Kent Nagano focuses the symphony's repertoire on programs featuring works by Beethoven, Bach, Brahms, and Mahler. It has programs for children 5 to 12 and special prices for people 34 and under, 25 and under, and 17 and under. *Place des Arts, Maison symphonique de Montréal. 1600 rue St-Urbain, www.osm.ca.* ☎ 888/842-9951 or 514/842-9951 for tickets. Tickets from C$42; discounts available for various age groups. Métro: Place-des-Arts. Map p 118.

Orchestre Métropolitain du Grand Montréal QUARTIER DES SPECTACLES

This is a world-caliber orchestra of more than 60 professional musicians who mostly trained in the province. It performs more than 70 concerts a year primarily at Place des Arts but also in 10 Montréal boroughs. Its program ranges from Slavik masters, to Bach and his successors, and beyond. *Place des Arts, Maison symphonique de Montréal. 1600 rue St-Urbain, www.orchestremetropolitain.com.* ☎ 866/842-2112 or 514/842-2112. Tickets from C$29. Métro: Place-des-Arts. Map p 118.

Pollack Concert Hall DOWNTOWN

A stone statue of Queen Victoria perched on her throne guards the entrance to this 1908 landmark building on the McGill University campus, where many classical concerts and recitals are staged. Because most of the concerts are performed by McGill students or alumni, tickets are modest—in fact, most are free. *555 rue Sherbrooke*

The crowd-pleasing Just For Laughs comedy festival.

ouest. www.music.mcgill.ca. ☎ 514/398-4547. Tickets free to C$30. Métro: McGill. Map p 118.

Comedy

The Festival Juste pour Rire (Just for Laughs Festival)

is the largest comedy festival in the world and has been going strong for nearly 35 years. In 2015, Dave Chappelle did six performances, and comedy galas were hosted by Wanda Sykes, Neil Patrick Harris, and Jane Lynch. Other recently featured comedians include Kevin Hart, Lewis Black, Kate McKinnon, Don Rickles, and Aziz Ansari. Held throughout the month of July. *Visit www.hahaha.com or call* ☎ 888/244-3155 or 514/845-2322.

The Comedy Nest DOWNTOWN

This long-running club entertains patrons with a full range of performers. Some nights feature newbie comics and other nights sell out for world-class headliners. The venue is housed at the Forum (former home of the Canadiens, where they won 24 Stanley Cups), west of Vieux-Montréal. *2313 Ste-Catherine ouest, in Forum de Montréal, 3rd floor. www.comedynest.com.* ☎ 514/932-6378. Cover from C$5. Métro: Atwater. Map p 118.

Les Grands Ballets showcases a diverse range of balletic forms.

Dance

★★ Les Grands Ballets Canadiens QUARTIER DES SPECTACLES   Founded in 1957, this prestigious touring company performs both a classical and a modern repertoire and has developed a following far beyond national borders. In the process, it has brought prominence to many gifted Canadian choreographers and composers. The troupe's production of "The Nutcracker" is always a big event each winter. Performances are held October through May. *Place des Arts, 175 rue Ste-Catherine ouest, www.grandsballets.com.* ☎ *866/842-2112 or 514/842-2112 for information and tickets. Tickets from C$53. Métro: Place-des-Arts. Map p 118.*

Film

In Montréal, English-language films are usually presented with French subtitles. However, when the letters *VF* (for *version française*) follow the title of a non-Francophone movie,

it means that the movie has been dubbed into French. Policies vary regarding English subtitles on non-English-language films, so ask at the box office.

★ IMAX Theatre VIEUX-PORT Images and special effects are way larger than life and visually dazzling on this screen in the Centre des Sciences de Montréal (p. 58). Recent films have highlighted underwater expeditions and pandas (both in 3-D). Running time is usually less than an hour. There's one screening per day in English. Tickets can be ordered online. *Quai King Edward, Vieux-Port. www. montrealsciencecentre.com.* ☎ *877/496-4724 or 514/496-4724. Movie tickets C$12 adults, with discounts for children and seniors, and free for children 3 and under. Shows daily. Métro: Place d'Armes or Champ-de-Mars. Map p 118.*

Sports & Rock Venues

Centre Bell DOWNTOWN   Seating 21,273 for most events, Centre Bell is the home of the Montréal Canadiens hockey team and host to the biggest international rock and pop stars traveling through the city, including Québec native Céline Dion. There are guided tours and a Montréal Canadiens

Madonna performs at La Centre Bell, home to many of the city's concerts and its beloved Canadiens.

Percival-Molson Memorial Stadium is within walking distance of downtown.

Hall of Fame (www.hall.canadiens. com). *1909 avenue des Canadiens-de-Montréal. www.centrebell.ca.* ☎ *877/668-8269 or 514/790-2525. Métro: Bonaventure. Map p 118.*

Percival-Molson Memorial Stadium DOWNTOWN American-style football is played here. During the Canadian Football League season, the stadium gets incredibly loud thanks to the die-hard, chest-painting fans of the Montréal Alouettes (that's French for "larks"). The team is popular, and tickets to games sell out quickly. *Top of rue University at McGill University campus. www.montreal alouettes.com.* ☎ *514/787-2525 for Alouettes ticket info. Tickets from C$25. Métro: McGill. Map p 118.*

Theater

★ **Centaur Theatre** VIEUX-MONTRÉAL The city's principal English-language theater is housed in a former stock-exchange building from 1903. It presents a mix of classics, foreign adaptations, and works by Canadian playwrights. Its reputation for showcasing some of the city's finest productions makes it a hot spot for tourists, and tickets to major plays are often hard to come by. *453 rue St-Francois-Xavier. www.centaurtheatre.com.* ☎ *514/ 288-3161. Tickets from C$29. Métro: Place d'Armes. Map p 118.*

Segal Centre for Performing Arts at the Saidye PLATEAU From about 1900 to 1930, Yiddish was Montréal's third most-common language. That status has since been usurped by any number of languages, but its dominance lives on here, one of the few North American theaters that still presents plays in Yiddish. *5170 Côte-Ste-Catherine. www.segal centre.org.* ☎ *514/739-7944. Tickets from C$25. Métro: Côte-Ste-Catherine or Snowdon. Map p 118.*

★ **Théâtre de Verdure** PARC LA FONTAINE This beloved open-air amphitheater has been a draw for free outdoor theater, music, and tango dancing, but it fell into disrepair and was closed for the 2014–16 seasons. However, major renovations were designed to restore the venue to its former glory so that it could re-open in 2017 as part of Montréal's 375th anniversary celebrations. Performances in the past were held from June to August, and many in the audience brought picnic dinners. Check with the tourism office (p 156) for updated information. *Parc La Fontaine. Métro: Sherbrooke. Map p 118.* ●

Theatrical performances are staged in both Yiddish and English at the Segal Centre for Performing Arts at the Saidye.

Hotel Best Bets

Start the day in style with a light breakfast at the restaurant Bonaparte, complimentary for the Auberge's guests.

Best **Luxury Hotel**
★★★ Ritz-Carlton Montréal $$$$
1228 rue Sherbrooke ouest (p 132)

Best **Romantic Hotel**
★★ Auberge du Vieux-Port $$$
97 rue de la Commune est (p 127)

Best **Family Hotels**
★★★ Le Saint-Sulpice Hôtel
Montréal $$ *414 rue St-Sulpice*
(p 131); ★★ Hôtel Bonaventure
Montréal $$ *900 rue de la Gauchet-*
iere ouest (p 129); ★★ Le Square
Phillips Hôtel & Suites $$ *1193*
Square Phillips (p 132)

Best **Value Hotel**
★ Hôtel Le Dauphin Montréal-
Downtown $ *1025 rue de Bleury*
(p 130)

Best **New Boutique Hotel**
★★ Hôtel ÉPIK Montréal $$ *171*
rue St-Paul ouest (p 129)

Best **High Design Hotel**
★★ Hôtel Gault $$ *449 rue*
Ste-Hélène (p 130)

Best **Full-Service Boutique
Hotel**
★★ Hôtel Nelligan $$$ *106 rue*
St-Paul ouest (p 131)

Best **Casual Cozy Hotel**
★★ Auberge de La Fontaine $$
1301 rue Rachel est (p 127)

Best **Step Back to the 18th
Century**
Hostellerie Pierre du Calvet $$$
405 rue Bonsecours (p 128)

Best **Nightclub-Like Hotel**
★ Le St-Martin Hôtel $$ *980 boul.*
de Maisonneuve ouest (p 132)

Best **Rooftop Pool & Jacuzzi**
★★ Hôtel Le Crystal $$ *1100 rue*
de la Montagne (p 130)

Best **In-House Dining**
★★★ Hôtel de l'Institut $$ *3535*
rue Saint-Denis (p 129)

Previous page: The Ritz-Carlton Montréal is one of the city's most splurge-worthy hotels.

Accommodations in Vieux-Montréal

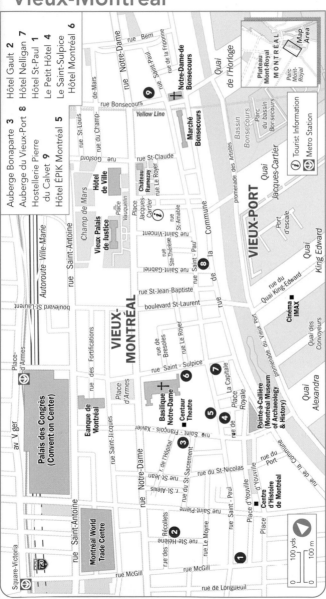

Auberge Bonaparte **3**
Auberge du Vieux-Port **8**
Hostellerie Pierre du Calvet **9**
Hôtel ÉPIK Montréal **5**
Hôtel Gault **2**
Hôtel Nelligan **7**
Hôtel St-Paul **1**
Le Petit Hôtel **4**
Le Saint-Sulpice Hôtel Montréal **6**

(i) Tourist Information
🅜 Metro Station

Accommodations in Downtown Montréal & the Plateau

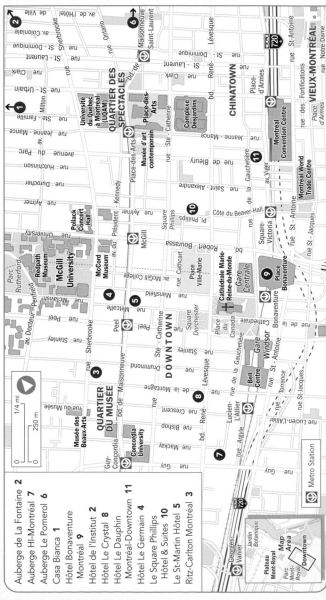

Auberge de La Fontaine **2**

Auberge HI-Montréal **7**

Auberge Le Pomerol **6**

Casa Bianca **1**

Hôtel Bonaventure Montréal **9**

Hôtel de l'Institut **2**

Hôtel Le Crystal **8**

Hôtel Le Dauphin Montréal-Downtown **11**

Hôtel Le Germain **4**

Le Square Phillips Hôtel & Suites **10**

Le St-Martin Hôtel **5**

Ritz-Carlton Montréal **3**

Hotels **A to Z**

Auberge de La Fontaine is out of the tourist orbit and one of the authors' favorite places to stay.

★★ Auberge Bonaparte VIEUX-MONTREAL   Rooms at the lowest price point are small but comfortable, and square footage increases as you move up in price. Some rooms feature gorgeous exposed brick walls. Rooms on the courtyard side have an appealing view of the Basilique Notre-Dame, which can also be seen from a rooftop terrace accessible to all guests. Complimentary breakfast is served in the graceful **Bonaparte** restaurant, expanded in 2013 with a new bar and more dining space. At night, the restaurant dishes out classic French cuisine, with the Dover sole meunière especially recommended. *447 rue St-François-Xavier.* ☎ *514/844-1448. www.bonaparte.com. 31 units. Doubles C$150–C$240. Métro: Place d'Armes. Map p 125.*

★★ Auberge de La Fontaine PLATEAU   For visitors who plan to spend time at the restaurants and bars of Plateau Mont-Royal and want a casual option, La Fontaine can't be beat. It feels like a cheerful hostel (although all the rooms are private) and bedrooms are done up in bright, funky colors. It's located directly on the lovely Parc La Fontaine and one of the city's central bike paths, and has a third floor terrace overlooking the park. The breakfast buffet (pastries, cereals, yogurt, fresh fruit, local cheeses) is one reason guests return to this *auberge* time and time again. Families are warmly accommodated. *1301 rue Rachel est. www.auberge delafontaine.com.* ☎ *800/597-0597 or 514/597-0166. 21 units. Doubles C$122–C$157. Métro: Mont-Royal. Map p 126.*

★★ Auberge du Vieux-Port VIEUX-MONTREAL   Terrifically romantic. This luxury inn in an 1882 building faces the waterfront, and many rooms as well as a rooftop terrace offer unobstructed views of Vieux-Port, a particular treat on summer nights when there are fireworks on the river. In addition to modern comforts, you'll find stone walls and wooden beams. The owners also offer a selection of studio, 1-, and 2-bedroom loft style apartments not far from the hotel, ideal for families and long-term stays. *97 rue de la Commune est.* ☎ *www. aubergeduvieuxport.com.* ☎ *888/ 660-7678 or 514/876-0081. 45 units. Doubles C$190–C$340. Métro: Champ-de-Mars. Map p 125.*

Your glass awaits on the terrace at Auberge du Vieux-Port hotel.

Auberge HI-Montréal DOWN-TOWN   A member of Hosteling International, HI-Montréal offers both shared accommodations and private rooms. Like most hostels, it features a communal kitchen, but this being Montréal, it also has a bar, organized pub crawls, and ice skating trips for guests. The raucous bar scene of rue Crescent is only 2 blocks away. *1030 rue Mackay. www.hostellingmontreal. com.* ☎ *866/843-3317 or 514/843-3317. 240 beds. Single bed in a shared room C$15–C$50; private room C$100. Métro: Lucien-L'Allier. Map p 126.*

Auberge Le Pomerol QUARTIER LATIN   The lower end of the Plateau flows into the Quartier Latin, and while we don't recommend staying in that neighborhood for a first visit—it lacks the charm of other parts of the city—return visitors who are familiar with all its messiness might find its central location appealing. Auberge Le Pomerol is a competent option in this neighborhood: Staff is friendly and there's a cozy shared living room and breakfast room. Executive rooms offer a little more space. *819 de Maisonneuve est. www. aubergelepomerol.com.* ☎ *514/526-5511. 27 units. Doubles C$110–C$215. Métro: Berri-UQAM. Map p 126.*

The independently owned Hôtel Bonaventure Montréal is a great choice for families in any season.

Bed & Breakfasts & Airbnb

B&Bs boast cozy settings and are often (but not always) less expensive than comparable hotels. They also give visitors an opportunity to meet a Montréaler. The city tourism office, **Tourisme Montréal,** has a select list of B&Bs that it recommends. They're listed at www. tourisme-montreal.org. **Airbnb** lists over 300 rentals of single rooms and whole apartments in Montréal. Find the listings at www.airbnb. com/s/Montreal.

★★ **Casa Bianca** PLATEAU   This elegant B&B is an architectural landmark. It's on the corner of a tree-lined residential street in Montréal's hip Plateau neighborhood, adjacent to Parc Jeanne-Mance and a stone's throw from Parc du Mont-Royal. If the weather is cooperating, the organic breakfast is served on a breezy patio. Yoga instruction can be planned in advance with an in-house yoga instructor. Rooms are spacious with antique touches, and many have claw-foot bathtubs that add to the homey feel. If you're looking to do some shopping, it's close to the shops and boutiques along boulevard St-Laurent and avenue Mont-Royal. *4351 av. de L'Esplanade. www.casabianca.ca.* ☎ *866/775-4431 or 514/312-3837. 5 units. Doubles C$119–C$269. Métro: Mont Royal. Map p 126.*

Hostellerie Pierre du Calvet VIEUX-MONTREAL   Fans of Masterpiece Theatre and faded old-world bric-a-brac, this quirky hotel could be for you. Step from cobblestone streets into an opulent 18th-century home boasting gold-leafed writing desks and four-poster beds of teak mahogany. In warm months, an outdoor courtyard is a hideaway

dining terrace. *405 rue Bonsecours. www.pierreducalvet.ca.* ☎ *866/544-1725 or 514/282-1725. 10 units. Doubles from C$295. Métro: Champ-de-Mars. Map p 125.*

★★ kids **Hôtel Bonaventure Montréal** DOWNTOWN The Bonaventure calls itself a "penthouse hotel," and that's accurate: It takes up the top floor of a concrete monster of an office building. Don't be put off by the building's brutalist exerior. The hotel is lovely: The 395 rooms and suites all have either expansive views of the city or a peek at delightful rooftop gardens that feature a resident family of ducks (and ducklings in spring), small walking paths, and a corker of a pool—outdoor, heated, and open year-round. Now independently owned, the hotel was part of the Hilton chain until 2015 and so far has retained some signature Hilton touches: a competent in-house restaurant and bar, long hallways with attached conference rooms, and conference attendees. Splurge for a package that includes access to the Executive Lounge, a private dining room where a deluxe continental breakfast buffet is put out each morning, snacks and desserts are served late afternoon, and drinks are available all day. *900 rue de la Gauchetiere ouest. www.hotel bonaventure.com.* ☎ *888/267-2575 or 514/878-2332. 395 units. Doubles C$159–C$349. Metro: Bonaventure. Map p 126.*

Hôtel Gault's minimalist style and mod furniture mix sleek style and colorful whimsy.

★★★ **Hôtel de l'Institut** PLATEAU For visitors who've "done" Old Montréal and want access to the Plateau's buzz of everyday Montréal life, there is no better option. Primely located and well priced, this elegant hotel is expertly run by hospitality students who are learning the Province's signature style. Rooms are up to date, tidy, and spacious. There's a work desk if needed, but better to throw open the curtains and catch a sunset from the 8th floor, ideally on a Mont Royal–facing terrace. Each stay includes breakfast in the student-run **Restaurant de l'Institut,** a fine choice for any meal, even amidst the plethora of neighborhood spots. *3535 rue Saint-Denis. www.ithq.qc.ca/en/hotel.* ☎ *855/229-8189 or 514/282-5120. 42 units. Doubles from C$129. Métro: Sherbrooke. Map p 126.*

★★ **Hôtel ÉPIK Montréal** VIEUX-MONTRÉAL Located smack dab in the center of Vieux-Montréal, this 1723 building was formerly the Auberge Les Passants du Sans Soucy, a longtime Frommer's favorite. New owners took over in 2014, and the building has undergone significant renovations for a sleek, modern feel. The lobby was expanded to make room for a cafe and there's also a 30-seat Mediterranean restaurant. The upper floors have been turned into a luxe two-bedroom penthouse. *171 rue St-Paul ouest. www.epik montreal.com.* ☎ *877/841-2634. 10 units. Doubles from C$160. Métro: Place d'Armes. Map p 125.*

Vieux-Montréal's rustic charm softens the crisp lines in a loft at Hôtel ÉPIK.

Hôtel Le Crystal is a luxurious choice near Le Centre Bell and rue Ste-Catherine.

★★ Hôtel Gault VIEUX-MONTREAL

Gault explores the far reaches of minimalism, and design aficionados will likely love it. With raw, monumental concrete walls, its structural austerity is stark but tempered by lollipop-colored contemporary furniture and photography by local artists. Large bedrooms are loft style, with cool concrete floors and polished steel architect lamps. Rooms on the top floor all have balconies. *449 rue Ste-Hélène. www.hotelgault.com.* ☎ *866/904-1616 or 514/904-1616. 30 units. Doubles C$179–C$249. Métro: Square Victoria. Map p 125.*

★★ Hôtel Le Crystal DOWN-TOWN

The Crystal is boutique hotel in a neighborhood not known for them (most are in Vieux-Montréal), and is a welcome option for downtown. Its location close to the Centre Bell arena (home to the Canadiens hockey team and venue for big touring musical events) means that many visitors are taking in (or performing at) these shows. A top-floor pool (indoor, ringed by glass windows) and outdoor all-season Jacuzzi and terrace are a big part of the Crystal's appeal. All the rooms are suites and the smallest, the "Urban Suite," is certainly ample for most guests: 495 square feet, with separate living and sleeping areas and a kitchenette. Enveloping sheets and luxurious mattresses are part of the mix, of course. The raucousness of rue Crescent and the endless shopping of rue Ste-Catherine are steps away. *1100 rue de la Montagne. www.hotellecrystal. com.* ☎ *877/861-5550 or 514/861-5550. 131 units. From C$229 suite. Métro: Lucien L'Allier. Map p 126.*

★ kids Hôtel Le Dauphin Montréal-Downtown DOWN-TOWN

The little Dauphin tries so hard and succeeds so well. It attracts both business people on a budget—it's right next door to the convention center—and families. Rooms are simple, but still modern (think Ikea), and kept in tip-top shape. All rooms are the same size, but with different bed configurations. A few have two beds, about a quarter have kings, and the rest have queens. There are also four junior suites. The modest breakfast room where the free continental breakfast is served has a genial hostel feeling. The location is generally quiet except nights when there are big festivals at the convention center, and it's about a 15-minute walk to Vieux-Montréal in one direction and the Quartier des Spectacles in the other. *1025 rue de Bleury. www.hoteldauphin.ca.* ☎ *888/784-3888 or 514/788-3889. 72 units. C$130–C$180 single; C$10 for a second person. Métro Place d'Armes. Map p 126.*

A guest room in Hôtel Nelligan.

The lobby of Le Petit Hôtel doubles as breakfast nook and bar.

★★ **Hôtel Le Germain** DOWN-TOWN Stylish design, comfortable beds, large bathrooms, and a location on a quiet street just steps from main thoroughfares—those are four big pluses in this trim hotel's favor. The Germain creates a cozy-chic atmosphere, drawing a mix of business people, vacationers, and families of students at McGill University, which is just up the street. *2050 rue Mansfield. www.germainmontreal.com.* ☎ *877/333-2050 or 514/849-2050. 101 units. Doubles from C$210. Métro: Peel. Map p 126.*

★★ **Hôtel Nelligan** VIEUX-MONTREAL Many of the Nelligan's bedrooms are dark-wooded, masculine retreats, with heaps of pillows and quality mattresses. The common spaces create a communal feel that will make you want to stay all day—certainly doable considering the many private corners for reading or enjoying a cocktail from either the atrium bar or rooftop terrace. *106 rue St-Paul ouest. www.hotelnelligan.com.* ☎ *877/788-2040 or 514/788-2040. 105 units. Doubles from C$250. Métro: Place d'Armes. Map p 125.*

★★ **Hôtel St-Paul** VIEUX-MONTREAL The chic St-Paul has been a star to design and architecture aficionados since its 2001 opening. Minimalism pervades, with simple lines and muted colors. This being Canada, pops of texture come from pelt rugs. Many rooms face Vieux-Montréal's less-touristed western edge, with its visually appealing stone and brick buildings. *355 rue McGill. www.hotelstpaul.com.* ☎ *866/380-2202 or 514/380-2222. 120 units. Doubles from C$210. Métro: Square Victoria. Map p 125.*

★ **Le Petit Hôtel** VIEUX-MONTREAL Le Petit Hôtel is a chic and trendy standout in Old Montréal's hospitality landscape. Everything—from the funky artwork to the music playing in the lobby—skews toward a younger demographic. Stone walls provide a dramatic backdrop throughout, and rooms vary in size from tiny to extra large, so pick what suits your needs. Breakfast is served in the lobby cafe, which also serves bakery items and doubles as a bar. *168 rue St-Paul ouest. www.petithotelmontreal.com.* ☎ *877/530-0360 or 514/940-0360. 28 units. Doubles C$209–C$299. Métro: Place d'Armes. Map p 125.*

★★★ **kids** **Le Saint-Sulpice Hôtel Montréal** VIEUX-MONTREAL Each unit at this top-notch, mid-sized boutique hotel is a suite with fully equipped kitchen. Even the smallest units are spacious and feel like decked-out efficiency apartments, ideal for families. The lobby has a well-stocked bar, and the hotel's **Sinclair Restaurant,** which focuses on contemporary French cuisine, serves in both an outdoor terrace and full indoor dining room. Customer service is of the highest order here, as the concierge staff are all members of the prestigious Clefs d'Or organization. *414 rue St-Sulpice. www.lesaintsulpice.com.* ☎ *877/785-7423 or 514/288-1000. 108 units. Suites from C$189. Métro: Place d'Armes. Map p 125.*

Le St-Martin Hôtel is one of downtown's few hotels with an outdoor heated lap pool.

★★ kids Le Square Phillips Hôtel & Suites DOWNTOWN

One of the great downtown hotel options for families, especially on weekends when business travelers have cleared out. Even the smallest of rooms are decent-sized studios, with a full kitchen including a large fridge and stove, and the bed separated from the living area. The warehouse walls are handy for muffling the noise: rooms here are close to a lot of action (both the busy shopping street rue Ste-Catherine and the Quartier des Spectacles arts district are around the corner), but seem totally insulated from the outside world. There's an indoor rooftop pool and a laundry room available. *1193 Square Phillips. www.squarephillips.com.* ☎ *866/393-1193 or 514/393-1193. 160 units. Studios from C$140. Métro: McGill. Map p 126.*

★ Le St-Martin Hôtel DOWN-

TOWN   Opened in 2010, the St-Martin has nightclubby feel, with its neon pink and cobalt blue accent lighting, chic in-house restaurant, and outdoor lap pool looking out over the city. Some rooms have unique glass corner windows, while others have modern-design standalone bathtubs or electric fireplaces. High-rises on this downtown block are tall, so rooms don't have much of a view, but that won't matter for most guests. The in-house **Bistro L'Aromate** serves inventive bistro-style cuisine with many French classics getting modern twists—look for the Wagyu beef *tartare* or the unique version of the sugar pie, served as bite-sized nuggets coated in nut flour and accompanied by caramel ice cream. The restaurant spills out to a sidewalk terrace for al fresco dining. *980 boul. de Maisonneuve ouest. www.lestmartinmontreal. com.* ☎ *877/843-3003 or 514/843-3000. 123 units. Doubles from C$209. Métro: Peel. Map p 126.*

★★★ Ritz-Carlton Montréal

DOWNTOWN   Since its launch in 1912, this luxe hotel has been a favorite for both accommodations and dining. Afternoon tea is served in the graceful Palm Court, and **Maison Boulud** features modern French cuisine. The hotel underwent a top to bottom renovation in 2010, sprucing up the grand ballroom and replacing nearly everything else. Today it's fresh, elegant, and earning raves from visitors. *1228 rue Sherbrooke ouest. www.ritzmontreal. com.* ☎ *800/363-0366 or 514/842-4212. 129 units. Doubles from C$430. Métro: Peel. Map p 126.* ●

A junior suite at the posh Ritz-Carlton Montréal.

9 The Best Day Trips & Excursions

Québec City

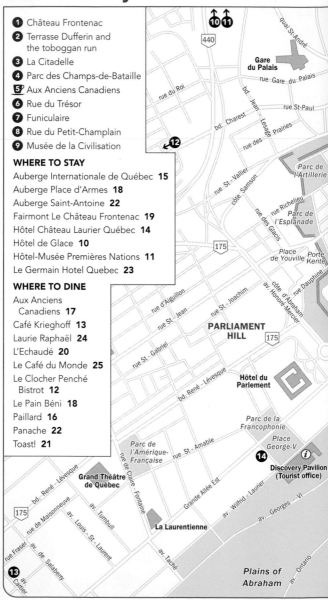

1. Château Frontenac
2. Terrasse Dufferin and the toboggan run
3. La Citadelle
4. Parc des Champs-de-Bataille
5. Aux Anciens Canadiens
6. Rue du Trésor
7. Funiculaire
8. Rue du Petit-Champlain
9. Musée de la Civilisation

WHERE TO STAY

Auberge Internationale de Québec **15**
Auberge Place d'Armes **18**
Auberge Saint-Antoine **22**
Fairmont Le Château Frontenac **19**
Hôtel Château Laurier Québec **14**
Hôtel de Glace **10**
Hôtel-Musée Premières Nations **11**
Le Germain Hotel Quebec **23**

WHERE TO DINE

Aux Anciens Canadiens **17**
Café Krieghoff **13**
Laurie Raphaël **24**
L'Echaudé **20**
Le Café du Monde **25**
Le Clocher Penché Bistrot **12**
Le Pain Béni **18**
Paillard **16**
Panache **22**
Toast! **21**

Previous page: Ice skating at Manoir Hovey.

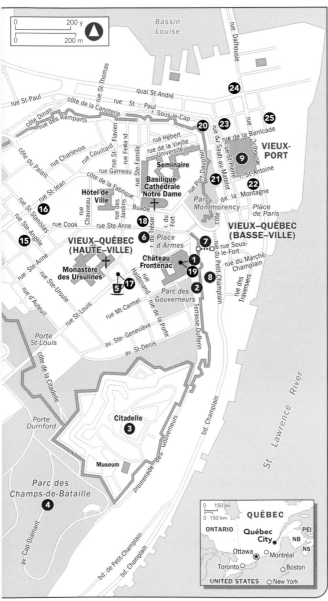

Bassin
Louise

rue Dalhousie

200 y
200 m

quai St-André
St - Paul
côte de la Canoterie
r. Sous-le-Cap

rue St-Paul
côte Dinan
rue des Remparts

rue St-Thomas

rue Hébert
rue de la Vieille
Université

côte du Palais

rue Charlevoix

rue Couillard
rue Ferland
rue St-Flavien

rue Garneau
rue Ste-Famille

VIEUX-
PORT

20

23

25

rue de la Barricade

rue du Sault-au-Matelot

rue St-Pierre

9

côte de la Fabrique

Seminaire

Basilique-
Cathédrale
Notre Dame

21

r. St-Antoine

22

rue St-Jean

Hôtel de
Ville

16

rue St-Stanislas

rue Ste-Angèle

15

rue Cook

rue Chauveau

rue des
Jardins

Buade

rue Ste-Anne

18

r. du
Trésor

6

Place
d'Armes

7

Parc de la
Montagne

Place
de Paris

VIEUX-QUÉBEC
(BASSE-VILLE)

rue Sous-
le-Fort

rue du Marché-
Champlain

VIEUX-QUÉBEC
(HAUTE-VILLE)

Monastère
des Ursulines

rue Ste-Anne

rue Ste-Ursule

rue Haldimand

Château
Frontenac

1

19

8

2

rue du Petit-Champlain

rue des
Traversiers

5

17

Parc des
Gouverneurs

rue d'Auteuil

rue St-Louis

rue Mt-Carmel

rue de la Porte

Terrasse Dufferin

av. Ste-Geneviève

Porte
St-Louis

av. St-Denis

côte de la Citadelle

Citadelle

3

promenade des Gouverneurs

bd. Champlain

St. Lawrence River

Porte
Durnford

Museum

Parc des
Champs-de-Bataille

4

av. Cap-Diamant

bd. de Petit-Champlain

bd. Champlain

150 mi
150 km

QUÉBEC

ONTARIO

Québec
City

PEI

NB

NS

Ottawa

Montréal

Toronto

Boston

UNITED STATES

New York

Québec City seduces from first view. Situated along the majestic Fleuve Saint-Laurent (St. Lawrence River), much of the oldest part of the city—Vieux-Québec, or, in English, Old Québec—sits atop Cap Diamant, a rock bluff that once provided military defense. Fortress walls still encase the upper city, and the soaring Château Frontenac, a hotel with castlelike turrets, dominates the landscape. A revitalized Lower Town, by the water, is thick with boutique hotels and cafes. The city is almost entirely French in feeling, spirit, and language: Almost everyone—95% of the population—is Francophone, or French speaking. But many of the area's 677,000 residents do know some English, especially those who work in hotels, restaurants, and shops. START: **A full day stroll can take in the sites below in the order presented. Start at Place d'Armes, the central plaza in the upper city.**

The striking Château Frontenac is the most photographed hotel in the world.

❶ ★★★ Château Frontenac. The original section of the famous edifice that defines the Québec City skyline was built as a hotel from 1892 to 1893 by the Canadian Pacific Railway Co. The architect, an American named Bruce Price, raised his creation on the site of the governor's mansion and named it after Louis de Buade, comte de Frontenac, an early governor general of New France. Fifty-minute guided tours discuss the famous people and historic events that influenced Frontenac (C$10 for guests through the concierge and C$18 for non-guests through www.cicerone.ca; ☎ 855/977-8977); the hotel also created a free app that offers a 15-minute interactive historical tour (at www.fairmont.com/frontenac-quebec).

❷ ★ kids Terrasse Dufferin and the toboggan run. In the warm months, this boardwalk promenade, with its green-and-white-topped gazebos, looks much as it did 100 years ago, when ladies with

Québec City 101

High season in Québec City is from June 24 (Jean-Baptiste Day) through Labour Day (the first Mon in Sept, as in the U.S.). Almost all of a visit can be spent on foot in the old Upper Town, atop Cap Diamant (Cape Diamond), and in the old Lower Town, which hugs the river below the bluff. There's a central tourist information center in Upper Town on Place d'Armes. Centre Infotouriste de Québec (12 rue Ste-Anne; www.bonjourquebec.com; ☎ 877/266-5687) is run by Québec province's tourism department and is open from 9am to 6pm daily from late June through August and from 9am to 5pm daily the rest of the year. The city's own tourism website is www.quebecregion.com.

parasols and gentlemen with top hats and canes strolled along it on sunny afternoons. The terrace offers vistas of river, watercraft, and distant mountains, and is particularly romantic at sunset. In winter, an old-fashioned toboggan run called Les Glissades de la Terrasse is set up right in the city on the steep wooden staircase at Terrasse Dufferin's south end. The slide extends almost to the Château Frontenac. Next to the ticket booth, a little sugar shack sells hot chocolate and traditional maple taffy. *Toboggan information: www.au1884.ca.* ☎ *418/528-1884. Cost is C$3 per person.*

❸ ★★ kids **La Citadelle.** The duke of Wellington had this partially star-shaped fortress built at the south end of the city walls in anticipation of American attacks after the War of 1812 (attacks that never came). The facility has never actually exchanged fire with an invader but continues its vigil for the state. It's now a national historic site, and since 1920 has been home to Québec's Royal 22e Régiment, the only fully Francophone unit in Canada's armed forces. That makes it North America's largest fortified group of buildings still occupied by troops. Entrance is by guided tour only. If you're inclined, try to time a

The long staircase running from La Citadelle to Terrasse Dufferin is converted into a toboggan run in winter.

Aerial view of the star-shaped fortress, La Citadelle.

visit to include the ceremonies of the changing of the guard (daily at 10am July 24–Sept 6.) *1 Côte de la Citadelle. www.lacitadelle.qc.ca.* ☎ *418/694-2815. Admission C$16 adults, C$13 seniors and students, C$6 children 7–17, free for children 7 and under; families C$32. June 24– Sept 6 daily 9am–5pm, shorter hours rest of the year. Changing of the guard ceremony may be canceled in the event of rain.*

④ ★★★ kids Parc des Champs-de-Bataille. Covering 108 hectares (267 acres) of grassy hills, sunken gardens, monuments, fountains, and trees, Québec's Battlefields Park was Canada's first national urban park. A section called the Plains of Abraham is where Britain's general James Wolfe and France's Louis-Joseph, marquis de Montcalm,

A quiet stroll in the Parc des Champs-de-Bataille.

engaged in their short but crucial battle in 1759, which resulted in the British defeat of France. It's also where the national anthem, *O Canada*, was first performed. The park is a favorite place for Québécois when they want sunshine or a bit of exercise during all seasons of the year. *Parc des Champs-de-Bataille. www. ccbn-nbc.gc.ca.* ☎ *888/497-4322 or 418/644-9841.*

Try Québécois home cooking right at **⑤ ★★ Aux Anciens Canadiens,** a venerable restaurant with costumed servers is in what's probably the city's oldest (1677) house. Prices are generally high but the restaurant's afternoon table d'hôte special, from noon to 5:45pm, is a terrific bargain: soup, a main course, a dessert, and a glass of beer or wine for C$26. Consider caribou in blueberry-wine sauce or Québéc meat pie, and don't pass up the maple sugar pie with cream. See p 142.

⑥ Rue du Trésor. Artists hang their prints and paintings of Québec scenes on both sides of this narrow pedestrian lane. In decent weather, it's busy with browsers and sellers. Artists are often happy to have a chat about their work.

⑦ ★ kids Funiculaire. To get from Upper Town to Lower Town, you can take streets, staircases, or this cliffside elevator, known as the

Value Meals, Québec Style

When dining out, always look for a *table d'hôte* option. These are fixed-price menus with three or four courses, and they usually cost little more than the price of a single a la carte main course. Restaurants at all price ranges offer them, and they present the best way to try out gourmet food for moderate prices. When offered at lunch, they are even less expensive.

funiculaire. It operates along an inclined 64m (210-ft.) track and offers excellent aerial views during its short trip. The upper station is on Place d'Armes. It operates daily 7:30am until 11pm (until midnight in high season). Wheelchairs and strollers can be accommodated. The one-way fare is C$2.25. *www. funiculaire-quebec.com*.

❽ ★ **kids** **Rue du Petit-Champlain.** This tiny, pedestrian-only shopping street is allegedly North America's oldest lane. It swarms with cafe sitters, strolling couples, and gaggles of schoolchildren in the warm months. In winter, it's a snowy wonderland with ice statues and twinkling white lights. If you're hungry, Le Lapin Saute (52 rue du Petit-Champlain; www.lapinsaute. com; ☎ 418/692-5325), is a country-cozy bistro that has hearty food and a lovely terrace overlooking a small garden. *www.quartierpetit champlain.com*.

❾ ★★★ **kids** **Musée de la Civilisation.** This wonderful museum may be housed in a lackluster gray-block building, but there is nothing plain about it once you enter. Spacious and airy, it has ingeniously arranged multidimensional exhibits. If time is short, definitely take in People of Québec Then and Now, a permanent exhibit that is a sprawling examination of Québec history, from the province's roots as a fur-trading colony to the turbulent movement for independence that started in the 1960s. *85 rue Dalhousie. www. mcq.org.* ☎ *866/710-8031 or 418/643-2158. Admission C$16 adults, C$15 seniors, C$10 students, C$5 children 12–16, free for children 11 and under; free for all on Tues Nov–Mar and Sat 10am–noon Jan– Feb. Late June to early Sept daily 9am–6pm, rest of the year Tues–Sun 10am–5pm.*

The colorful gardens of the Musée de la Civilisation.

Québec City: **Where to Stay**

★ kids **Auberge Internationale de Québec** There are 277 beds in this centrally located, affordable youth hostel. Most are in the dorm layouts standard to Hostelling International (HI), while others are in modest private rooms for one to five people, with either shared or private bathrooms. *19 rue. Ste-Ursule. www.aubergeinternationaledequebec.com.* ☎ *866/694-0950 or 418/694-0755. 25 private rooms, 277 beds. C$86–C$137 private room for 2 with bathroom; C$25–C$35 per person for shared dorm room. Discount available for HI members. Rates for private rooms include breakfast.*

★★ **Auberge Place d'Armes** This high-end (yet well-priced) *auberge* has carefully renovated guest rooms that feature everything from exposed stone walls dating from 1640 to modern rain showers with jets, flatscreen TVs, and fine furnishings. This section of rue Ste-Anne is pedestrian-only (though you can drive up to drop off your bags) and lined with outdoor dining options—great for people-watching. Breakfast is included and served at the in-house restaurant, **Le Pain Béni** (p 143). **Note:** You need to use stairs to reach all guest rooms. *24 rue Ste-Anne. www.aubergeplacedarmes.com.* ☎ *866/333-9485 or 418/694-9485. 21 units. Doubles C$150–C$280. Rates include breakfast.*

★★★ **Auberge Saint-Antoine** This is one of the most memorable and splurge-worthy hotels in Québec

The striking and elegant Auberge Saint-Antoine.

Charming Hôtel Château Laurier Québec is well located, on Parliament Hill.

City. Artifacts unearthed during a large-scale archeological dig are displayed throughout the hotel with curatorial care. Rooms are luxurious and spacious. Staff extends a warm welcome and will go out of their way to meet your needs, especially during the off-season. **Panache** (p 143), where breakfast is served, offers some of the city's finest dining. This hotel picks up annual national and international awards and is a member of the prestigious Relais & Châteaux luxury group. Free tours are available to guests upon request. *8 rue St-Antoine. www.saint-antoine. com.* ☎ *888/692-2211 or 418/692-2211. 95 units. Doubles C$189–C$439.*

★★★ kids **Fairmont Le Château Frontenac** Québec's magical "castle" opened in 1893 and has been wowing guests ever since. Many rooms are full-on luxurious, outfitted with elegant château furnishings and marble bathrooms. Prices depend on size, location, and view, with river views garnering top dollar. Lower-priced rooms overlooking the inner courtyard face gabled roofs, and children might imagine Harry Potter swooping by in a Quidditch match. *1 rue des Carrières (at Place d'Armes). www.fairmont.com/frontenac-quebec.* ☎ *866/540-4460 or 418/692-3861. 611 units. Doubles from C$399.*

★★ Hôtel Château Laurier Québec

Sandwiched between the scenic oasis of the Plains of Abraham—the site of many city festivals—and the frenetic, club-lined Grande-Allée, Château Laurier is many different hotels in one. Families choose it for location and pool, but there are there are six room categories that vary in age, style, and price, including an abundance of wheelchair-accessible rooms. Château Laurier distinguishes itself as both a "Franco-responsible" hotel (French music plays in the hallways, for example) and an eco-responsible hotel (the pool is saltwater, surplus food is delivered to food banks, recycling is de rigeur, and there's an electric car recharging station on site). *1220 Place Georges-V ouest. www.hotelchateaulaurier.com. ☎ 877/522-8108 or 418/522-8108. 282 units. Doubles C\$174–C\$279.*

★ Hôtel de Glace

Meticulously crafted each winter from 500 tons of ice, Québec's seasonal ice hotel is unlike anything you've experienced (unless you've slept on a slab of ice) and just 10 minutes from downtown. You can visit by day for C\$18 or take one of the rooms from 9pm until 8am, before the next day's visitors arrive, starting at C\$189 per person. It's open January through March. *9530 rue de la Faune. www.hoteldeglace-canada.com. ☎ 877/505-0423 or 418/623-2888. 44 units. Basic overnight package with dinner, breakfast, and cocktail from C\$799 for 2.*

★ Hôtel-Musée Premières Nations

Every room in this relaxing, earthy resort features a private

Chill out at Québec's seasonal Hôtel de Glace.

The refined yet cozy lobby of Le Germain Hôtel Québec.

balcony that overlooks the Akiawenrahk River. The hotel is situated on a forested section of the First Nations reservation called Wendake, just 15 minutes from Québec City by car. Once here, you'll find everything you need to decompress. There's an onsite "multisensory" Nation-Santé Spa (C\$35 per person; non-guests can come for the day). The high-end La Traite restaurant specializes in First Nations–inspired cuisine such as red deer, dried seal, or smoked mackerel (table d'hote menus start at C\$45 per person). An afternoon could be spent poking around the handful of shops and galleries in Wendake, hiking the adjacent trails, or admiring the nearby Kabir Kouba waterfall. *5 Place de la Rencontre, Wendake, Québec. www.hotel premieresnations.ca. ☎ 866/551-9222 or 418/847-2222. 55 units. Doubles C\$159–C\$209.*

★★★ Le Germain Hôtel Québec

Urban elegance is the ruling principle in one of the city's most refined boutique hotels. Built in 1912, the building formerly housed Dominion Fish & Fruit Limited and became a hotel in 1997. Part of a small chain, the rooms here are furnished with exceptionally comfortable beds and sheets that are downright heavenly. The continental breakfast (which includes delicious espresso) can be taken on the leafy outdoor terrace in the summer or near the lobby fireplace in colder months. *126 rue St-Pierre. www.legermainhotels.com/en/ quebec. ☎ 888/833-5253 or 418/692-2224. 60 units. Doubles C\$199–C\$335. Rates include continental breakfast.*

Québec City: **Where to Dine**

★★ Aux Anciens Canadiens

TRADITIONAL QUEBECOIS One of the best places in La Belle Province at which to sample cooking that has its roots in New France's earliest years. Québec's favorite dessert, sugar pie, reaches its apogee at this admittedly tourist-heavy venue in central Upper Town. Think maple syrup with a crust, or pecan pie without the pecans. *34 rue St-Louis. www.auxancienscanadiens. qc.ca.* ☎ *418/692-1627. Entrees C$36–C$64. Lunch and dinner daily.*

★★★ kids Café Krieghoff

LIGHT FARE Café Krieghoff may not wow or woo those seeking haute cuisine, but it can make you feel like you're taking an afternoon off from tourists and settling in to a low-profile Québécois way of life. Partly it's the Montcalm neighborhood, just 10 minutes walk from the Parliament building down Grande-Allée, a right turn on avenue Cartier. And partly it's the great coffee (included with most breakfasts), reliable cooking, friendly service, and chance to sit outside. *1089 av. Cartier. www.cafekrieghoff.qc.ca.* ☎ *418/ 522-3711. Most items under C$19. Breakfast, lunch, and dinner daily.*

★★ Laurie Raphaël

CONTEMPORARY QUEBECOIS Dining in this part of town can be very expensive, especially at accomplished restaurants like Laurie

Enjoy a casual meal in Montcalm at Café Krieghoff.

Laurie Raphaël's signature eggs with lobster and sautéed chanterelles.

Raphaël. However, there there's an exceptional three-course "chef chef" lunch for C$29 per person. On sunny days, it's ideal to reserve a table on the corner terrace. While the food is ultra-gourmet, the service is generous and easygoing. Dinner here can be an extraordinary culinary experience to add to a Québec City vacation. *117 rue Dalhousie. www.laurieraphael.com.* ☎ *418/692-4555. Entrees C$45– C$54. Lunch and dinner Tues–Fri, dinner Sat.*

★ L'Echaudé

BISTRO In a city that specializes in the informal bistro tradition, L'Echaudé is a star. The classic dishes are all in place, from confit de canard to steak frites, and the tone is casual sophistication. A late-night discount kicks in after 9pm when la carte menu items are 21% off. *73 rue Sault-au-Matelot. www.echaude.com.* ☎ *418/ 692-1299. Entrees C$25–C$35. Lunch and dinner daily.*

★ kids Le Café du Monde

TRADITIONAL FRENCH Large (it seats more than 200) and jovial, this very Parisian-style restaurant manages the nearly impossible: classic French food and fast service without a compromise in quality—even on crowded holiday weekends. *84*

rue Dalhousie. www.lecafedumonde.
com. ☎ 418/692-4455. Entrees
C$17–C$39. Lunch and dinner daily,
breakfast Sat–Sun and holidays.

★★★ Le Clocher Penché Bistrot

BISTRO The development of
this unpretentious St-Roch neighborhood bistro parallels the polish-
ing up of the overall area. With its
caramel-toned woods, tall ceilings,
and walls serving as gallery space
for local artists, Clocher Penché has
laid-back European class. Service
reflects the food—amiable and without flourishes. 203 rue St-Joseph est.
www.clocherpenche.ca. ☎ 418/640-
0597. Entrees C$21–C$27. Lunch and
dinner Tues–Sat, brunch Sun.

★ Le Pain Béni

CONTEMPO-
RARY QUEBECOIS If you want to
sit outdoors on the touristy, pedestrian-only part of rue Ste-Anne, find
an open table at Le Pain Béni. It
pegs its menu as "bistronomique,"
a mix of high and low, with traditional French fare punctuated by
avant-garde experimentation.
Indoor seating is also a fine choice,
with exposed stone and brick walls
from the 1600s. 24 rue Ste-Anne.
www.painbeni.com. ☎ 418/694-
9485. Entrees C$21–C$36. Breakfast,
lunch, and dinner daily May–Oct;
breakfast daily, lunch, and dinner
Tues–Sat Nov–Apr.

Another excellent dish served without
pretense at Le Clocher Penché Bistrot.

Foie gras poêle at Toast!

★★★ kids Paillard

LIGHT FARE
Paillard has a high-end fast-food feel
to it, but it's one of a kind, and thor-
oughly Québec. The bread is crusty
and sometimes piping hot, either
used on sandwiches or served with
soups that are (and taste) homemade. It's perfect for an affordable
lunch or dinner that doesn't take
hours, or for a coffee break with a
formidable macaron. There are also
salads and gelati. 1097 rue St-Jean.
www.paillard.ca. ☎ 418/692-1221.
Most items under C$10. Breakfast,
lunch, and dinner daily.

★★ Panache

CONTEMPORARY
QUEBECOIS The restaurant of
the superb Auberge Saint-Antoine
(p 140) is housed in a former 19th-
century warehouse delineated by
massive wood beams and rough
stone walls. It is the most romantic
of the city. The frequently changing
menu is heavy on locally sourced
game, duck, and fish. 10 rue St-
Antoine. www.saint-antoine.com.
☎ 418/692-1022. Entrees C$42–
C$56. Breakfast and dinner daily,
lunch Mon–Fri.

★ Toast!

CONTEMPORARY QUE-
BECOIS On summer nights the
outdoor dining terrace in back, with
wrought-iron furniture and big leafy
trees overhead, is an oasis. The
interior room glows crimson from a
wall of fire-engine-red tiles, retro-
modern lights, and red Plexiglas
window paneling. 17 rue Sault-
au-Matelot. www.restauranttoast.
com. ☎ 418/692-1334. Entrees
C$25–C$45, or C$85. Dinner daily.

The Laurentians

1 St-Sauveur

2 Val David

3 Mont-Tremblant Pedestrian Village

4 A Day at the Spa

WHERE TO STAY

Château Beauvallon **10**

Fairmont Mont-Tremblant **8**

Hôtel Mont-Tremblant **5**

Quintessence **7**

WHERE TO DINE

Crêperie Catherine **6**

Microbrasserie La Diable **9**

The Laurentian Mountains (also known as the Laurentides) provide year-round recreational opportunities. Skiing and snow-boarding are the most popular activities, but in the warmer months the mountains thaw and open up a new array of options. The highest peak, Mont-Tremblant, is 968m (3,176 ft.) high and located 129km (80 miles) northwest of Montréal. Closer to the city, the terrain resembles a rumpled quilt, its folds and hollows cupping a multitude of lakes. Come for a day or stay for a week. Note that as you head north, you're more likely to find venues whose proprietors and websites are French only. START: **Drive north out of Montréal on Autoroute 15. For an orientation to the region, stop at the information center, well marked from the highway, at exit 51. Tourisme Laurentides (☎ 800/561-6673; www.laurentides.com) shares a building with a McDonald's.**

An autumn scene at Mont St-Sauveur.

① St-Sauveur. Only 60km (37 miles) north of Montréal, the village of St-Sauveur is flush with outlet malls and the carloads of shoppers they attract, while a few blocks farther north, the older village square bustles with less-frenzied activity. Dining and snacking on everything from crepes to hot dogs are big activities here, evidenced by the many beckoning cafes. If you want a picnic, Chez Bernard (407 rue Principale; www.chezbernard.com; ☎ 450/240-0000), is a pretty store that sells fragrant cheeses, crusty breads, savory tarts, pâtés, sausages, and prepared meals. You'll want to fill up before heading to Parc Aquatique du Mont St-Sauveur (www.parc aquatique.com; ☎ 450/227-4671). It features rafting, a wave pool, a tidal-wave river, and slides, including one which you travel to by chairlift and ride down in a tube. Full-day tickets are C$18 to C$38, with half-day and family rates also available. For 10 days in August, the Festival

des Art de St-Sauveur (www.fass.ca; ☎ 450/227-0427) presents music and dance performances along with jazz and chamber concerts. The schedule always includes a number of free events.

② Val David. This is the region's faintly bohemian enclave, conjuring up images of cabin hideaways set among ponds and lakes, while creeks tumble through fragrant forests. There are hectares of breathtaking trails for mountain bikers and hikers (and, in winter, snowshoers and cross-country skiers), and Val David is one of the villages along the bike path called P'Tit Train du Nord, built on a former railroad track (see "Biker's Paradise: The Route Verte," on p 154). Residents boast that Val David is the birthplace of rock climbing in Eastern Canada, and climbing enthusiasts flock to the nearby Dufresne Regional Park (www.parcregional dufresne.com) to explore its 650 rated routes. Unlike the heavily visited Mont-Tremblant, where cheesy souvenir stores are plentiful, Val David is home to a handful of stylish little stores that sell well-made, authentic crafts. If you're in the area from mid-July to mid-August, check out the village's huge ceramic art festival (www.1001pots.com; ☎ 819/322-6868). Sculptors and

Biker's Paradise: The Route Verte

Québec is bike crazy, and it's got the goods to justify it. The Route Verte (Green Route) is a 5,000km (3,107-mile) bike network that stretches from one end of the province to the other, linking all regions and cities. The idea was modeled on the Rails-to-Trails program in the U.S. and cycling routes in Denmark, Great Britain, and along the Danube and Rhine rivers. Within a year, the National Geographic Society had declared it one of the 10 best bicycle routes in the world.

Included in the network is the popular P'tit Train du Nord bike trail through the Laurentian Mountains. It's built on a former railway track and passes through the villages of Ste-Adèle, Val David, and Mont-Tremblant. Cyclists can get food and bike repairs at renovated railway stations along the way and hop on for a day trip or a longer tour. The trail is free to ride on. The Route Verte website (www.routeverte.com) provides maps and an "accommodations" link that lists places to rent bikes as well as B&Bs, campsites, and hotels that are especially focused on serving travelers. The annual official tourist guide to the Laurentians published by the regional tourist office (www.laurentides.com; ☎ 800/561-6673 or 450/224-7007) always has a big section on biking. If you plan a trip, keep in mind Autobus le Petit Train du Nord (www.autobuslepetittraindunord.com; ☎ 888/893-8356 or 450/569-5596), which provides baggage transport and ride planning.

ceramicists, along with painters, jewelers, pewter smiths, and other craftspeople display their work; and there are concerts and other outdoor activities including pottery workshops for children on weekends. *Tourist office at 2579 rue de l'Église. www.valdavid.com. ☎ 888/322-7030.*

❸ **Mont-Tremblant Pedestrian Village.** The Mont-Tremblant area is a kind of Aspen meets Disneyland. A terrific ski mountain boasts an ever-expanding resort village at the bottom of its slope and is a prime destination in the province in all four seasons. The Mont-Tremblant ski resort (www.tremblant.ca) draws the biggest downhill crowds in the Laurentians and is repeatedly ranked as the top resort in eastern North America by *Ski Magazine*

(see "Skiing in the Laurentians," below). There are some well-regarded cultural offerings here, too, including the Tremblant International Blues Festival (www.tremblantblues.com), which puts on up to 100 shows, many free, for 10 days in July. The village itself has the prefabricated look of a theme park, but at least planners used the Québécois architectural style of pitched roofs in bright colors, not ersatz Bavarian Alpine flourishes. For a sweeping view, take the panoramic gondola from the bottom of the village to the top (C$17 for adults with discounts for youth). There are dozens of restaurants, bars, and shops here, and most are open year-round. *Tourisme de Mont-Tremblant, 5080 Montee Ryan. www.tourismemonttremblant.com. ☎ 819/425-2434.*

❹ A Day at the Spa. Spas are big business around here. They're the most popular new features at hotels, especially in the Mont-Tremblant area, where people are looking for new ways to pamper themselves beyond dropping a lot of money on skiing. In the Québec province, the organization Spas Relais Santé distinguishes between day spas, which offer massages and *esthétique* services such as facials; destination spas, which often involve overnight stays and healthy cuisine; and Nordic spas, which are built around a natural water source and include outdoor and indoor spaces.

If you've never experienced a European-style Nordic spa before, try to set aside 3 hours for a visit to Le Scandinave Spa (4280 Montée Ryan, Mont-Tremblant; www.scandinave.com; ☎ 888/537-2263 or 891/425-5524). It's a tranquil complex of small buildings tucked among evergreen trees on the Diable River shore, and is as chic as it is

Mont-Tremblant village offers a bustling town and fantastic ski slopes.

rustic. For C$48 visitors (18 and older only) have the run of the facility. Options include outdoor hot tubs designed to look like natural pools (one is set under a man-made waterfall); a Norwegian steam bath thick with eucalyptus scent; indoor relaxation areas with super-comfortable, low-slung chairs; and the river itself, which the heartiest of folk dip into even on frigid winter days. (A heat lamp keeps a small square of river open on the iciest of days.) The idea is to move from hot to cold to hot, which supposedly purges toxins and invigorates your skin. Bathing suits are required, and men and women share all spaces except the changing rooms. For extra fees, massages and yoga classes are offered.

Skiing in the Laurentians

Founded in 1939 by a Philadelphia millionaire named Joe Ryan, the Mont-Tremblant ski resort pioneered the development of trails on both sides of a mountain and was the second mountain in the world to install a chairlift. Today, the vertical drop is 645m (2,116 ft.), and there are 96 downhill runs and trails. Half are expert terrain, about a third are intermediate, and the rest beginner.

When the snow is deep, skiers here like to follow the sun around the mountain, making the run down slopes with an eastern exposure in the morning and down the western-facing ones in the afternoon. There are higher mountains elsewhere with longer runs and steeper pitches, but something about Mont-Tremblant compels people to return time and again.

Cross-country skiers have many options. Parc National du Mont-Tremblant maintains six loops (43km/26 miles) of groomed track in the Diable sector, and there's another 112km (69 miles) available for backcountry skiing in both the Diable and the Pimbina sectors. Visit www.sepaq.com to locate visitor centers, warming huts, and a variety of accommodations, including yurts.

The Laurentians: **Where to Stay in Mont-Tremblant**

The Fairmont's heated pools are a big draw after a day on the slopes.

★ kids Château Beauvallon

Since opening in 2005, Beauvallon has become the region's premiere property for families who want to stay near but off the ski mountain. The 70-suite operation positions itself as an affordable high-end retreat for seasoned travelers, and delivers with a relaxed elegance. *6385 Montée Ryan. www.chateau beauvallon.com.* ☎ *888/681-6611 or 819/681-6611. 70 units. 1 bedroom suite C$179–C$249.*

★★ kids Fairmont Mont-Tremblant

The name-brand resort for families who want to stay directly on the mountain. The Fairmont stands on a crest above the pedestrian village and offers year-round outdoor and indoor pools, a 38-person outdoor Jacuzzi, and ski-in, ski-out accessibility to the chairlifts. *3045 chemin de la Chapelle.*

Ice skating is another popular winter sport in Mont-Tremblant.

www.fairmont.com/tremblant. ☎ *800/257-7544 or 819/681-7000. 314 units. Doubles C$239–C$499.*

Hôtel Mont-Tremblant

Located in the old village of Mont-Tremblant 5km (3 miles) northwest of the pedestrian village, this modest hotel is popular with skiers who want to avoid the resort village's higher prices and cyclists who appreciate the location directly on the Route Verte bike path. Rates include breakfast. *1900 chemin du Village (Rte. 327). www.hotel-monttremblant.com.* ☎ *888/887-1111 or 819/425-3232. 22 units. Doubles C$99–C$126.*

Lounging poolside at the swanky Quintessence.

★★★ Quintessence

The region's luxury property. Every room is a suite, accommodations are hugely comfortable, there's an outdoor infinity pool, and the spa is reserved for hotel guests only. Lavish dinners can be started in the cozy, fire-lit wine bar then continued in the La Quintessence dining room or outdoors near the pool. *3004 chemin de la Chapelle. www. hotelquintessence.com.* ☎ *866/425-3400 or 819/425-3400. 30 units. Suites C$399–C$622.*

The Laurentians: **Where to Dine in Mont-Tremblant**

Go sweet or savory at Crêperie Catherine—but do go.

★★ Crêperie Catherine
BREAKFAST/BRUNCH This delectable breakfast spot is worth the trek off mountain and into the Centre-Ville of Mont-Tremblant. In addition to both savory and sweet crepes made before your eyes, Crêperie Catherine offers *sucre a la crème* (a concoction of brown sugar and butter). We suggest you slather it on—as if you were on vacation. *977 rue Labelle, Centre-Ville Tremblant. www.creperiecatherine. ca.* ☎ *819/681-4888. Entrees C$12–C$17, dessert crepes from C$4.95. Breakfast, lunch, and dinner daily.*

★ Microbrasserie La Diable
LIGHT FARE Set in a free-standing chalet, this microbrewery offers several home brews, plus reliable basics such as burgers, sausage with homemade sauerkraut, and a veggie sauté. *117 chemin Kandahar (in the pedestrian village). www. microladiable.com.* ☎ *819/681-4544. Entrees C$11–C$28. Lunch and dinner daily.*

Cantons-de-l'Est

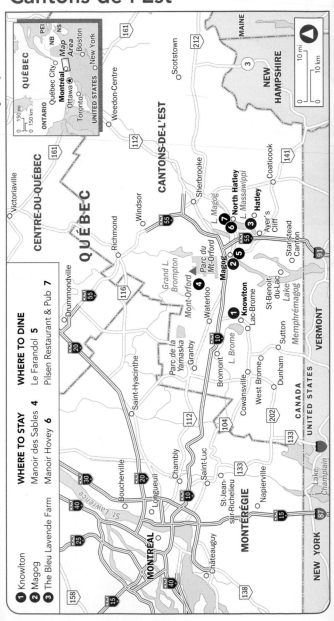

WHERE TO STAY

Manoir des Sables **4**
Manoir Hovey **6**

WHERE TO DINE

Le Farandol **5**
Pilsen Restaurant & Pub **7**

1 Knowlton
2 Magog
3 The Bleu Lavende Farm

The rolling countryside of Cantons-de-l'Est is largely pastoral, marked by rolling hills, small villages, a smattering of vineyards, and the 792m (2,598-ft.) peak of Mont-Orford, the centerpiece of a provincial park. Serene glacial lakes attract summer swimmers, boaters, and bicyclists who loop around them. In winter, skiers who don't head north to the Laurentians come this direction. Still referred to by most Anglophones as the Eastern Townships, the southern edge of the region borders Vermont, New Hampshire, and Maine. **START: Leave Montréal by Pont Champlain, the bridge which funnels into arrow-straight Autoroute 10, and head east toward Sherbrooke.**

The lovely Abbaye de Saint-Benoît-du-Lac is home to 30 monks who make and sell a variety of popular cheeses.

❶ **Knowlton.** For a good confluence of countryside, cafes, and antiquing, head to the town of Knowlton, at Brome Lake's southeast corner. It's part of the seven-village municipality known as Lac Brome. From Autoroute 10, take exit 90, heading south on Rte. 243. Two main shopping streets (Lakeside and Knowlton) have about three dozen boutiques and antiques stores that reveal the creeping chic influence of refugees from Montréal. The city has an historic walking tour online at www.knowltonquebec.ca.

❷ **Magog.** Confusingly, the town of Magog is not adjacent to Lac Magog. That lake is about 13km (8 miles) north. Instead, the town is positioned at the northernmost end of the long Lac Memphrémagog, which spills across the U.S.-Canadian border into Vermont on its southern end. Croisière Memphrémagog (www.croisiere-memphremagog.com; ☎ 888/842-8068 or 819/843-8068)

Cabanes à Sucre: A Little Old Place Where We Can Get Together

Throughout Canada's history, maple syrup has been an economic and cultural boon for the Québec province. In March and April, maple trees around Montréal are tapped and *cabanes à sucre* (sugar shacks) open up in rural areas. Some just sell maple syrup and candies, while many serve full meals and even stage entertainment.

A particularly fun tradition is *tire sur la neige*, where hot maple syrup is poured onto a clean layer of snow. Guests pick up the semisoft confection before it hardens and enjoy what's known as "maple toffee."

Wine (& *Cidre de Glace*) Country

Canada is known more for its beers than its wines, but that hasn't stopped agriculturists from giving wine a shot. In Cantons-de-l'Est, vintners are concentrated around Dunham, about 103km (64 miles) southeast of Montréal, with several vineyards along Rte. 202. A stop for a snack or a facility tour makes for a pleasant afternoon, and if you're really gung-ho, follow the established Route des Vins (www.laroutedesvins.ca), which passes 21 vintners. One farm on the route is Vignoble de l'Orpailleur (1086 Rte. 202, Dunham; www.orpailleur.ca; ☎ 450/295-2763), which has guided tours daily from June through October. Its L'Orpailleur Classique is popular on Montréal restaurant menus.

Ice cider and ice wine are two regional products that may be new to visitors. They're made from apples and grapes left on trees and vines past the first frost, and are served ice-cold with cheese, foie gras, or dessert. A top producer is Domaine Pinnacle (150 Richford Rd., Frelighsburg; www.icecider.com; ☎ 450/298-1226), about 13km (8 miles) south of Dunham. Its *cidre de glace* is a regular gold medalist in international competitions. The farm's tasting room and boutique are open daily from 10am to 5pm May through October.

offers lake cruises leaving from Point Merry Park, the focal point for many of the town's outdoor activities. Several firms rent sailboats, motorboats, kayaks, and windsurfers. The town is one of the largest in the region, with about 25,000 people and lots of boutiques and chic restaurants. Not far from here is **Abbaye de Saint-Benoît-du-Lac** (www.st-benoit-du-lac.com; ☎ 819/843-4080), a monastery that's home to about 30 monks who live largely in silence. They support themselves by making cheeses and products from their apple orchards, which are sold on-site in a small shop. Visitors also can attend services that feature Gregorian chant.

❸ The Bleu Lavende Farm. Canada's largest producer of lavender also happens to be one of the region's most popular destinations. Bleu Lavende (www.bleulavande.ca;

Vineyards in Dunham, where local specialties include ice cider and ice wine.

☎ 888/876-5851 or 819/876-5851) is a huge farm, an agricultural discovery center, and a place to buy products infused with lavandula: chocolate, cleaning products, sprays, and other goodies. Located on 891 Narrow Rd., 4.4km (2.7 miles) from Rte. 247 in Stanstead, it can attract more than 2,000 visitors per day during peak season (guided tours cost C$10 during peak), when the lavender blooms in July and August. The boutique is open daily from May to October.

Cantons-de-l'Est: **Where to Stay**

★★ Manoir des Sables

ORFORD This facility is one of the region's most complete resort hotels, and its unofficial motto could be "we have something for everyone." It serves couples, families, golfers, skiers, skaters, fitness enthusiasts, tennis players, and kayakers, and offers up snowshoeing, on-site ice skating, and Saturday-night horse-drawn sleigh rides in winter, with canoeing and fishing in the hotel's lake in summer. *90 av. des Jardins. www.manoirdessables. com. ☎ 800/567-3514 or 819/847-4747. 141 units. Doubles C$199–C$311.*

Pretty Manoir Hovey is perfect for a pampering weekend away.

★★★ Manoir Hovey NORTH

HATLEY This manor, a member of the exclusive Relais & Châteaux group, manages to maintain a magical balance of feeling between a genteel estate for a private getaway and a grand resort for a weekend's pampering. Aristocratic touches include a carefully manicured English garden, and a massive stone hearth in a library lounge. Its restaurant is the most esteemed in the region. *575 chemin Hovey. www.manoirhovey.com. ☎ 800/661-2421 or 819/842-2421. 41 units. Doubles C$340–C$420. Rates include breakfast, 3-course dinner, gratuities, and use of most recreational facilities.*

Kayaking on the lake at Manoir des Sables.

Cantons-de-l'Est: **Where to Dine**

Le Farandol is the setting for fine French dining.

★ **Le Farandol** MAGOG
FRENCH Originally a bakery and restaurant called Owl's Bread Boulangerie, now the two have dedicated spaces. The chef of Le Farandol restaurant brings unique flair to foie gras, cassoulet, and a vegetarian dish with spiced lentils. The shop's signature fresh-baked bread and mouthwatering pastries are part of his menu and can also be purchased at the newly located Owl's Bread Boulangerie, down the road at 2389 rue Principale ouest. *428 rue Principale ouest. www. lefarandol.com.* ☎ *819/769-0314. Entrees C$25–C$34. Lunch and dinner Wed–Sun.*

Pilsen Restaurant & Pub
NORTH HATLEY *INTERNATIONAL* Featuring a deck over a narrow river, this former horse-carriage manufacturing shop fills up quickly on warm days with patrons dining on burgers, pulled pork sandwiches, and a variety of panini, including a signature offering with duck confit. Best washed down by local microbrew Massawippi Blonde. *55 rue Main. www.pilsen.ca.* ☎ *819/842-2971. Entrees C$12–C$27. Lunch and dinner daily mid-May to Nov, Thurs–Sun rest of the year.* ●

The
Savvy Traveler

Before **You Go**

Government Tourist Offices

In Montréal: Downtown Montréal boasts a large **Infotouriste Centre** (1255 rue Peel; ☎ 877/266-5687 or 514/873-2015; info@bonjourquebec.com. The city of Montréal maintains a terrific website at **www.tourisme-montreal.org**.

The Best Times to Go

The summer months—late June through August—are when Montréal is at its busiest. You'll pay the most for a hotel room in this period, and it can be hot and humid, but the city is in full bloom. In May and early June it's easier to get accommodations and the weather is often more comfortable, although you'll miss out on the big festivals. September and October are less hectic months and the perfect time for autumn hikes and seeing the region's beautiful fall foliage. Winter in Montréal is cold and snowy, but people still get out and play. Early spring and late fall, when the weather can get iffy and not much is happening, are quieter times in the city.

Festivals & Special Events

Montréal celebrates its **375th anniversary in 2017,** and special events are planned all year. Details are at www.375mtl.com.

JANUARY. La Fête des Neiges (Snow Festival) ☎ 514/872-6120; www.fetedesneiges.com) is the city's premier winter festival and features outdoor events such as dog-sled runs, a human foosball court, and tobogganing. It's held four weekends in January and the beginning of February.

FEBRUARY. Festival Montréal en Lumière (Montréal High Lights Festival) (☎ 855/864-3737 or 514/288-9955; www.montrealhighlights.com) is a deep-winter food fest with culinary competitions and wine tastings, multimedia light shows, classical and pop concerts, and the "*Nuit blanche*" all-night party where everyone dresses in white and heads to a free breakfast at dawn.

MAY. Montréal Museums Day (www.museesmontreal.org), usually on the last Sunday in May, is a day of free admission to most of the city's museums. There even are free buses to get visitors from place to place.

MAY–JUNE. Montréal Bike Fest (☎ 800/567-8356 or 514/521-8356; www.velo.qc.ca) brings out tens of thousands of cyclists for races of varying degrees of length and difficulty over 8 days—in the Tour de l'Île de Montréal, Tour la Nuit and Metropolitan Challenge. Over 100,000 spectators line the streets to watch.

JUNE. Les FrancoFolies de Montréal (☎ 855/372-6267 or 514/876-8989; www.francofolies.com) is a music fest that features French-language pop, hip-hop, electronic, world beat, and *chanson*. It's based at the Quartier des Spectacles downtown, with shows both outdoors on the plaza and inside the many theater halls in the area.

JUNE–JULY. Hordes of sightseers and music fans make the **Festival International de Jazz de Montréal** (☎ 888/299-3378 or 514/871-1881; www.montrealjazzfest.com) one of the most exciting and acclaimed music festivals in the world.

Previous page: Ice skating is a favorite winter pastime in Montréal.

MONTREAL'S AVERAGE MONTHLY TEMPERATURES (°F/°C)

	JAN	FEB	MAR	APR	MAY	JUNE
High (°F)	21	24	35	51	65	73
High (°C)	–6	–4	1	10	18	22
Low (°F)	7	10	21	35	47	56
Low (°C)	–13	–12	–6	1	8	13

	JULY	AUG	SEPT	OCT	NOV	DEC
High (°F)	79	76	66	54	41	27
High (°C)	26	24	18	12	5	–2
Low (°F)	61	59	50	39	29	13
Low (°C)	16	15	10	3	–1	–10

JULY. For eight evenings, **L'International des Feux Loto-Québec** (International Fireworks Competition; ☎ 514/397-2000; www.laronde.com/fr/larondefr/linternational-des-feux/accueil) lights up the skies with a truly spectacular fireworks shows. (*Insider tip:* The Jacques Cartier bridge closes to traffic during the fireworks and offers an unblocked, up-close view.) Also in July, **Festival Juste pour Rire** (Just for Laughs festival; ☎ 888/244-3155 or 514/845-2322; www.hahaha.com) brings improvisational comedy by big and lesser-known names to town. Also in July, **Montréal Complètement Cirque** (☎ 855/770-3434 or 514/285-9175; montrealcirquefest.com) is a festival of circus arts founded in 2010 in part by the Cirque du Soleil. Indoor shows, outdoor shows, and special family performances take place at the TOHU center in the north of the city and throughout Quartier des Spectacles downtown.

AUGUST–SEPTEMBER. The **Festival des Films du Monde** (☎ 514/848-3883; www.ffm-montreal.org) is a must for movie buffs, with hundreds of films from across the globe.

SEPTEMBER. Early fall is the perfect time to view the changing foliage in the city's parks and the surrounding region, especially the northern Laurentian Mountains (p 145).

DECEMBER. Celebrating the holidays *a la française* is a particular treat in Vieux-Montréal, where the streets are nearly always banked with snow and the ancient buildings sport wreaths, decorated fir trees, and glittery white lights.

The Weather

Montréal is a city of weather extremes, with two main seasons: a hot summer and a bitterly cold winter. About 3 weeks each of pleasant spring and crisp fall take place in between.

Québécois who live through half-year-long winters know how to dress for the cold. Layers are essential and practicality trumps fashion. A dark wool or down coat can serve both gods, but sporty ski clothes also work throughout the province. Pack a hat, gloves, scarf, thermal socks, and waterproof boots with traction in the cold months. Long underwear is probably only needed for outdoor activities. A second pair of shoes, if the primary ones get soaked, can save a vacation.

Weather forecasts from the Canadian government are at **weather.gc.ca**.

Useful Websites

- **www.tourisme-montreal.org**: The slick official site of the city has up-to-the-minute details about venues, festivals, neighborhoods, and hotel deals. It has a special section for gay and lesbian travelers, who make up a big part of city tourism business.

- **www.lavitrine.com**: La Vitrine is a ticket office for Montréal's cultural events, accessible both online and in a centrally located office at the Place des Arts, at 2 rue Ste-Catherine est (☎ 866/924-5538 or 514/285-4545). It sells last-minute bargain tickets as well as full-price tickets.

- **www.cultmontreal.com**: Cult Montréal has, in English, up to the minute previews of music, nightlife, and arts events.

- **www.montrealgazette.com**: The city's English-language newspaper. The Gazette is heavy on tabloid-style reporting but still a useful source of restaurant and cultural happenings.

- **www.stm.info**: The website for Montréal's public transportation system has detailed route maps of bus and Métro lines, information on service interruptions, and a useful trip planner.

Car Rentals

If you're arriving in town by train or plane, you won't need a car in Montréal unless you plan on taking day trips outside the city limits.

All the major car-rental companies are represented in Montréal. You'll find rental agencies downtown as well as at Montréal-Trudeau airport. The best deals are usually found online at rental-car company websites, although all the major online travel agencies also offer rental-car reservations services. Websites for car-rental agencies are listed later in this chapter.

Québec province mandates that residents have radial snow tires on their cars in winter, from mid-December until March 15. Rental-car agencies are required to provide snow tires on car rentals during that period, and many charge an extra, nonnegotiable fee. The minimum driving age is 16 in Québec, but some car-rental companies will not rent to people under 25. Others charge higher rates for drivers under the age of 21.

Mobil Phones

Cellphone service is good in Québec cities and sometimes spotty in areas beyond city borders. Visitors from the U.S. should be able to get roaming service or a short-term international data plan to use their cellphones in Canada. Ask your provider for options. Europeans and most Australians are on the GSM (Global System for Mobile Communications) network with removable plastic SIM cards. Call your wireless provider for information about traveling. You may be able to purchase pay-as-you-go SIM cards in Canada with local providers such as Rogers (www.rogers.com).

Prepaid phone services are an option. With OneSuite.com (**www.onesuite.com**), for instance, you prepay an online account for as little as US$10. You then dial a toll-free or local access number (from, say, a hotel phone), enter your PIN, and dial the number you're calling. Calls from Canada to mainland U.S. cost just US2.5¢ per minute. Some hotels charge for local and even toll-free calls, so check before dialing.

Cheaper still are calls over the Web on a service such as Skype (**www.skype.com**). Skype can be used from computers or an app on a smartphone. Calls to people who also have the program are free. You can call people who don't have the service, although modest fees apply.

Getting **There**

By Plane

Montréal's main airport is **Aéroport International Pierre-Elliot-Trudeau de Montréal** (airport code YUL; ☎ 800/465-1213 or 514/394-7377; www.admtl.com), known better as Montréal-Trudeau airport. It's 21km (13 miles) southwest of downtown Montréal.

The airport is well served by the city's **Express Bus 747** (www.stm. info/info/747.htm), which travels between the airport and downtown, with 11 designated stops, mostly along boulevard René-Lévesque. The bus operates 24 hours a day, 7 days a week. A trip takes 45 to 60 minutes, depending on traffic, and buses leave every 20 to 30 minutes. One-way fares are C$10 for adults. They are sold at the airport from machines at the international arrivals level (good for 24 hours use on all subways and buses) at on the city at Métro stations and the Stationnement de Montréal street parking pay stations (for use within 2 hours). You can also pay with cash on the bus (coins only, exact change).

A taxi trip to downtown Montréal costs a flat fare of C$40 plus tip (C$4–C$6). Call ☎ 514/394-7377 for more information.

By Car

Many visitors from the mid-Atlantic and New England regions of the United States and eastern sections of Canada drive to Montréal. All international drivers must carry a valid driver's license from their country of residence. A U.S. license is sufficient as long as you are a visitor and actually are a U.S. resident. A U.K. license is sufficient as well. If the driver's license is in a language other than French or English, an International Driver's Permit is required in conjunction with the country of residence driver's license.

Driving north to Montréal from the U.S., the entire journey is on expressways. From New York City, all but the last 40 or so miles of the 603km (375-mile) journey are within New York State on I-87. I-87 links up with Canada's Autoroute 15 at the border, which goes straight to Montréal. From Boston, the trip is 518km (322 miles).

By Train

Montréal is a major terminus on Canada's **VIA Rail** network (www. viarail.ca; ☎ 888/842-7245 or 514/989-2626;). Its station, **Gare Centrale** (895 rue de la Gauchetière ouest; ☎ 514/989-2626), is centrally located in a busy, safe part of downtown. The station is adjacent to the Métro subway stop **Bonaventure Station.** (The older Gare Windsor, the city's former train station, is down the block and still on some city maps. The castle-like building is now used for offices.) VIA Rail trains are comfortable—all major routes have Wi-Fi, and some trains are equipped with dining cars and sleeping cars.

The U.S. train system, **Amtrak** (www.amtrak.com; ☎ 800/872-7245) has one train per day into Montréal from New York that makes intermediate stops. Called the *Adirondack,* it's very slow: 11 hours if all goes well, although delays aren't unusual. Its scenic route passes along the Hudson River's eastern shore and west of Lake Champlain.

The train ride between Montréal and Quèbec City takes about 3 hours.

By Bus

Montréal's central bus station, called **Gare d'autocars de Montréal** (www.gamtl.com; ☎ 514/842-2281), is at 1717 rue Berri, near the corner of rue Ontario est. It replaced the city's old bus station in 2011. Connected to the terminal is one of the city's major Métro stations, **Berri-UQAM Station.** Several Métro lines pass through the station. UQAM—pronounced "Oo-kahm"—stands for Université de Québec à Montréal, a public university that has a large urban campus here. **Taxis** usually line up outside the terminal building.

By Boat

Both Montréal and Québec City to the north are stops for cruise ships that travel along the St. Lawrence River (in French, Fleuve St-Laurent). The Port of Montréal, where ships dock, is part of the lively Vieux-Port (Old Port) neighborhood and walking distance from restaurants and shops.

Getting **Around**

By Foot, Wheelchair & Stroller

Montréal is a terrific city to experience outdoors. All the sites and neighborhoods listed in this book are compact enough to be experienced by foot. Travelers in wheelchairs or using strollers will find the city alternately accommodating and maddening. Many sidewalks have curb cuts for easy passage onto the streets, but many buildings and Métro stops are not accessible. In wintertime, sidewalks and roadways can be extremely icy.

By Public Transportation

For speed and economy, nothing beats Montréal's underground **Métro** system (www.stm.info; ☎ 514/786-4636). Stations are marked on the street by blue-and-white signs that show a circle enclosing a down-pointing arrow. The Métro is relatively clean (its first new cars in 40 years came into service in early 2016), and quiet trains whisk passengers through a decent network. It runs from about 5:30am to 12:30am, Sunday through Friday, and until about 1am Sun morning.

Fares are set by the ride, not by distance. A single ride, on either the bus or Métro, costs C$3.25 (reduced fare of C$2.25 for ages 6–17 and 65 and older). Automatic vending machines take credit cards. You can purchase tickets for cash only from a booth attendant at a Métro station. Tickets serve as proof of payment, so hold onto them for the duration of your trip. Transit police make periodic checks at transfer points or upon exiting and the fine for not having a ticket can run as high as C$500.

Single tickets can be purchased as a set of 10 tickets for C$27. If you plan to use the Métro more than twice a day, **1-day or 3-day passes** are a good deal. Passes are available at select stations listed at www.stm.info.

To pay, some tickets simply need to be tapped at the turnstile on the card reader. Others need to be slid through a slot in the turnstile and removed as it comes out. You can also show your pass to the booth attendant. A single paper ticket acts as its own transfer ticket; there are 2 hours from the time a ticket is first validated to transfer, and you insert the ticket into the machine of the next bus or Métro train.

Tap Your Own Pedal Power

Montréal is bike crazy, and it's got the goods to justify it. The city helps people indulge their passions by overseeing an ever-expanding network of about **600km (373 miles) of cycling paths** and year-round bike lanes. From April to November, car lanes in heavily biked areas are blocked off with concrete barriers, turning the passages into two-way lanes for bikers. Most Métro stations have large bike racks, and in some neighborhoods sections of the street where cars would normally park are fenced off for bike parking.

If you're serious about cycling, get in touch with the nonprofit biking organization **Vélo Québec** (www.velo.qc.ca; ☎ 800/567-8356 or 514/521-8356). It has a host of information for cyclists (vélo means "bicycle" in French) and co-hosts a weeklong bike festival in late May each year (see p 156). Its main office, **La Maison des Cyclists** (1251 rue Rachel est), is located across the street from the pretty Parc La Fontaine and has a cafe, a boutique with books and bike gear, and staff to help arrange bike trips and tours.

Note: Métro accessibility is **severely limited for wheelchairs and strollers.** Only eight Métro stations, all along the orange line, have elevators, and even those are not always operating. Parents with strollers often have to put strollers on escalators (a practice not discouraged in Montréal' as it is throughout the U.S.) and often have only a staircase as an entrance or exit option. Traveling by bus can be the better option with a stroller.

Bus fares are the same as fares for Métro trains, and Métro tickets are good on buses, too. Exact change is required if you want to pay on the bus. Buses run throughout the city and give tourists the advantage of traveling aboveground, although they don't run as frequently or as swiftly as the Métro. All buses have front-door access ramps for wheelchairs and strollers.

By Bike
Montréal has an exceptionally good system of bike paths, and bicycling is as common for transportation as it is for recreation.

Since 2009, a self-service short-term bicycle rental program called **BIXI** (www.bixi.com; ☎ 877/820-2453 or 514/789-2494) has become a defining presence of the city. A combination of the words *bicyclette* and *taxi*, BIXI allows users to pick up bikes from special BIXI stands throughout the city and drop them off at any other stand, for a small fee. Some 5,200 bikes are in operation and available at 460 stations in Montréal's central boroughs from April through November. The program shuts down during the harsh winter months.

Visitors have three short-term options: a one-time use for C$2.75; a 24-hour access pass for C$5; or a 72-hour access pass for C$12. With the access passes, you can borrow bikes as many times as you want. For each trip, the first 30 minutes are free. Trips longer than 30 minutes incur additional charges. (Note that BIXI will place a security deposit of C$100 per bike on your credit card, which will stay there for 10 days.)

If you'll be using a bike for a full day, it may be cheaper to rent from a shop (you'll also get a helmet and lock, which BIXI doesn't provide). One option is **Ça Roule/Montréal on Wheels** (www.caroulemontreal. com; ☎ 877/866-0633 or 514/866-0633) at 27 rue de la Commune est, the waterfront road in Vieux-Port. All-day rentals there are C$30 on weekdays and C$35 on weekends.

By Taxi

Cabs come in a variety of colors and styles, so their principal distinguishing feature is the plastic sign on the roof. At night, the sign is illuminated when the cab is available. The initial charge is C$3.45. Each additional kilometer (½ mile) adds C$1.70, and each minute of waiting adds C63¢. A short ride downtown usually costs about C$8. Tip 10 to 20%. Not all drivers accept credit cards.

Members of hotel and restaurant staffs can call cabs. Taxis also line up outside most large hotels or can be hailed on the street.

Uber, the San Francisco–based company that coordinates drivers with customers, launched in

Montréal in 2014. As of early 2016 Uber was still under siege by the government, which has called the use of drivers who don't have taxi licenses illegal. Uber's local website, www.uber.com/cities/montreal, may have updated news.

By Car

Montréal is an easy city to navigate by car, although traffic during morning and late afternoon rush hour can be horrendous. All familiar rules apply, though turning right on red in the city is prohibited.

It can be difficult to park for free in downtown Montréal, but there are plenty of metered spaces. Traditional meters are set well back from the curb so they won't be buried by plowed snow in winter. Metered parking costs C$3 per hour, and meters are in effect daily until 9pm. If there are no parking meters in sight, look for computerized Pay 'N Go stations, which are rapidly replacing meters. They're black metal kiosks about 1.8m (6 ft.) tall with a white "P" in a blue circle. Press the "English" button, enter the letter from the space where you are parked, then pay with cash or a credit card, following the on-screen instructions.

Most downtown shopping complexes have underground parking lots, as do the big downtown hotels. Some of the hotels allow guests "in/out privileges" for free, which can save money if you plan to do some sightseeing by car.

Fast **Facts**

AREA CODES Montréal area codes are **514** and **438**. Outside of Montréal, the area codes are **450, 579, 819,** and **873.** You always need to dial the three-digit area code in addition to the seven-digit number.

Numbers that begin with **800, 866, 877,** or **888** are free to call from both Canada and the U.S.

ATMS/BANKS ATMs (*guichet automatique*) and banks are easy to find in all parts of the city. In Canada, some debit cards require a four-digit pin. If your card has a longer pin it might be declined.

AUTOMOBILE ORGANIZATIONS
Members of the American Automobile Association (AAA) are covered by the Canadian Automobile Association (CAA; www.caaquebec.com) while traveling in Canada. Bring your membership card and proof of insurance. The 24-hour hot line for emergency road service is ☎ 800/222-4357 or *222 on a mobile phone. The AAA card will also provide discounts at a wide variety of hotels and restaurants.

BABYSITTERS Many Montréal hotels offer some form of babysitting service. If not, your hotel's concierge should be able to help find a reliable sitter.

B&BS A handful of select bed and breakfasts are listed by neighborhood at www.tourisme-montreal.org.

BANKS Banks are generally open from 8 or 9am to 4pm Monday to Friday. Most major Canadian banks have branches on either rue Sherbrooke or rue Ste-Catherine.

BIKE RENTALS See p 161 for details on the self-service bicycle rental program **BIXI** (www.bixi.com) and for other rental options.

BUSINESS HOURS Most stores in the province are open from 9 or 10am until 5 or 6pm daily, with longer evening hours on Thursday and Friday. That said, the city is in the middle of an experiment (running through 2020) that allows stores in much of the city to remain open 24/7. Most stores were only expected to take advantage on of extended hours during major festival events.

CONSULATES & EMBASSIES Embassies are located in Ottawa, Canada's capital. The **U.S. Embassy** information line ☎ 613/688-5335

or 613/238-5335 for after-hours emergencies. The U.S. consulate in Montréal is at 315 Place d'Youville, Ste. 500 (☎ 514/398-9695) but visitors must first check in at 1155 Rue St-Alexandre; nonemergency American citizen services are provided here by appointment only. The **U.K. consulate** for the province is in Montréal at 2000 McGill College Ave., Ste. 1940 (☎ 514/866-5863). For contact information for other embassies and consulates, search for "foreign representatives in Canada" at www.international.gc.ca.

CURRENCY EXCHANGE Commercial exchange bureaus and hotels often have the highest transaction fees. The best rates will come from withdrawing money at an ATM. That said, you can find currency exchange booths all over the city as well as at larger train stations and hotels.

CUSTOMS International visitors can expect at least a probing question or two at the border or airport. Normal baggage and personal possessions should be no problem, but plants, animals, fireworks, and weapons are among the items that may be prohibited or require additional documents before they're allowed in. For specific information about Canadian rules, check with the **Canada Border Services Agency** (www.cbsa-asfc.gc.ca; ☎ 506/636-5064 from outside the country or 800/461-9999 within Canada). Search for "bsf5082" to get a full list of visitor information.

Tobacco and alcoholic beverages face strict import restrictions: Individuals 18 years or older are allowed to bring in 200 cigarettes, 50 cigars, or 200 grams of tobacco; and only one of the following amounts of alcohol: 1.14 liters of liquor, 1.5 liters of wine, or 8.5 liters of beer (24 12-ounce cans or bottles). Additional amounts face hefty taxes. Possession of a car radar detector is prohibited, whether or not it is connected. Police officers can confiscate it and fines may run as high as C$650. Visitors can temporarily bring recreational vehicles, such as snowmobiles, boats, and trailers, as well as outboard motors, for personal use.

If you're traveling with expensive items, such as laptops or musical equipment, consider registering them before you leave your country to avoid challenges at the border on your return.

For information on what you're allowed to bring home, contact one of the following agencies:

U.S. Citizens: U.S. Customs & Border Protection (CBP), 1300 Pennsylvania Ave., NW, Washington, DC 20229 (www.cbp.gov; ☎ 877/227-5511).

U.K. Citizens: www.hmrc.gov.uk or ☎ 0800/595-000.

Australian Citizens: Australian Customs Service, Customs House, 5 Constitution Ave., Canberra City, ACT 2601 (www.customs.gov.au; ☎ 1300/363-263 or 612/9313-3010 from outside Australia).

New Zealand Citizens: New Zealand Customs, the Customhouse, 1 Hinemoa St., Harbour Quays, P.O. Box 2218, Wellington, 6140 (www.customs.govt.nz; ☎ 0800/428-786 or 649/927-8036 from outside New Zealand).

DINING Restaurants are colloquially called "restos" in the Québec province. Many moderately priced bistros offer outstanding food, congenial surroundings, and amiable service at reasonable prices. Nearly all have menus posted outside, making it easy to do a little comparison shopping. While many restaurants are open all day between meals, some shut down between lunch and dinner. Most restaurants serve until 9:30pm or 10pm.

To dine for less, consider **table d'hôte (fixed-price) meals.** Many restaurants offer them. An entire two- to four-course meal, often with a beverage, can be had for little more than the price of an a la carte main course.

It's wise to make a reservation if you wish to dine at one of the city's top restaurants, especially on a Friday or Saturday evening. A hotel concierge can make the reservation, though nearly all restaurant hosts will switch immediately to English when they sense that a caller doesn't speak French. Except in a handful of luxury restaurants, there are no dress codes. But Montréalers are a fashionable lot and manage to look smart even in casual clothes.

DOCTORS See "Hospitals," below.

DRINKING LAWS The legal drinking age in the province is 18. All hard liquor and spirits in Québec are sold through official government stores operated by the Québec Société des Alcools (look for maroon signs with the acronym SAQ). Wine and beer are available in grocery stores and convenience stores, called *dépanneurs.* Bars can pour drinks as late as 3am, but often stay open later.

Penalties for drunk driving in Canada are heavy. Drivers caught under the influence face a maximum life sentence if they cause death, and a maximum 10-year sentence if they cause bodily harm.

DRUGSTORES A pharmacy is called a *pharmacie*; a drugstore is a *droguerie*. A large chain in Montréal is **Pharmaprix** (www.pharma prix.ca; ☎ 800/746-7737).

ELECTRICITY Like the U.S., Canada uses 110 to 120 volts AC (60 cycles), compared to the 220 to 240 volts

AC (50 cycles) used in most of Europe, Australia, and New Zealand. If your small appliances use 220 to 240 volts, you'll need a 110-volt transformer and a plug adapter with two flat parallel pins to operate them in Canada. They can be difficult to find in Canada, so bring one with you.

EMERGENCIES Dial ☎ 911 for police, firefighters, or an ambulance.

EVENT LISTINGS La Vitrine (www.lavitrine.com) is a ticket office for Montréal cultural events, accessible online and in the Place des Arts (see p 158). **Cult Montréal** (www.cultmontreal.com) has, in English, up-to-the-minute previews of music, nightlife, and arts events. Also see "Newspapers & Magazines," below.

FAMILY TRAVEL Montréal offers an abundance of family-oriented activities. Many of them are outdoors, even in winter. Watersports, river cruises, fort climbing, and fireworks displays are among summer's many attractions, with dog sledding and skiing top choices in snowy months. For accommodations, restaurants, and attractions that are particularly kid friendly, look for the "Kids" icon throughout this guide. Also see "Montréal with Kids" on p 56.

GASOLINE (PETROL) Gasoline in Canada is sold by the liter; 3.78 liters equals 1 gallon. In early 2016, the price of a liter in Montréal was approximately C$.97, the equivalent of about US$3.66 per gallon.

HEALTH Canada has a state-run health system, and Québec hospitals are modern and decently equipped, with well-trained staffs. You are unlikely to get sick from Canada's food or water.

Familiar over-the-counter medicines are widely available in Canada. If there is a possibility that you will run out of prescribed medicines during your visit, take along a prescription from your doctor. Bring medications in their original containers with pharmacy labels—otherwise, they may not make it through airport security. If you're entering Canada with syringes used for medical reasons, bring a medical certificate that shows they are for medical use and be sure to declare them to Canadian Customs officials.

HOLIDAYS Canada's important public holidays are New Year's Day (Jan 1); Good Friday and Easter Monday (Mar or Apr); Victoria Day (the Mon preceding May 25); St-Jean-Baptiste Day, Québec's "national" day (June 24); Canada Day (July 1); Labor Day (first Mon in Sept); Canadian Thanksgiving Day (second Mon in Oct); and Christmas (Dec 25).

HOSPITALS Hospitals with emergency rooms include **Hôpital Général de Montréal** (1650 rue Cedar; ☎ 514/934-1934) and **Hôpital Royal Victoria** (687 av. des Pins ouest; ☎ 514/934-1934). **Hôpital de Montréal pour Enfants** (2300 rue Tupper; ☎ 514/412-4400), is a children's hospital. All three are associated with McGill University.

INSURANCE Medical Insurance Medical treatment in Canada isn't free for foreigners, and hospitals make you pay your bills at the time of service. Check whether your insurance policy covers you while traveling in Canada, especially for hospitalization abroad. Carry details of your insurance plan with you, and leave a copy with a friend at home.

Travel Insurance Some $2 billion in travel insurance is sold each year, covering costs from natural disasters to last-minute cancellations to personal medical emergencies. Should you buy it? In his 2014 book "How to Be the World's Smartest Traveler," consumer advocate and *National Geographic Traveler* editor-at-large Christopher Elliot recommends that it makes sense to buy insurance if you're spending over $5,000, if you have a complex itinerary, if you're leaving the country, or if you're simply a nervous traveler and want the peace of mind. *Consumer Reports* recommends not buying insurance through a travel agent, who might be selling a particular policy because of their sales commission. Instead, check out insurance marketplaces such as **www.InsureMyTrip.com** or **www.SquareMouth.com**, which offer insurance from many carriers. Elliot notes that the prices of travel insurance policies will vary according to a customer's age, state of residence, and types of coverage (for instance, a medical travel-insurance policy might be prudent if your regular insurance doesn't cover medical costs during foreign travel). A policy typically costs between 4% and 8% of the vacation's nonrefundable cost.

Trip-Cancellation Insurance
Trip-cancellation insurance will help retrieve your money if you have to back out of a trip or depart early, or if your travel supplier goes bankrupt. *Consumer Reports* notes that concerns about trip cancellation (before you leave) and trip interruption (during your trip) are the key reasons people buy insurance, and that 80% of claims are related to medical problems. "Unexpected injury and illnesses are, of course, covered," writes the magazine. "But if you consulted your doctor about a problem 60 to 180 days before your trip and that problem comes home to roost after you buy your travel, that would be an excludable pre-existing condition." Ask a sales rep about whether

pre-existing conditions could be covered and how, and ask him or her to point out the language in the policy's fine print that proves the coverage.

For more information on medical insurance while traveling, travel insurance, and trip-cancellation insurance, please visit www.frommers.com/planning.

INTERNET ACCESS   Nearly all hotels and auberges, as well as most cafes, offer Wi-Fi. Some hotels still offer high-speed Internet access through cable connections. Except at the larger hotels, Wi-Fi is generally free. Many hotels maintain business centers with computers for use by guests, or have a computer available for guest use. Again, except at the larger hotels, this access is often free. Many public spaces now have free Wi-Fi.

LANGUAGE   Canada is officially bilingual, but the Québec province has laws that make French mandatory in signage. About 65% of Montréal's population has French as its first language (and about 95% of Québec City's population does). Still, an estimated four out of five Francophones (French speakers) speak at least some English. Hotel desk staff, sales clerks, and telephone operators nearly always greet people initially in French, but usually switch to English quickly if necessary. Outside of Montréal, visitors are more likely to encounter residents who don't speak English. If smiles and sign language don't work, look around for a young person—most of them study English in school.

LGBTQ TRAVELERS   The province of Québec is a destination for international LGBTQ travelers. Gay life here is generally open and accepted (gay marriage is legal throughout the province), and gay travelers are heavily marketed to.

Travelers will often find the rainbow flag prominently displayed on the doors and websites of hotels and restaurants.

Many LGBTQ travelers head straight to the Gay Village (also known simply as "the Village"), a neighborhood east of downtown located primarily along rue Ste-Catherine est between rue St-Hubert and rue Papineau. The Village is action central on any night, but it especially picks up during **Montréal Pride** (www.fierte montrealpride.com) in August and the **Black & Blue Festival** (www. bbcm.org) in October, which is one of the world's largest circuit parties. **"Fugues"** magazine (www.fugues. com) lists events and gay-friendly lodgings, clubs, and other resources.

The Village Tourism Informa-tion Centre, at 1307 rue Ste-Cath-erine est (☎ 888/647-2247), is open June to August from noon to 6pm (days vary; call in advance). It's operated by the **Québec Gay Chamber of Commerce** (www. ccgq.ca).

LEGAL AID If you are arrested, your country's embassy or consulate can provide the names of attorneys who speak English. See "Consul-ates & Embassies," above.

MAIL & POSTAGE English-language services are offered at about one out of four offices of **Canada Post** (www.canadapost.ca; ☎ 866/607-6301) in the city, including at 157 rue St-Antoine ouest in Vieux-Mon-tréal and 800 René-Lévesque ouest in downtown. A letter or postcard to the U.S. costs C$1.20. A letter or postcard to anywhere else outside of Canada costs C$2.50. A letter to a Canadian address costs C85¢. **FedEx** (☎ 800/463-3339; www. fedex.com/ca) also offers service from Canada.

MEDICAL REQUIREMENTS Unless you're arriving from an area known to be suffering from an epidemic (particularly cholera or yellow fever), inoculations or vaccinations are not required for entry into Canada.

MONEY Canadian money comes in graduated denominations of dollars and cents. Bills have security strips and bold colors, and start at C$5 and go up. Coins include one-dol-lar and two-dollar denominations, nicknamed the Loonie (for a one-dollar coin) and the Toonie (for a two-dollar coin).

Credit or debit cards are accepted at almost all shops, restaurants, and hotels, but you should always keep some cash on hand for small venues that don't take plastic.

NEWSPAPERS & MAGAZINES "The Globe and Mail" (www.theglobe andmail.com) is Canada's national English-language paper. The **"Montréal Gazette"** (www. montrealgazette.com) is the city's primary English-language paper.

PARKING See "By Car" in the "Getting Around" section, earlier in this chapter.

PASSES Montréal Museums Pass (www.montrealmuseums.org) is an excellent option for ambitious sightseers. It grants entry to over 40 museums and attractions. The C$80 pass is good for 3 consecutive days plus unlimited access to public transportation (including the airport shuttle, bus no. 747); the C$75 pass is good for any 3 days within a 3-week period and does not include public transport. Look for the pass at museums or the tourist office at 1255 rue Peel (downtown).

PASSPORTS For country-specific passport information, contact the following agencies:

For Residents of Australia Contact the Australian **Passport**

Information Service. Visit www. passports.gov.au or call ☎ 131-232.

For Residents of Ireland Contact the **Passport Office,** Frederick Buildings, Molesworth Street, Dublin 2 (www.dfa.ie; ☎ 01/671-1633).

For Residents of New Zealand Contact the **Passports Office,** Department of Internal Affairs, Level 3, 109 Featherston Street, P.O. Box 1568, Wellington 6011 (www.passports.govt.nz; ☎ 0800/22-50-50 in New Zealand or 04/463-9360).

For Residents of the United Kingdom Visit your nearest passport office, major post office, or travel agency, or contact the **Identity and Passport Service** (IPS), 4th floor, Peel Building, 2 Marsham St., London, SW1P 4DF (www.ips.gov.uk; ☎ 0300/222-0000).

For Residents of the United States To find your regional passport office, check the **U.S. State Department** website (http://travel.state.gov) or call the **National Passport Information Center** (☎ 877/487-2778) for automated information.

Make a copy of your passport's information page and keep it separate from your passport in case of loss or theft. For emergency passport replacement, contact your country's embassy or consulate (see "Consulates & Embassies," p 163).

POLICE Dial ☎ 911 for police, firefighters, or an ambulance.

SAFETY Montréal is a safe city. Still, common sense insists that visitors stay alert and observe the usual urban precautions. It's best to stay out of parks at night and to take a taxi when returning from a late dinner or nightclub.

SENIOR TRAVELERS Mention that you're a senior when you make your travel reservations; many Québec hotels offer discounts for older travelers. As well, ask about reduced admission for theaters, museums, and other attractions, which are often available for visitors 60-plus.

SMOKING Smoking was banned in the province's bars, restaurants, clubs, casinos, and some other public spaces in 2006. Most inns and hotels are now entirely smoke-free as well. Check before you book if you're looking for a room in which you can smoke.

SPECTATOR SPORTS Montréal hockey fans are a passionate bunch, and many travelers plan their trip around attending a home game. The city's beloved NHL **Montréal Canadiens** (www. canadiens.com; ☎ 877/668-8269 or 514/790-2525) have won 24 Stanley Cups, and devoted fans pack the Centre Bell to cheer on *Les Habitants.*

TAXES Most goods and services in Canada are taxed 5% by the federal government (the GST/TPS) and 9.975% by the province of Québec (the TVQ). In Montréal, hotel bills have an additional 3.5% accommodations tax.

TAXIS See "By Taxi" in the "Getting Around" section, p 162.

TELEPHONES The Canadian telephone system is operated by Bell Canada. All **operators speak English and French.** In Canada, dial ☎ 0 to reach an operator.

When making a local call within the province of Québec, you must dial the area code before the seven-digit number. Phone numbers that begin with 800, 866, 877, and 888 are **toll-free** within Canada and from the U.S. You need to dial 1 first.

To call Montréal from the U.S.: Dial 1, then the three-digit area code, then the seven-digit number.

To call Montréal from the U.K./ Ireland/Australia/New Zealand: Dial the international access code 00 (from Australia, 0011), then the Canadian country code 1, then the area code, and then the seven-digit number.

To call the U.S. from Montréal: Dial 1, then the three-digit area code and seven-digit number.

To call the U.K./Ireland/Australia/ New Zealand from Montréal: Dial 011, then the country code (U.K. 44, Ireland 353, Australia 61, New Zealand 64), then the number.

For directory information, dial ☎ 411.

TICKETS Call venues individually for specific ticket information. Tickets at large stadiums are often handled by outside ticket companies and have large fees associated with them. For last-minute as well as future-event tickets, visit **La Vitrine** online or in person (see p 158).

TIPPING In restaurants, bars, and nightclubs, tip waiters 15% to 20% of the check, tip checkroom attendants C$1 per garment, and tip valet-parking attendants C$1 per vehicle. In hotels, tip bellhops C$1 per bag and tip the chamber staff C$3 to C$5 per day. Tip taxi drivers 15% of the fare; tip skycaps at airports C$1 per bag; and tip hairdressers and barbers 15% to 20%.

TOILETS You won't find public toilets on the streets in Montréal or Québec City, but they can be found in tourist offices, museums, railway and bus stations, and large shopping complexes. Restaurants and bars often reserve their restrooms for patrons.

TOURIST OFFICES The main tourist office is the **Infotouriste Centre** (1255 rue Peel; ☎ 877/266-5687 or 514/873-2015; Métro: Peel). It's open daily and the bilingual staff can provide suggestions for

accommodations, dining, car rentals, and attractions. In Vieux-Montréal, there's a small tourist information office at 174 rue Notre-Dame est, at the corner of Place Jacques-Cartier (Métro: Champ-de-Mars). It's open daily May through October and closed the rest of the year.

TOURS An introductory guided tour is an efficient way to begin exploring a new city, and can give you a good lay of the land and overview of Montréal's history. **Gray Line** (www.grayline.com; ☎ 800/472-9546) offers commercial guided tours in air-conditioned motorcoach buses daily year-round. The basic city tour takes 3½ hours. There's also a shorter 2-hour "Hop-on-Hop-Off" tour on a London-style double-decker bus. **Amphi-Bus** (www.montreal-amphibus-tour.com; ☎ 514/849-5181) is something a little different: It tours Vieux-Montréal much like any other bus until it waddles into the waters of the harbor for a dramatic finish. **Le Bateau-Mouche** (www.bateau mouche.ca; ☎ 800/361-9952 or 514/849-9952) is a glass-enclosed vessel reminiscent of those on the Seine in Paris. It plies the St. Lawrence River from mid-May to mid-October, taking passengers on a route inaccessible by traditional vessels and providing sweeping views of the city.

Tours by foot and by bike are offered by **Fitz & Follwell Co.** (www.fitzandfollwell.co; ☎ 514/ 840-0739) and **Guidatour** (www. guidatour.qc.ca; ☎ 800/363-4021 or 514/844-4021), and include culinary tours with stops for espresso and bagels.

For a complete listing of tours and tour operators, check under "Guided Tours" in the *Montréal Official Tourist Guide*, available at the downtown Infotouriste Centre

(1255 rue Peel; ☎ 877/266-5687 or 514/873-2015; Métro: Peel).

TRAVELERS WITH WHEELCHAIRS, STROLLERS, OR RESTRICTED MOBILITY Québec regulations regarding wheelchair accessibility are similar to those in the U.S. and the rest of Canada, including requirements for curb cuts, entrance ramps, designated parking spaces, and specially equipped bathrooms. That said, while the more modern parts of the cities are fully wheelchair accessible, access to the restaurants and inns housed in 18th- and 19th-century buildings, especially in Vieux-Montréal, is often difficult or impossible. Montréal's underground Métro system has only eight stations with elevators; the rest have escalators or just stairs.

Information on accessibility of specific accommodations and tourist sites is online at **www.bonjour quebec.com**, the official website of the Québec government. Search for "Kéroul," the organization that Tourisme Québec collaborates with to update the database. Kéroul also provides information at its own websites, **www.keroul.qc.ca** and **www.larouteaccessible.com**.

Montréal: **A Brief History**

1535 A community of Iroquois establishes the village of Hochelaga in what's now called Montréal, living in 50 homes and farming the land. French explorer Jacques Cartier visits the village that year. When the French return in 1603, the village is empty. Other First Nations people, including the Algonquins and Hurons, also inhabit the region.

1608 Samuel de Champlain arrives in Québec City motivated by the burgeoning fur trade, obsessed with finding a route to China, and determined to settle "New France." Three years later, he establishes a fur trading post in Montréal where the Pointe-à-Callière now stands.

1617 Parisian apothecary Louis Hérbert and Mary Rollet become the first colonists in Québec City to live off the produce of their own farm.

1642 Ville-Marie is founded by Paul de Chomedy de Maisonneuve, who installs a wood cross at the top of Mont-Royal.

1670 Hudson Bay Company is incorporated by British royal charter, and the competition around the fur trade in the Québec province heightens tension between France and England.

1759 After over a century of conflict about who would rule the new world, the British defeat the French in Québec City and enter Montréal.

1760 Montréal falls to the British.

1763 The king of France cedes all of Canada to the king of England in the Treaty of Paris, ending the Seven Years' War.

1775 U.S. general George Washington and the U.S. Continental Congress decide to extend their rebellion north and take the Québec province and the St. Lawrence River from the British, assuming that French-Canadians would happily join their cause. They predict wrongly. American Revolutionary forces occupy Montréal and Québec City after battles in 1775 and 1776 and then withdraw after a few months.

1821 English-speaking McGill University is established.

1824 The Lachine Canal opens after 3 years of construction, helping turn Montréal into a major port.

1833 Jacques Viger, born in Montréal in 1787, becomes the first mayor of Montréal.

1844 The Parliament of Canada is established in Montréal, though it later moves to Ottawa.

1852 The most devastating fire the city has experienced, known later as the Great Montréal Fire, leaves as many as 10,000 of the city's 57,000 inhabitants homeless and thousands without jobs in the middle of the hot, dry summer.

1857 The Gradual Civilization Act helps establish the Indian residential school system, a program of forced assimilation of First Nations children.

1859 Victoria Bridge is completed.

1924 A new, illuminated cross is unveiled on Mont-Royal on Christmas Day.

1933 Marché Atwater opens.

1939 The National Film Board is established.

1962 The city begins construction of the Métro system, which opens in 1966.

1962 With the construction of Place Ville-Marie, the Underground City is born.

1967 The Montréal World Exposition (Expo 67) is held and puts the city on glorious display to the world. The event is a major benchmark in the city's modern history.

1968 Parti Québécois is founded.

1968 Canadian soldiers take to the streets of Québec City to quell unrest by separatists.

1969 Montréal Expos, a Major League Baseball team, is established. The franchise later is relocated to Washington, D.C., in 2004, where it becomes the Washington Nationals.

1976 Montréal hosts the athletically successful but financially disastrous Summer Olympics, sending the city into years of monstrous debt.

1977 Bill 101 passes, all but banning the use of English on public signage in the Québec province.

1979 The Festival International de Jazz de Montréal is founded.

1985 Bill C-31 gives First Nations women the right to marry white men and keep their Indian status, a right long held by First Nations men.

1992 Montréal celebrates its 350th birthday.

1998 A January ice storm cripples the region, cutting off power to millions, causing massive damage to trees and property, and leaving a thick layer of ice across streets, buildings, and roofs.

1999 The definition of "spouse" is changed in 39 laws and regulations, eliminating all legal distinctions between same-sex and heterosexual couples and recognizing the legal status of same-sex civil unions.

2001 The federal and provincial government and the Cree Nation sign La Paix des Braves (The Peace of the Braves) allowing Hydro-Québec to set up hydroelectric plants on Cree land in exchange for C$3.5 billion.

2002 Construction of Palais des Congrès (Convention Center) is completed. It's an unlikely design triumph featuring transparent glass exterior walls in a crazy quilt of pink, yellow, blue, green, red, and purple rectangles.

2005 Gay marriage becomes legal in all Canadian provinces and territories.

2006 UNESCO, the United Nations Educational, Scientific and Cultural Organization, designates Montréal a UNESCO City of Design for "its ability to inspire synergy between public and private players" and reputation for design innovation.

2008 A report on provincial angst over so-called reasonable accommodation of minority religious practices declares, "Québec is at a turning point . . . The identity inherited from the French-Canadian past is perfectly legitimate and it must survive,

but it can no longer occupy alone the Québec identity space."

2014 Pauline Marois, then the Québec Premier and the leader of the Parti Québécois, oversteps: Confident about gaining a parliamentary majority, she calls for elections. Heated campaign conversation focuses around Marois' proposed "charter of values," which would have restricted headscarves worn by Muslim public employees, among other provisions. Another prominent PQ candidate declares his focus on the independence of Québec. These two things prove a self-destructive one-two punch, and the party is trounced in its worst defeat since 1970. The Liberal party, strongly anti-secession, takes power, with Philippe Couillard as the province's new premier.

The Politics of **Language & Identity**

Montréal and Québec City, the twin cities of the province of Québec, have a stronger European flavor than Canada's other municipalities. Most residents' first language is French, and a strong affiliation with France continues to be a central facet of the region's personality.

Many in Québec stayed committed to the French language and culture after British rule was imposed in 1759. Even with later waves of other immigrant populations pouring in over the cities, there was still a kind of bedrock loyalty held by many to the province's Gallic roots. Many Québécois continue to look across the Atlantic for inspiration in fashion, food, and the arts. Culturally and linguistically,

it is that tenacious French connection that gives the province its special character.

In 1867, the British North America Act created the federation of the provinces of Québec, Ontario, Nova Scotia, and New Brunswick. It was a kind of independence for the region from Britain, but was unsettling for many French-Canadians, who wanted full autonomy. In 1883, *Je me souviens*—an ominous "I remember"—became the province's official motto.

In 1968, the Parti Québécois (PQ) was founded by René Lévesque, and the separatist movement began in earnest. One attempt to smooth ruffled Francophones (French speakers) was made in 1969, when federal legislation stipulated that all services across Canada were henceforth to be offered in both English and French, in effect declaring the nation bilingual.

That didn't assuage militant Québécois, however. They undertook to guarantee the primacy of French in their own province. To prevent dilution by newcomers, the children of immigrants were required to enroll in French-language schools, even if English or a third language was spoken in the home. This is still the case today. In 1977, Bill 101 passed, all but banning the use of English on public signage. The bill funded the establishment of enforcement units, a virtual language police who let no nit go unpicked. The resulting backlash provoked the flight of an estimated 400,000 Anglophones to other parts of Canada.

Support for the secessionist cause burgeoned again in Québec in the early 1990s, fueled by an election that firmly placed the PQ back in control of the provincial government. A referendum held in 1995 narrowly defeated succession from the Canadian union, but the vote settled nothing. The issue continued to divide families and dominate political discourse.

In 2014, Pauline Marois, then the Québec Premier and the leader of the Parti Québécois, was voted out of office after a campaign that highlighted her proposed "charter of values," which would have restricted headscarves worn by Muslim public employees, among other provisions. The Liberal party, which is strongly anti-secession, took power, and Philippe Couillard became the province's new premier.

In the past 15 years, Montréal has become probably the most bilingual city in the world. Most people are comfortable speaking French, English, and a kind of Franglish patois that combines both.

Two other important cultural phenomena have emerged over the past 15 years. The first is an institutional acceptance of homosexuality. By changing the definition of "spouse" in 39 laws and regulations in 1999, Québec's government eliminated all legal distinctions between same-sex and heterosexual couples and became Canada's first province to recognize the legal status of same-sex civil unions. Gay marriage became legal in all of Canada's provinces and territories in 2005. Montréal, in particular, has transformed into one of North America's most welcoming cities for gay people.

The second phenomenon is an influx of even more immigrants into the province's melting pot. Québec welcomed over 50,000 permanent residents in 2010, with over 46,000 of them settling in Montréal.

Together with 70,000 aboriginal people from 11 First Nations tribes who live in the province, immigrants help make the region as vibrant and alive as any on the continent.

Useful **Phrases & Menu Terms**

A word or two of even halting French can go a long way in encouraging a French speaker to help you out. After all, you're asking your hosts to meet you much more than halfway in communicating. At the very least, practice basic greetings and the introductory phrase, *Parlez-vous anglais?* (Do you speak English?).

Useful Words & Phrases

ENGLISH	FRENCH	PRONUNCIATION
Yes/No	Oui/Non	wee/noh
Okay	D'accord	dah-core
Please	S'il vous plaît	seel voo play
Thank you	Merci	mair-see
You're welcome	De rien	duh ree-ehn
Hello (during daylight)	Bonjour	bohn-jhoor
Hello (at night)	Bonsoir	bohn-swahr
Goodbye	Au revoir	o vwahr
What's your name?	Comment vous appellez-vous?	kuh-mahn voo za-pell-ay-voo?
My name is	Je m'appelle	jhuh ma-pell
How are you?	Comment allez-vous?	kuh-mahn tahl-ay-voo?
So-so	Comme ci, comme ça	kum-see, kum-sah
I'm sorry/Excuse me	Pardon	pahr-dohn
Do you speak English?	Parlez-vous anglais?	par-lay-voo zahn-glay?
I don't speak French	Je ne parle pas français	jhuh ne parl pah frahn-say
I don't understand	Je ne comprends pas	jhuh ne kohm-prahn pas
Where is . . . ?	Où est . . . ?	ooh eh . . . ?
Why?	Pourquoi?	poor-kwah?
here/there	ici/là	ee-see/lah
left/right	à gauche/à droite	a goash/a drwaht
straight ahead	tout droit	too drwah
I want to get off at . . .	Je voudrais descendre à . . .	jhe voo-dray day-son-drah ah . . .
airport	l'aéroport	lair-o-por
bridge	pont	pohn
bus station	la gare d'autobus	lah gar duh aw-toh-boos
bus stop	l'arrêt de bus	lah-ray duh boohss
cathedral	cathedral	ka-tay-dral
church	église	ay-gleez
hospital	l'hôpital	low-pee-tahl
museum	le musée	luh mew-zay
police	la police	lah po-lees
one-way ticket	aller simple	ah-lay sam-pluh
round-trip ticket	aller-retour	ah-lay re-toor
ticket	un billet	uh bee-yay
toilets	les toilettes	lay twa-lets

In Your Hotel

ENGLISH	FRENCH	PRONUNCIATION
bathtub	une baignoire	ewn bayn-nwar
hot and cold water	l'eau chaude et froide	low showed ay fwad
Is breakfast included?	déjeuner inclus?	day-jheun-ay ehn-klu?

ENGLISH	FRENCH	PRONUNCIATION
room	une chambre	ewn shawm-bruh
shower	une douche	ewn dooch
sink	un lavabo	uh la-va-bow

The Calendar

ENGLISH	FRENCH	PRONUNCIATION
Sunday	dimanche	dee-mahnsh
Monday	lundi	luhn-dee
Tuesday	mardi	mahr-dee
Wednesday	mercredi	mair-kruh-dee
Thursday	jeudi	jheu-dee
Friday	vendredi	vawn-druh-dee
Saturday	samedi	sahm-dee
yesterday	hier	ee-air
today	aujourd'hui	o-jhord-dwee
this morning/this afternoon	ce matin/cet après-midi	suh ma-tan/set ah-preh mee-dee
tonight	ce soir	suh swahr
tomorrow	demain	de-man

Food, Menu & Restaurant Terms

ENGLISH	FRENCH	PRONUNCIATION
I would like to eat	Je voudrais manger	jhe voo-dray mahn-jhay
Please give me	Donnez-moi, s'il voo play	doe-nay-mwah, seel vous plaît
a bottle of	une bouteille de	ewn boo-tay duh
a cup of	une tasse de	ewn tass duh
a glass of	un verre de	uh vair duh
a cocktail	un apéritif	uh ah-pay-ree-teef
the check/bill	l'addition/la note	la-dee-see-ohn/la noat
a knife	un couteau	uh koo-toe
a napkin	une serviette	ewn sair-vee-et
a spoon	une cuillère	ewn kwee-air
a fork	une fourchette	ewn four-shet
fixed-price menu	table d'hôte	tab-lah dote
Is the tip/service included?	Est-ce que le service est compris?	ess-ke luh ser-vees eh com-pree?
Waiter!/Waitress!	Monsieur!/Mademoiselle!	mun-syuh/mad-mwa-zel
wine list	une carte des vins	ewn cart day van
appetizer	une entrée	ewn en-tray
main course	un plat principal	uh plah pran-see-pahl
tip included	service compris	sehr-vees cohm-pree
tasting/chef's menu	menu dégustation	may-new day-gus-ta-see-on

Numbers

ENGLISH	FRENCH	PRONUNCIATION
0	zéro	zeh-roh
1	un	uhn
2	deux	duh
3	trois	twah
4	quatre	kah-truh
5	cinq	sank
6	six	seess
7	sept	set
8	huit	weet
9	neuf	nuhf
10	dix	deess
11	onze	ohnz
12	douze	dooz
13	treize	trehz
14	quatorze	kah-torz
15	quinze	kanz
16	seize	sez
17	dix-sept	deez-set
18	dix-huit	deez-weet
19	dix-neuf	deez-noof
20	vingt	vehn
30	trente	trahnt
40	quarante	kah-rahnt
50	cinquante	sang-kahnt
100	cent	sahn
1,000	mille	meel

Websites

Airlines

AIR CANADA
www.aircanada.ca
AIR FRANCE
www.airfrance.com
AMERICAN AIRLINES
www.aa.com
BRITISH AIRWAYS
www.british-airways.com
DELTA AIR LINES
www.delta.com
KLM ROYAL DUTCH AIRLINES
www.delta.com
LUFTHANSA
www.lufthansa.com
PORTER AIRLINES
www.flyporter.com

SWISS AIR
www.swiss.com
UNITED AIRLINES
www.united.com

Car-Rental Agencies

ALAMO
www.alamo.com
AVIS
www.avis.com
BUDGET
www.budget.com
DOLLAR
www.dollar.com
ENTERPRISE
www.enterprise.com

Websites

HERTZ
www.hertz.com
NATIONAL
www.nationalcar.com
THRIFTY
www.thrifty.com

Major Hotel & Motel Chains
BEST WESTERN
www.bestwestern.com
CLARION
www.choicehotels.com/clarion
COURTYARD BY MARRIOTT
www.marriott.com/courtyard
CROWNE PLAZA HOTELS
www.ichotelsgroup.com/crowneplaza
DAYS INN
www.daysinn.com
ECONO LODGE
www.choicehotels.com/econo-lodge
EMBASSY SUITES
www.embassysuites.com
FAIRMONT HOTELS & RESORTS
www.fairmont.com
FAIRFIELD INN BY MARRIOTT
www.fairfield.marriott.com
LE GERMAIN & ALT HOTELS
www.legermainhotels.com

HAMPTON INN
http://hamptoninn1.hilton.com
HILTON HOTELS
www.hilton.com
HOLIDAY INN
www.holidayinn.com
HYATT
www.hyatt.com
INTERCONTINENTAL HOTELS & RESORTS
www.intercontinental.com
LOEWS HOTELS
www.loewshotels.com
MARRIOTT
www.marriott.com
OMNI HOTELS
www.omnihotels.com
RESIDENCE INN BY MARRIOTT
www.marriott.com/residenceinn
RITZ CARLTON
www.ritzcarlton.com
SHERATON HOTELS & RESORTS
www.starwoodhotels.com/sheraton
SOFITEL
www.sofitel.com
TRAVELODGE
www.travelodge.com
WESTIN HOTELS & RESORTS
www.starwoodhotels.com/westin

Index

Index

See also Accommodations and Restaurant indexes, below.

A

AAA (American Automobile Association), 163
Abbaye de Saint-Benoît-du-Lac, 152
Accommodations, 127–132.
    See also Accommodations Index
        best bets, 124
        Cantons-de-l'Est, 153
        Mont-Tremblant, 148
        Québec City, 140–141
Aéroport International Pierre-Elliot-Trudeau de Montréal, 159
Airbnb, 128
Air travel, 159
American Automobile Association (AAA), 163
Antique Alley, 33, 85
Archambault, 90
Area codes, 162
Arthur Quentin, 90
Arts and entertainment, 117–122
        best bets, 116
ATMs/banks, 162–163
Autobus le Petit Train du Nord, 146
Avenue Laurier, 84, 87

B

Babysitters, 163
Bagels, 37
Bagg Street Shul, 75
Banks, 163
Banque de Montréal, 63
Bar Furco, 110
Bar Henrietta, 110
Bars, 110–113
Basilique-Cathédrale Marie-Reine-du-Monde, 68
Basilique Notre-Dame de Montréal, 6, 11, 63
Beach volleyball, 54
Beatnick's, 90
Beaver Lake (Lac des Castors), 79
Bed & breakfasts (B&Bs), 128, 163
Biftek, 110

Biking, 6, 48, 52–53, 161–162
    Montréal Bike Fest, 156
    Route Verte (Green Route), 146
    tours, 53
Bilboquet, 58
Bill 101, 29
Bílý Kůň, 47, 110
Biodôme de Montréal, 21, 60
BIXI, 48, 161–162
Bleu Lavende Farm (Stanstead), 152
Boating, 53–54
Boat travel, 160
Bota Bota, 40–41
Boulevard René-Lévesque, 68
Boulevard St-Laurent (the Main), 10, 19, 74
Bourgeoys, Marguerite, 27, 64
Bourget, Bishop Ignace, 68
Brasserie Harricana, 110
Brutopia, 111
Business hours, 163
Bus travel, 160
    Autobus le Petit Train du Nord, 146
Buvette Chez Simone, 111

C

Cabanes à sucre (sugar shacks), 151
Cabaret Mado, 113
Calvet, Pierre du, 64
Canadian Automobile Association (CAA), 163
Cantons-de-l'Est, 151
ÇaRoule/Montréal on Wheels, 10
Car rentals, 158
Cartier, Jacques, 26
Car travel, 159, 162
Casa del Popolo, 47, 113
Casino de Montréal, 117
Cathédrale Christ Church, 69, 92
Cellphones, 158
Centaur Theatre, 122
Centre Bell, 121
Centre des Sciences de Montréal, 9, 58, 121
Centre Infotouriste de Québec (Québec City), 137
Chalet du Mont-Royal, 80
Champlain, Samuel de, 28
Chapelle Notre-Dame-de-Bon-Secours, 27, 64
Château Frontenac (Québec City), 136
Cheeses, 104

Chemin Olmsted, 78
Chez Bernard (St-Sauveur), 145
Children, 5, 58–60, 165
Chinese Garden, 21–22
Chomedey, Paul de, Sieur de Maisonneuve, 63, 80
Cidre de glace, 152
Cimetière Mont-Royal, 80
5 à 7 (happy hour), 6
Circus, 117
Cirque du Soleil, 5, 116, 117
City Hall (Hôtel de Ville), 64
Classical music, 117
Club Monaco, 87
Club Soda, 113–114
Comedy, 120
The Comedy Nest, 120–121
Complex Les Ailes, 92
Consulates, 163
Crocs, 87
Croisière Memphrémagog, 151–152
Croisières AML Cruises, 53
Croix du Mont-Royal, 80
Cross-country skiing, 53
    Parc National du Mont-Tremblant, 147
Currency exchange, 163
Customs regulations, 163–164

D

Dance clubs, 113
Darling Foundry, 45
De Gaulle, Charles, 64
De Maisonneuve, Sieur, Paul de Chomedey, 63
Department stores, 86–87
Dieu du Ciel, 111
Dining, 98–104, 164. See also Restaurant Index
        best bets, 94
        Cantons-de-l'Est, 154
        Mont-Tremblant, 149
        Québec City, 142–143
        table d'hôte option, 103, 139
Divan Orange, 114
Domaine Pinnacle, 90, 152
Drawn & Quarterly, 85
Drinking laws, 164
Drugstores, 164
Dufresne Regional Park, 145
Dunham, 152

E

Eaton Centre, 91
Edibles, 88–90
Edifice Aldred, 63

Electricity, 164–165
Embassies and consulates, 163
Emergencies, 165
Event listings, 165
Expo 67, 44–45

F

Fairmont Bagel, 37
Fall foliage, 157
Families with children, 5, 58–60, 165
Fashion (clothing), 87–88
Fashion & Design Festival, 44
Festival des Art de St-Sauveur, 145
Festival des Films du Monde, 157
Festival International de Jazz de Montréal, 22, 156
Festival Juste pour Rire (Just for Laughs Festival), 120
Festival Juste pour Rire (Just for Laughs festival), 157
Festival Montréal en Lumière (Montréal High Lights Festival), 156
Festivals and special events, 156–157
Films, 121–122
Fireworks, 59, 157
First Nations, 26
Fourrures Dubarry Furs, 87
FrancoFolies de Montréal, 156
Franklin, Benjamin, 28, 64
Frenco, 88
Frisbee games, 54–55
Funiculaire (Québec City), 138–139

G

Gagné, Mariouche, 45
Gasoline, 165
Golden Square Mile, 13
Guilde Canadienne des Métiers d'Art, 85

H

Habitat 67, 44–45
Happy hour (5 à 7), 6
Harricana, 45, 88
Harry Rosen, 88
Health, 165
Henry Birks et Fils, 69
Historic Montréal, 24–29
Hochelaga, 26, 170
Hockey, 54
Holidays, 165
Holt Renfrew, 86
Horse-drawn carriages (calèches), 4, 68

Hospitals, 165
Hôtel de Ville (City Hall), 64
Hotels, 127–132
  best bets, 124
Housewares, 90
H2O Adventures, 54
Hurley's Irish Pub, 114

I

Ice cider, 152
Ice skating, 53, 59
Ice wine, 152
The Illuminated Crowd (sculpture), 70–71
IMAX Theatre, 121
Insectarium de Montréal, 22, 60
Insurance, 165–166
International Fireworks Competition, 157
International Sculpture Symposium sculptures, 79
Internet and Wi-Fi, 166

J

Japanese Garden, 22, 40
Jardin Botanique, 5, 21–22, 39, 40
Jardin Nelson, 65
Jazz, 5, 65
Jean-Noël Desmarais Pavilion, 32
Jewish Montréal, 75
Jewish Public Library, 75
Joseph, General Louis, 28
Just for Laughs Festival (Festival Juste pour Rire), 120, 157

K

Kaliyana, 73, 88
Kanehsatake: 270 Years of Resistance (film), 26
Kanuk, 73, 88
Kids, 5, 58–60, 165
Knowlton, 151

L

La Baie (The Bay), 69, 86
La Biosphère, 44
Labo Culinaire (Foodlab), 111
La Cage Brasserie Sportive, 111
Lac Brome, 151
Lac des Castors (Beaver Lake), 79
Lachine Canal, 6, 10
Lachine Canal bike path, 52–53
La Citadelle (Québec City), 137–138

Lac Magog, 151
Lac Memphrémagog, 151
La Fête des Neiges (Snow Festival), 156
La Maison des Cyclists, 161
La Maison Pierre du Calvet, 64
Language, 166
La Ronde Amusement Park, 59
LARPers (Live Action Role Players), 54
La Sala Rossa, 47, 114
Laurentian Mountains (the Laurentides), 145–149
La Vieille Europe, 89
La Vitrine, 165
Le Bateau-Mouche, 53
Le Centre Eaton, 91
Legal aid, 167
Le Grand Magasin Ailes de la Mode, 92
Le Jardin Nelson, 111–112
Leonowens, Anna, 80
Le Scandinave Spa (Mont-Tremblant), 147
Les Chocolats de Chloé, 41, 89
Les Cours Mont-Royal, 91–92
Les FrancoFolies de Montréal, 22, 156
Les Glissades de la Terrasse (Québec City), 137
Les Grands Ballets Canadiens, 121
Les Promenade de la Cathédrale, 92
Lévesque, René, 29
LGBTQ travelers, 166–167
L'International des Feux Loto-Québec, 59, 157
L'Opera de Montréal, 117, 120
L'Oratoire St-Joseph, 18
L'Orchestre Symphonique de Montréal (OSM), 120

M

McCord Museum, 70
McGill University, 13, 70
McTavish, 54
Magog, 151
Mail and postage, 167
The Main. See Boulevard St-Laurent
Maison du Jazz, 14, 114
Maisonneuve, Sieur de, 63, 80
Maison Smith, 19, 79
Maple syrup, 151
Marché Atwater, 35, 89

Marché Bonsecours, 10, 65

Marché Jean-Talon, 89

Mason, Raymond, 70–71

Méchant Boeuf, 112

Medical requirements, 167

Métro, 160–161

Mobile phones, 158

Money, 167

Montréal Bike Fest, 22, 156

Montréal Canadiens, 168

Montréal Complètement Cirque, 157

Montréal High Lights Festival (Festival Montréal en Lumière), 157

Montréal Holocaust Memorial Centre, 75

Montréal Museum of Archaeology and History (Pointe-à-Callière), 4, 11, 26

Montréal Museums Day, 156

Montréal Museums Pass, 167

Montréal Science Centre, 58

Mont Royal Cemetery, 80

Mont-Tremblant, 145–147
   accommodations, 148
   restaurants, 149

Mont-Tremblant Pedestrian Village, 146

Musée d'Art Contemporain de Montréal, 32, 44, 48

Musée de la Civilisation (Québec City), 139

Musée des Beaux-Arts Boutique, 90

Musée des Beaux-Arts de Montréal (Museum of Fine Arts), 13–14, 32, 71

Musée du Château Ramezay, 27–29

Musée Grévin Montréal, 15

Musée Marguerite-Bourgeoys, 27, 64–65

Musée McCord, 13, 25

Museum of Fine Arts (Musée des Beaux-Arts de Montréal), 13–14, 32, 71

Music stores, 90

Music venues, 113–114

N

National Film Board of Canada, 26

Neighborhood walks, 62–80
   downtown Montréal, 68–71
   Parc du Mont-Royal, 78–80
   Plateau Mont-Royal, 73–75
   Vieux-Montréal, 63–65

Newspapers and magazines, 167

Nightlife, 110–114
   best bets, 106

Notre-Dame-des-Neiges Cemetery (Our Lady of the Snows Cemetery), 79–80

O

Obomsawin, Alanis, 26

O Canada (national anthem), 138

Ogilvy, 86–87

Olmsted, Frederick Law, 18–19, 78

Orchestre Métropolitain du Grand Montréal, 120

OSM (L'Orchestre Symphonique de Montréal), 120

Our Lady of the Snows Cemetery (Notre-Dame-des-Neiges Cemetery), 79–80

Outremont, 59

P

Palais des Congrès, 43

Paragraphe, 85

Parc Albert-Saint-Martin, 59

Parc Aquatique du Mont St-Sauveur, 145

Parc des Champs-de-Bataille (Québec City), 138

Parc du Mont-Royal, 18, 54
   neighborhood walk, 78–80

Parc Jean-Drapeau, 59

Parc Jeanne-Mance, 54

Parc La Fontaine, 20, 55, 60, 74

Parc Mont-Royal, 41

Parc National du Mont-Tremblant, 147

Parc Rutherford, 54

Parking, 162

Parks, 52–55

Passes, 167

Passports, 167–168

Pei, I.M., 69, 91

Percival-Molson Memorial Stadium, 122

Petrol, 165

Philémon, 112

Picnic, Parc La Fontaine, 60

Place d'Armes, 63

Place des Arts, 32

Place Jacques-Cartier, 10, 64

Place Ville-Marie, 69, 91

Plateau Mont-Royal, 5, 48, 72, 73
   neighborhood walk, 73–75

Playgrounds, 59

Pointe-à-Callière (Montréal Museum of Archaeology and History), 4, 11, 26–27

Point Merry Park (Magog), 152

Police, 168

Politics, 172–173

Pollack Concert Hall, 120

Poutine, 4–5, 37, 74

Première Moisson, 89, 102

P'tit Train du Nord bike trail, 145, 146

Pullman, 112

Q

Quadricycle bike-buggies, 52

Quartier des Spectacles, 32

Québec City, 28, 136–143

Québec City
   accommodations, 140–141
   high season, 137
   restaurants, 139, 142–143

R

Ramezay, Claude de, 27

Raplapla, 85

Redpath Museum, 13

Renaud-Bray, 73, 85

The Réservoir, 54

Restaurants, 98–104, 164. See also Restaurant Index
   best bets, 94
   Cantons-de-l'Est, 154
   Mont-Tremblant, 149
   Québec City, 142–143
   table d'hôte option, 103, 139

Rock climbing, 145

Roots, 88

Route des Vins, 152

Route Verte (Green Route), 146

Royal 22e Régiment (Québec City), 137–138

Rue Crescent, 14

Rue Duluth, 74

Rue du Petit-Champlain (Québec City), 139

Rue du Trésor (Québec City), 138

Rue Prince-Arthur, 74–75

Rue Sherbrooke, 13, 70

Rue St-Antoine, 9

Rue St-Denis, 20, 73

Rue Ste-Catherine, 69
Rue St-Paul, 10
Ryan, Joe, 147

S
Safdie, Moshe, 32, 44
Safety, 168
Sailors' Church (Chapelle
    Notre-Dame-de-Bon-
    Secours), 64–65
St. Lawrence River, 10
St-Sauveur, 145
St-Viateur Bagels, 37
SAQ Signature, 89–90
Seasons, 80, 156
Segal Centre for Performing
    Arts, 75
Segal Centre for Performing
    Arts at the Saidye, 122
Senior travelers, 168
Separatist movement, 29
Shopping, 82–92
        antiques, arts & crafts
            and galleries, 85
        best bets, 84
        books and toys, 85–86
        department stores,
            86–87
        edibles, 88–90
        fashion (clothing),
            87–88
        housewares, 90
        music, 90
Simons, 87
Sir Winston Churchill Pub,
    112
Skiing, Mont-Tremblant
    area, 146, 147
Sklavos, Yerassimos, 79
Sky Club & Pub, 113
Skype, 158
Smoking, 168
Snow Festival (La Fête des
    Neiges), 156
Spas, Mont-Tremblant area,
    147
Spas Relais Santé, 147
Spectator sports, 168
Square Dorchester, 68
Sugar shacks (cabanes à
    sucre), 151
Suite 88 Chocolatier, 90
Summer, 80

T
21 Balançoires, 32
Tam Tams, 6, 54
Taxes, 168
Taxis, 159, 162

Telephones, 168–169
Temperatures, average
    monthly, 157
Tennis, 55
Terrasse Dufferin (Québec
    City), 136–137
Theater, 122
Théâtre de Verdure, 55, 122
Tipping, 169
Tire sur la neige, 151
Toboggan run (Québec
    City), 137
Toilets, 169
Tourist information, 156, 169
    Québec City, 137
Tours, 169–170
Train travel, 159
Transportation, 160–162
Tremblant International
    Blues Festival, 146
Trip-cancellation insurance,
    166

U
Underground City, 6, 91
    shopping, 86
Upstairs Jazz Bar & Grill, 14,
    114

V
Val David, 145
Vélo Québec, 161
Velvet, 112–113
Vices & Versa, 113
Vieux-Montréal, neighbor-
    hood walk, 63–65
Vieux Palais de Justice, 64
Vieux-Port, 9, 52
Vignoble de l'Orpailleur
    (Dunham), 152
Visitor information, 156, 169
    Québec City, 137

W
Walking, 160. See also
    Neighborhood walks
Weather, 157
Websites, 158
Wheelchair accessibility,
    160, 170
White, Stanford, 63
Wines, 152
Winter, 80
Wolfe, James, 28, 138

Z
Zone, 73, 90

Accommodations
Auberge Bonaparte, 127
Auberge de La Fontaine,
    127
Auberge du Vieux-Port,
    41, 127
Auberge HI-Montréal, 128
Auberge Internationale de
    Québec (Québec City),
    140
Auberge Le Pomerol, 128
Auberge Place d'Armes
    (Québec City), 140
Auberge Saint-Antoine
    (Québec City), 140
Casa Bianca, 128
Château Beauvallon (Mont-
    Tremblant), 148
Fairmont Le Château Fron-
    tenac (Québec City), 140
Fairmont Mont-Tremblant,
    148
Hostellerie Pierre du Calvet,
    128–129
Hôtel Bonaventure
    Montréal, 129
Hôtel Château Laurier
    Québec (Québec
    City), 141
Hôtel de Glace (Québec
    City), 141
Hôtel de l'Institut, 129
Hôtel ÉPIK Montréal,
    129–130
Hôtel Gault, 43, 130
Hôtel Le Crystal, 130
Hôtel Le Dauphin Mon-
    tréal-Downtown, 130
Hôtel Le Germain, 131
Hôtel Mont-Tremblant, 148
Hôtel-Musée Premières
    Nations (Québec City),
    141
Hôtel Nelligan, 131
Hôtel St-Paul, 131
Le Germain Hôtel Québec
    (Québec City), 141
Le Petit Hôtel, 131
Le Saint-Sulpice Hôtel Mon-
    tréal, 131
Le Square Phillips Hôtel &
    Suites, 132
Le St-Martin Hôtel, 132
Manoir des Sables (Orford),
    153
Manoir Hovey (North
    Hatley), 153
Quintessence (Mont-
    Tremblant), 148
Ritz-Carlton Montréal, 132

Restaurants

Au Pied de Cochon, 36, 98
Aux Anciens Canadiens, 138
Aux Anciens Canadiens (Québec City), 142
Aux Vivres, 47, 59, 98
Beauty's Luncheonette, 98
Birks Café, 69
Bonaparte Restaurant, 11, 127
Brasserie T, 33, 98
Brutopia, 71
Café des Amis, 79
Café Krieghoff (Québec City), 142
Café Vasco Da Gama, 71
Chez l'Épicier, 98–99
Crêperie Catherine (Mont-Tremblant), 149
Deville Dinerbar, 14
Eggspectation, 64, 99
Espace La Fontaine, 55
Europea, 99
Fairmount Bagel, 37, 75, 99
Ferreira Café, 35, 99–100

Gandhi, 100
Graziella, 100
Hôtel Herman, 100
Jardin Nelson, 65
Java U, 70
Joe Beef, 49
Juliette et Chocolat, 20
La Banquise, 37, 74, 100
Laurie Raphaël (Québec City), 142
Lawrence, 100–101
Le Balmoral, 101
Le Café du Monde (Québec City), 142–143
L'Echaudé (Québec City), 142
Le Clocher Penché Bistrot (Québec City), 143
Le Club Chasse et Pêche, 101
Le Farandol (Magog), 154
Le Garde Manger, 102
Le Pain Béni (Québec City), 143
Les Glaceurs, 58

L'Express, 20, 101–102
Magpie Pizzeria, 102
Marché de la Villette, 27
Microbrasserie La Diable (Mont-Tremblant), 149
Modavie, 102
Olive + Gourmando, 10, 41, 94, 102
Paillard (Québec City), 143
Panache (Québec City), 143
Pilsen Restaurant & Pub (North Hatley), 154
Première Moisson, 89, 102
Resto Vego, 15, 103
Reuben's, 15
Ritz-Carlton Montréal, 40
St-Viateur Bagel & Café, 73, 75
St-Viateur Bagels, 37
Schwartz's, 5, 36, 74, 75, 103
Stash Café, 104
Taverne F, 33
Toast! (Québec City), 143
Toqué!, 35, 104
Wilensky Light Lunch, 75

Photo **Credits**

Museum of Fine Arts; p 73, top: © Alice Gao/Commission Canadienne du Tourisme; p 73, bottom: © Tourisme Montréal, Mario Melillo; p 74, top: Courtesy of La Banquise/Cyril PERROT BOTELLA; p 74, bottom: © Tourisme Montréal, Mario Melillo; p 78, top: © La Compagnie du Cimetière du Mont-Royal, Michael Slobodian; p 78, bottom: © Tourisme Montréal; p 79, top: © Tourisme Montréal, Stéphan Poulin; p 79, bottom: © Les amis de la montagne/S. Montigné, 2008; p 80: © Tourisme Montréal, Susan Moss; p 81: Courtesy of Suite 88; p 84: © Canadian Guild of Crafts, Studio du Ruisseau, SMQ; p 85: Courtesy of Drawn and Quarterly; p 86: Sandra Cohen-Rose and Colin Rose; p 87: Sandra Cohen-Rose and Colin Rose; p 88, top: Courtesy of Dubarry Furs; p 88, bottom: Courtesy of Kaliyana; p 89: Phil Roeder; p 90: © Tourisme Montréal; p 91: © The Montréal Eaton Centre, Stéphan Poulin; p 93: Courtesy of Olive + Gourmando; p 94: Courtesy of Brasserie T/Hans Laurendeau; p 99: Henry; p 100: Chun Yip So; p 101, top: Courtesy of Hotel Herman; p 101, bottom: Courtesy of La Banquise/Cyril PERROT BOTELLA; p 102: Courtesy of Lawrence; p 103: Courtesy of Olive et Gourmando; p 104: yawper; p 105: Courtesy of Montréal Jazz Festival/Benoit Rousseau; p 106: Courtesy of Bar Furco; p 110: Courtesy of Bar Henrietta; p 111: © Sébastien Roy; p 112: © Méchant Boeuf Bar-Brasserie; p 113, top: Courtesy of Sir Winston Churchill Pub; p 113, bottom: Courtesy of Montréal Jazz Festival/Benoit Rousseau; p 114, top: Courtesy of Club Soda/Empay Photographe; p 114, bottom: Courtesy of Upstairs Jazz Bar/Alain Mercier; p 115: ©Pierre-Étienne Bergeron; p 116: © Société des casinos du Québec; p 117, top: © Andrew Miller; p 117, bottom: Courtesy of Orchestre Metropolitain du Grand Montréal/Pierre Dury; p 120: © Just For Laughs Festival; p 121, top: Jean-laurent Ratel/Les Grands Ballets; p 121, bottom: proacguy1; p 122, top: © MTTQ/ André Rider; p 122, bottom: Jean-François Hamelin; p 123: Courtesy of the Ritz Carlton; p 124: Courtesy of Auberge Bonaparte; p 127, top: Courtesy of Auberge de la Fontaine; p 127, bottom: Courtesy of Auberge du Vieux Port Hotel/Alexi Hobbs; p 128: Courtesy of Hôtel Bonaventure Montréal; p 129, top: Courtesy of Gault Montréal; p 129, bottom: Courtesy of EPIK/REVERSE PROJECT; p 130, top: Courtesy of Hotel Le Crystal; p 130, bottoom: Courtesy of Nelligan/Alexi Hobbs; p 131: Courtesy of Le Petit Hotel/Alexi Hobbs; p 132, top: Courtesy of Le St-Martin Hôtel; p 132, bottom: Courtesy of the Ritz Carlton; p 133: VBoudrias; p 136: Rob Crandall/Shutterstock.com; p 137: bill_comstock; p 138, top: Caporal David Robert; p 138, bottom: Guillaume Cattiaux; p 139: jacme31; p 140, top: Courtesy of Hôtel Château Laurier Québec; p 140, bottom: Courtesy of Saint Antoine/ Guillaume D. Cyr; p 141, top: Courtesy of Groupe Germain Hôtels; p 141, bottom: © Renaud Philippe; p 142, top: Courtesy of Laurie Raphael; p 142, bottom: Courtesy of Café Krieghoff; p 143, top: Courtesy of Toast!; p 143, bottom: Catherine Côté; p 145: Richard Cavalleri; p 147: Sean Murphy; p 148, top: Courtesy of Fairmont Tremblant; p 148, middle: Courtesy of Hotel Quintessence/Yves Lefebvre; p 148, bottom: Albert Pego/ Shutterstock.com; p 149: Courtesy of Creperie Catherine; p 151: Sandra Cohen-Rose and Colin Rose; p 152: Jean-François Renaud; p 153, top: EM info@manoirhovey.com; p 153, bottom: EM info@hotelsvillegia.com; p 154: EM info@lefarandol.com; p 155: © Fitz and Follwell